Hyperion
and
the Hobbyhorse

"Barnsley Main Seam," George Hector, 1959. York Minster, York, U.K.

Hyperion
and
the Hobbyhorse

Studies in
Carnivalesque Subversion

Arthur Lindley

DELAWARE

Newark: University of Delaware Press
London: Associated University Presses

Associated University Presses
440 Forsgate Drive
Cranbury, NJ 08512

Associated University Presses
16 Barter Street
London WC1A 2AH, England

Associated University Presses
P.O. Box 338, Port Credit
Mississauga, Ontario
Canada L5G 4L8

The paper used in this publication meets the requirements of the American National Standard for Permanence of Paper for Printed Library Materials Z39.48–1984.

Library of Congress Cataloging-in-Publication Data

Lindley, Arthur, 1941–
  Hyperion and the hobbyhorse : studies in carnivalesque subversion / Arthur Lindley.
    p. cm.
  Includes bibliographical references and index.
  ISBN 0-87413-588-5 (alk. paper)
  1. English drama—Early modern and Elizabethan, 1500–1600—History and criticism. 2. Social problems in literature. 3. English poetry—Middle English, 1100–1500—History and criticism.
  4. Shakespeare, William, 1564–1616. Antony and Cleopatra.
  5. Chaucer, Geoffrey, d. 1400—Characters—Wife of Bath.
  6. Marlowe, Christopher 1564–1593—Characters—Heroes.
  7. Shakespeare, William, 1564–1616. Hamlet. 8. Literature and society—England—History. 9. Gawain and the Grene Knight.
  10. Carnival in literature. 11. Revenge in literature. I. Title.
PR658.S5L56   1996
820.9'355—dc20   96-2971
                                                              CIP

For Judith and Ian

Contents

Preface: "Barnsley Main Seam"

THE least prepossessing monument in a grandly prepossessing building is tucked into the back of the south wall of the choir of York Minster, between the base of a pillar and the stairs that lead down to the crypt (see frontispiece). It is called "Barnsley Main Seam," and it is labeled "an offering to the Minster from the miners of Yorkshire, modelled and presented by George Hector, 1959." I will try to describe it with some care.

An image of the givers, the model shows a miner at work on a coal seam. The image is one of oppressive and multiple enclosure. There is a picture frame, the bottom of which is submerged in the cathedral floor. Within that is another frame of grey imitation rock, itself framed by a structure of pipe-metal supports, like the frame of a soccer goal. Within that is a band of rough stone ceiling that fills the top one-fifth of this inner frame, creating a space so low that the miner has to bend until his back is nearly horizontal to the floor. The construction itself is placed so low that the viewer has to adopt a similar posture to see into it. When you do, you find the figure staring back at you from within a further cagelike enclosure made up of four pipe supports. His posture, with both arms dangling, is apelike, not because the man is—if he could stand erect he would be tallish and conventionally handsome—but because the space forces the posture upon him. He is assimilated to what he works in: Even his shirt is the color of the stone around him. His space is named, he is not.

The image is hellish, not just in the conventional, Labour-conference, dead-metaphoric sense, but in a sense peculiarly appropriate to its location in a cathedral. We see that contorted posture elsewhere, in images of demons in torment; the low, dark, painful space suggests a hell waiting to be harrowed. At the same time, however, this is a figure in a niche, unmistakably suggestive of icons and images of saints, not to mention the relief sculptures of dignitaries on the facing wall. The dark enclosure is uncannily like the underchurch directly below it, a place of massive foundation stones and low ceilings. Men built this cathedral, working in conditions and with materials strikingly similar to the miner's.

9

More directly, the worker's space is metonymic of the cathedral crypt just below and behind it. As such, it suggests not only the human body in the grave, but also Christ in the tomb.

Aggressively plain, the image does not so much decorate the building as interrogate it, asking implicit questions about sainthood and its relation to ordinary humanity. The image belongs to the cathedral but, to the extent that it inscribes the image of the builders, the cathedral belongs to it. Perhaps accidentally, perhaps significantly, it faces away from altar and choir. Necessarily, it poses some fundamental problems: about the relation between marginal and central; between what is "high" and what is "low"; what is dark and what is illuminated; what is named and what is nameless; what is displayed and what is hidden. (The construction itself is placed below eye level, and most visitors pass without noticing it.) The image, as placed, invites consideration of the complex, hierarchical structure of authority represented by a cathedral, especially a flag-hung national one like this. It reminds you of those otherwise excluded from a building full of memorials. *Et in cathedra ego.*

Needless to say, this conflation of images has a remarkable leveling effect, whether you read it in religious or political terms. Religiously, it asserts the real or potential equality in significance of savior, saint, sinner, demon, and undifferentiated man; or if you prefer, a familiar Augustinian lesson in the way different levels and orders of creation reflect one another. Politically, it asserts the equality of nameless workers with the effusively named soldiers, aristocrats, and clergy whose memorial space it shares and whose authority you might read it as indicting. To the extent that it compels your attention, of course, it literally forces you to lower your eyes. It rearranges the verticals that structure the building. It offers the implicit possibility of a carnivalesque inversion of the power that weighs down on that figure: Here is the saint, here is the center. A commonplace example of the Christian heroic, celebrating the patient suffering of the humble, is also an example of the Christian mock-heroic. Every cathedral is necessarily an act of idolatry as well as an act of worship.

And, of course, the sculpture is also an offering. You are free to read it as a reassuring Christian commonplace: The poor in spirit worship Him, too. In the same way—I say this almost without irony—you can read *Dr. Faustus* as orthodox Augustinianism, the *Wife of Bath's Prologue* as an indictment of the unnaturalness of female aggression, and *Hamlet* as an argument for stable monarchy. The texts that I discuss in the book that follows likewise encode subversive possibilities within orthodox gestures, as the Fool registers loyalty to Lear by mocking him, as carnival mock-kings testify to the authority of real kings. The manuscript of *Sir Gawain and the Green Knight* ends, famously, with the motto that became that of the order of the garter and with a perfectly conventional prayer. Even more richly than George Hector's ingenious construction, however, they observe the pieties of their culture while subjecting it to pervasive and critical if ultimately ambivalent scrutiny. Like it, they devastate and leave intact. Like it, they reflect the clerical orthodoxies of, in their case, the fundamentally Augustinian culture of the later middle ages and the early Renaissance. But they also reflect a demotic and critical response to it, a response, like this little sculpture, at once serious and gnomicly playful, saint disguised as gargoyle and gargoyle as saint. The interaction of clerical and demotic is largely the subject of this book.

In what follows, I have concentrated on a small number of works—*The Wife of Bath's Prologue and Tale, Sir Gawain and the Green Knight,* the plays of Marlowe, *Hamlet* and revenge tragedy, *Antony and Cleopatra*—which are not only indisputably major, seminal and so forth, but which also give the justified impression of gathering, defining, and evaluating extraordinarily vast stretches of the available culture. Anyone who has ever tried to explain to undergraduates approximately what *Sir Gawain and the Green Knight* is "about" will know how vast that culture is. The vastness of the culture-defining works is also an excuse for a study that, despite the ambitions implied by its title, does not pretend to coverage of a still vaster period. "My wyt is short ye may wel understond."[1] I hope that the echoes of the texts I am discussing will be audible in those I omit. *Pearl,* like Gawain, dramatizes the discovery that everything familiar and tangible in the protagonist's world is, in fact, unknown and mysterious. The expense of spirit in the pursuit of the material and external, the loss of soul through misdirected love, is as much the process of *The Canon's Yeoman's Tale* or *The Pardoner's Tale* as of the Wife's text. The deconstruction of warrior masculinity, with its assumptions of definitional clarity and psychological self-sufficiency, by feminine multiplicity and interdependency, which I describe in the chapter on *Sir Gawain,* is also the fundamental premise of *Antony and Cleopatra.* The starting point of the play's action, the lady introducing the hero to selves and narratives that he didn't know he had, is also the "comic" ending mooted for and rejected by Gawain. In both cases, the woman exposes and elaborates the theatricality of identity, erases gender boundaries—the Lady "captures" Gawain, Cleopatra wears Antony's "sword Philippan"—subverts sexual hierarchy, and opens closed male identity to multiple potentiality. In both cases, a heroic sense of the self as determined, fixed, complete, consciously directed is displaced and subverted (*degraded,* to use the Bakhtinian term) by a comic one. The long disappearance of the Cotton Nero A X manuscript, of course, precludes a connection through influence. Augustinian presumptions about the multiplicity of the self and carnivalesque delight in the subversive pleasures of women on top provide, I argue, all the connections one needs. For all that, however, I am temperamentally inclined to leave a significant number of connections and applications unstated. If my paradigm is valid, readers will find more and stranger uses for it than I have.

Acknowledgments

THE author would like to thank the editors and publishers involved for permission to reprint earlier versions of three of the chapters in this book. A substantial part of chapter 4 first appeared as "The Unbeing of the Overreacher: Proteanism and the Marlovian Hero" in the *Modern Language Review* 84, no. 1 (Jan. 1989), 1–17; of chapter 2 under its present title in *ELH* 59 (1992), 1–21; of chapter 3 also under its present title in *Exemplaria* 6, no. 1 (1994), 67–86.

The writing of this book was facilitated by sabbatical years at Birmingham and Cambridge. I would like to thank Susan Brock and her staff at the Shakespeare Institute, University of Birmingham, and the staff of the English Faculty Library and the University Library, Cambridge, for their hospitality and assistance.

Hyperion
and
the Hobbyhorse

1

The Varieties of *Ludus:* Augustinian Privation and the Carnivalesque

BAKHTINIAN CARNIVAL

As any number of critics and historians have figured out by now, it is no good trying to talk about the great first chapter of Bakhtin's *Rabelais and His World* as either history or—strictly speaking—literary interpretation.[1] Bakhtin's treatise is an exercise in myth-making and covert allegory, as much a program for subverting Stalinism (of which it is also an allegorical account in the fashion of *Animal Farm*) as it is a commentary on late-medieval literature and culture.[2] As a description of the social phenomenon of carnival, the chapter is frankly, if implicitly, fictional: it approaches the activities of the marketplace only through their literary reflections, and it attempts to recreate a version of medieval popular culture by extrapolating backward from early Renaissance literature.[3] Even in imagining that culture, Bakhtin's text notoriously creates a market from which all the unpleasantries of commerce have been banished along with the cruel and exclusionary aspects of folk humor. It imagines an oppressive establishment that also licenses rebellion. For that matter, it also creates a Rabelais without Christianity and a carnival season divorced from (and triumphant over) Lent rather than inextricably linked as mutually defining and supporting elements in the calendar of the church year.

The outline of Bakhtin's "history" of carnival will be groaningly familiar to students of critical theory. Carnival, for Bakhtin, is an embodiment of the liberated communality of the people in perennially renewed rebellion against the social and spiritual restrictions of the official order. It is marked by

> the suspension of all hierarchical precedence. . . . All were considered equal during carnival . . . such free familiar contacts were deeply felt and formed an essential element of the carnival spirit. People were . . .

reborn for new, purely human relations. . . . The utopian ideal and the realistic merged in this carnival experience.[4]

Carnival thus represents the people's "second life" (9), both an escape from and a critique of the static, oppressive hierarchy of class and economic relations embodied in what Bakhtin calls the "official feast" (9, 10). Carnival is the festive embodiment of change and disorder: "it celebrated temporary liberation from the prevailing truth. . . . Carnival was the true feast of becoming, change, and renewal" (10). (My shifting tenses, by the way, are those of Bakhtin, for whom carnival is both a lost past and a permanent principle.) It embodied the temporary rebellion not only of the lower classes, but also of the lower faculties, of instinct against reason, of flesh against spirit. Because "in this tradition woman is essentially related to the material bodily lower stratum," carnival also celebrates the dominance of the feminine: "womanhood is shown in contrast to the limitations of her partner. . . . [s]he represents in person the undoing of pretentiousness" (240). Carnival is the healthy assertion of the rights of the body, the material principle, at the expense of the spirit. Its humor "degrades" the high and disembodied only to reconnect it with the sources of life: "to degrade an object [is] to hurl it down to the reproductive stratum, the zone in which conception and a new birth take place" (21). In what Terry Castle has called "Bakhtin's lyrical theory of carnival," it is vital, proletarian energy expressing itself at the expense of dead, hierarchic form.[5]

The history of carnival is that of its triumph over and suppression by the official culture, to which it stands as positive to negative, living to dead, relative to absolute, liberating to enslaving, Dionysian to Apollonian (if I may cite one of Bakhtin's unacknowledged sources), and by which, at some indefinite point, it has been displaced. "Unlike the earlier and purer feast, the official feast asserted all that was stable, unchanging, perennial. . . . It was the triumph of a truth already established" (9). An official feast, "monolithically serious" (9), is a contradiction in terms, a travesty as well as a usurpation: "the state encroached upon festive life and turned it into a parade" (33); and "the true nature of human festivity was betrayed and distorted" (9). Under these (admittedly mythical) circumstances, carnival becomes a kind of revenge, "a parody of the extracarnival life" (11), but more specifically a parody—as in the boy bishops or mock-kings—of the official order. The pattern is a kind of double *ludus:* Pure festivity is displaced by a solemn travesty that in turn is exposed by parody, "legalized carnival licentiousness" (13). Cultural history is a revenger's comedy.

Bakhtin's history is also, however, in several senses a myth of loss. In one sense, true, popular carnival is—as the saying goes—always already lost by the time it has been transmuted into print. Historically speaking, genuine, medieval carnival has been lost to our stratified, official-ridden society, displaced in the later Renaissance by an (anti-body, antilife) "aesthetics of the beautiful" (29) intended to suppress the communal, erase the carnal, marginalize the grotesque, and debase the popular. An individualist, elitist aesthetic supports an authoritarian, bourgeois culture. The "power of regeneration" (38) in true carnival has been lost to us, but even that was a kind of memorialization, the survival of a primitive communism, that "purer feast," an Edenic original. The "utopian character" of carnival looks back to a lost original and forward to a future that has not happened. The "abstract and deadened ideal-ism" (22) that is buried by carnival triumphs in history.

It should be apparent by now that we are dealing less with history than with theology, a kind of materialist revivalism: "in carnival people were reborn" (10); "the carnival bonfire. . . renews the world" (17). "Utopian in the extreme," as Ken Hirschkop has written, carnival is "a vision rather than a programme."[6] To say that is not to dismiss or minimize the politics of Bakhtin's critical thought but rather to insist that his criticism is best understood as, in fact, a materialized form of Christian religiosity that, as we shall see, shows certain striking links to Augustinian theology. The great drive that Bakhtin sees in carnival and that we may see in his writing on it, is toward transcendence. As Caryl Emerson says, for Bakhtin, "authorship"—including both "formally aesthetic authorship and its 'everyday' real-life counterpart"—"is theological—a reenactment, writ small, of supreme authority creating humanity."[7] This myth is about saving souls, albeit material ones. Carnival "made a man renounce his official state as monk, cleric, scholar" (13) in order to experience a rapturous communalism freed from commerce, power relationships, and especially "the bourgeois conception of the completed, atomized man" (24). We are dead but in carnival we may be transformed and live. In the midst of death, like Augustine before his conversion, we are on the verge of life. To call carnival the people's "second life" is, of course, to offer it as an alternative afterlife. Carnival is true religiosity for Bakhtin because it is inverted religiosity, promising spiritual release through denial of the spirit and immersion in the material. "Bakhtin," Emerson adds, "reverses the traditional idea

underlying the wonder of resurrection. He stresses the inseparabil-
ity of body and soul not because the body has a soul but because
souls must have bodies; his is a religion not so much of resurrection
as of incarnation."[8] Implicit in Bakhtin's insistence on the primacy
of carnival and his close paralleling of it with theology is the assumption that Christianity travesties carnival's message of joy, liberation, renewal, community.[9] He reverses the apparent relation in
which carnival parodies official religion. The relationship is thus a
double *ludus* in which parody undoes travesty. The two modes of
salvation are inversely mirroring, however: two opposed ways to
the same end.

For Bakhtin, however, there is only one true way, just as there
is only one true medieval culture, the popular one. The official
feast exists only as a usurpation of the forms of community (an
assertion that better fits Bakhtin's subtext about Stalinism than his
ostensible text about medieval society); the official culture exists
only as a series of negatives. It is the principle of denial, censor-
ship, death: an evil figured as privation. The system Bakhtin has
constructed is neither dialectic nor dialogic, because the official,
being merely parasitic on the popular, has nothing positive to say
for itself.[10] As Aron Gurevich says, "the two cultures appeared
to Bakhtin as the opposition of motion and immobility, life and
mortification."[11] To see them in those terms is to separate two
things that, historically, must have been interactive. The grotesque
is, of course, incorporated into the official, as the imps on medieval
cathedrals or the marginal figures on medieval manuscripts remind
us. Rabelais was a cleric. Most of the records of medieval popular
culture on which Bakhtin depends were clerical. As Gurevich puts
it: "medieval grotesque was rooted in a specific kind of dualistic
view of the world" (*Medieval Popular Culture*, 183); it "is not opposed to the sacred" (207). A gargoyle, to (re)state the obvious, is
not antithetical to a cathedral, it is part of a cathedral. Carnival
was, of course, integrated into the church year, yielding to Lent
just as the boy bishops and other figures of mock authority yielded
their powers back to the official order.[12] Obviously, the official order would not have tolerated carnival if it were intolerable. Licensed rebellion is also a contradiction in terms. The proper
relation of the two orders is not oppositional but dialectical, each
supplying forms to the other, as carnival, for instance, took a my-
thology of death and rebirth from the official religion. The gargoyle
adorns the cathedral as the cathedral elevates the gargoyle.

The work of demolishing the historicity of Bakhtin's "history"
of festivity has already been done, if not overdone, by a rota of

contemporary authors, among whom the most notable are Emmanuel LeRoy Ladurie, Leah Marcus, Leonard Tennenhouse, Peter Stallybrass and Allon White, all committed in different ways to arguing against Bakhtin's essentialist view of carnival and showing, as Paul Strohm writes, that it historically has been "subject to varied appropriation and use."[13] Marcus, for example, has devoted a book on the "politics of mirth" to studying how Elizabeth and the Stuarts consciously incorporated festivity into royalist public relations—in such gestures as the Stuart sponsorship of the Cotswold Games—arguing that "the appeal to 'public mirth' in the Stuart period was an appeal to royal authority," a way of aligning crown with populace against parliament.[14] Tennenhouse describes how, in Shakespearean history plays, "the popular energy embodied in carnival legitimizes authority, provided that energy can be incorporated in the political body of the state," as Hal's tavern experience can be incorporated into his populist kingship.[15] Stallybrass and White, while endorsing the "demystifying potential" of carnival, also warn against "the false essentializing of carnivalesque transgression" as either "*intrinsically* radical or conservative."[16] "Carnival," they point out, frequently manifests exclusionary and xenophobic feelings and is liable to be directed at minorities and the powerless, "those who 'don't belong'" (19); for example, Jews and Gypsies. What is clear from a great deal of historical evidence is that carnival has no necessary political valence, despite its intensely political significance. As Ladurie's account of the 1580 events in Romans demonstrates, the forms of carnival are equally available to peasant and aristocrat, for revolution or reaction. In Romans, both parties had their own carnivals, but neither represented the poor, let alone the community as a whole. Carnival, like revenge, is dangerous, in spite of Bakhtin's attempts to minimize or defuse the violence of its disorder and the aggression of its mockery. Ladurie concludes that the bloodshed growing out of the rivalry of carnivals "may well have expressed the essence of the institution, founded on conflict, expulsions, and murders."[17]

I take most of this criticism as read, at least as regards the referential function of literature as a political instrument and a reflector of social conditions. I am not, however, primarily concerned with that function but with a more formal one: with events within texts. We need, I think to distinguish between "carnival"—roughly, "what happens in the marketplace" or at the Cotswold Games, for that matter—and "carnivalesque," roughly "what happens in *Hamlet*."[18] The former may be collective and unwritten; the latter is authored. Literary carnivalesque is derived from folk custom but in textual practice is necessarily used by an individual author, in drama at least, acting through an individual character. The literary user is thus always a mediator of carnival, not a spontaneous participant. She or he is in Rabelais's position; that is, in Hamlet's—evoking community rather than embodying it. That is to say that the carnivalesque author is in the position Bakhtin ascribed to Dostoevsky in his late revision of *The Problems of Dostoevsky's Art.*[19]

The carnivalesque survives as a concept of literary theory, not of social history. It does so because it describes an element, a process of demystification, manifestly present in a great range of Western literature, whatever the social sources or political consequences, if any, of that element may have been outside the texts. Bakhtin is not writing—at least not directly—about social behavior but about the ways in which social practice ("carnival") is refracted and reimagined in literary texts ("carnivalesque"). Studies such as that of Stallybrass and White, therefore, strike me as somewhat beside the carnivalesque point.

I have tried to illustrate the extent and persistence of that literary presence by a small, but strikingly varied, selection of unarguably major works of late-medieval and Renaissance texts: the *Canterbury Tales* and *Sir Gawain* on one side; the plays of Marlowe, *Hamlet* and revenge tragedy, *Antony and Cleopatra* on the other. Alisoun of Bath makes a career out of carnivalesque inversion; Bertilak's Lady makes narrative and drama out of carnivalesque subversion. Tamburlaine does, especially in *Part I,* mock and uncrown kings, whether we assume that Elizabethan audiences saw this as conservative warning or revolutionary incitement. When Hamlet tries to define Claudius's kingship, he reaches for the imagery of carnival, describing a "king of shreds and patches," a drunken mock-king enacting a grotesque parody of regal authority. When he contrasts his father's reign with his uncle's, he again thinks of carnival: "the hobby-horse is forgot."[20] On perhaps the sole occasion when he summons up an unidealized memory of the lost past, he remembers not his father but the jester at his father's feast. Yorick's role, as lunatic and mocking licensed fool, is, of course, among the most prominent of those Hamlet has appropriated for himself as the designated restorer of that past. As I will show in chapter five, the carnivalesque functions for Hamlet and the audience as both a myth and a metaphor. The myth, which startlingly anticipates Bakhtin's, is that of the death of carnival: the destruction of an old order of communal freedom and intimacy by a new order based on cold, isolated, treacherous self-interest. That destruction is symbolized most vividly by the burying of Ophelia in Yorick's vacated grave. This myth of historical transition is replayed again and again in Shakespearean tragedy, most elaborately and explicitly in the transition from Antony's Rome to Caesar's in *Antony and Cleopatra*.[21]

Metaphorically, the carnivalesque functions as a trope for the parodic subversion of social identity, as a political, psychological, and religious phenomenon. Carnival role-play breaks down distinctions between self and other, just as it breaks down the illusion of a singular identity: Gawain as the form signified by the pentangle or Hamlet as the idealized prince remembered by Ophelia. It subverts hierarchy by direct parody—for example, by the image of Claudius reflected in "The Mousetrap"—of the classifications on which hierarchy depends, the effect of handy-dandy inversions and conflations of, say, fool and king. More pervasively, as Terry Castle writes of eighteenth-century masquerade, the carnivalesque is "antitaxonomic"; it subverts the "vision of a classifiable cosmos" based on the "desire for firm conceptual boundaries."[22] In short, it uncrowns. To use an overly familiar but usefully flexible term, I am using carnival as a trope for a kind of deconstruction, especially of social authority and its supporting idealizations: the reduction of Hyperion to the satyr, but also the reduction (or expansion) of singularity into multiplicity; from the one king around which Denmark organized itself to the profusion of kings (Claudius, the Ghost, Hamlet, Fortinbras) under which it disorganizes itself. For reasons that will become clear, I hope, in the course of this chapter, this customarily takes the form of a double *ludus:* the travesty of genuine authority by what usurps it—Claudius's imitation of his brother's royal and familial authority in the first court scene, for instance—and the parody required to unmask that travesty, Hamlet's response to it. Faustus the magician parodies freedom, authority, philosophical investigation, while clowns and devils parody him. In both texts, of course, the parodic interrogation of authority goes beyond the individual figure to the concept itself. On an equally fundamental level carnival "degradation" interrogates the idea of a coherent self, as Hamlet finds in the graveyard. The democratizing tendency Bakhtin finds in the institution is precisely its erasure of the illusion of individualism. What we all are at the "lower bodily level" is interchangeable.[23]

Carnival, in other words, bequeathed to the carnivalesque something more important than scatology or holly bobs or even Alisoun's red-faced, gap-toothed, birthmarked embodiment of grotesque realism. It transmitted a way of seeing the official world as game and official and social identity as the arbitrary assignment of role (the king as "king") that is characteristic of games. Carnival, of course, revels in carnivality. As with the gloriously elaborated fantasticality of Rio carnival costumes, the instability or unreality of the show is the point of it and the most basic comment it makes on what it represents. It subverts the signs that construct the social self. In this strictly literary sense, the subversiveness of the carnivalesque—unlike that of carnival—does not depend on what follows from the performance (the political use, say, that could be made of a performance of *Julius Caesar*) nor on what resolution is imposed on carnival activity at the end of the text (Lovewit's return at the end of *The Alchemist,* say, or Fortinbras's coup). A subverted sign, unlike a government, stays subverted. King stays "king": Hamlet can become virtually anybody except that nameless, unselfconscious prince Ophelia remembers, the rose of her unfallen state. Self-consciousness, too, is permanent. If there is a process of remystification at the end of a carnivalesque text, it must take cognizance of the demystification that has preceded it, as Gawain's green "bende," the final sign of his *untrawthe,* takes indirect but pointed cognizance of the pentangle, the earlier sign of his *trawthe.* Fortinbras's first act as king is to fix Hamlet, in gloriously inappropriate form, by burying him as a soldier. Official forms are restored, whether discredited or not. Deconstruction, as we all know, is a potentially endless process; closure is something we impose out of the need for closure, to restart the game. All the texts I discuss, to the extent that they are carnivalesque, ironize closure just as they subvert other forms of authority and definition. Like carnival, the carnivalesque puts things into play.

In summary, whatever the historicity of carnival, the carnivalesque is undoubtedly real, a shaping element in major texts from the *Canterbury Tales* to *Paradise Lost* and beyond (for example, to Lovelace's attempts to carnivalize Clarissa Harlowe).[24] It does not operate, however, in the simply positive way that Bakhtin mythologizes. It is used more to interrogate dystopias than to establish utopias. In the carnivalesque, utopia is, *pace* Hirschkop, a dubious memory. The time of Yorick, as Hamlet knows, is dead and quite possibly imaginary. To remember your Hyperion-father as a hobby horse (let alone a forgotten one) is, of course, to question the validity of memory altogether and, with it, the coherence of the self in time. Hamlet is surrounded by forgetting, which is precisely what makes his memorializing a matter of desperate and self-ironized assertion. "Well said, old mole" is hardly a statement of serene

trust. Hamlet can remember an image of his parents' perfect marriage only in the knowledge that the image—an unverifiable memory and thus equally a fantasy—must in some sense have been
delusory. Thus his image of Gertrude's wifely devotion famously
shades over into an image of sickly and devouring lust: "she would
hang upon him, / As if increase of appetite had grown / By what
it fed on" (I.2.143–45). In the carnivalesque, "Hyperion" is always
a fiction of idealized authority that is customarily paired with its
counter-fiction, the hobby horse. Hamlet's honored father is also
"this fellow in the cellerage" (I.5.151): doubly or triply unreal; the
shade of a character imitated by an actor.

All this amounts, of course, to a fairly straightforward account
of the carnivalesque as a textual phenomenon. This demystifying
and "democratic" process has, however, a source and a context
that Bakhtin does not recognize and that has not, to my knowledge,
been noted and explained before, because that source is central to
the "official medieval culture" that Bakhtin characterizes as "intolerant, one-sided" and hostile to laughter (*Rabelais*73). That en-
abling source is Augustinian theology, its particular version of the
self and of the effects of privative evil on that self. The carnivalesque, I argue, is what happens when the popular practice of
carnival is read through Augustinian doctrine, defined by it, and
thus transmuted into textual practice. Literarily, Augustinianism
is the theory; carnivalesque is the practice. Put another way, the
doctrine authorizes the mode. The relationship is cooperative and
dialectic, not simply oppositional. The result is not what Bakhtin
says: the emergence of "a new, free and critical *historical* consciousness" (73), but the synthesis of two forms of consciousness
already long present in medieval culture.

AUGUSTINIAN PRIVATION

Augustine formulated and reformulated the doctrines of evil
that, in the form of what we might nonpejoratively call vulgar Augustinianism, have remained for sixteen hundred years the orthodoxy of the Catholic Church and have been passed through such
devout Augustinians as Luther and Calvin into the mainstream of
Protestant theology.[25] You find it incorporated by Aquinas into
the *Summa Theologiæ;* you find it restated in the *New Catholic
Encyclopedia,* s.v. "evil"; you find it in more elaborate and medi-
ated form in the work of the distinguished modern Thomist Charles
Journet.[26] In this formulation, evil is essentially negative: It is an

absence, as darkness is the absence of light: an omission, a defect, a privation. It is the *non* in front of *serviam*. Strictly or Platonically speaking, however, evil does not exist because it is fundamentally a turning away (*aversio*) from God conceived as the source of being, "existence in the supreme degree" (*City of God,* 12.2).[27] *Malum est non ens:* "There is no such entity in nature as 'evil'; 'evil' is merely a name for the privation of good" (*CG,* 11.22; cp. 12.3).[28] Paradoxically, evil has effects and accidents without having substance. Pain, for example, a natural evil, may be very real to us, but its reality is parasitic. It is, to Augustine at least, the absence of that health natural to the body. It is dis-ease, dis-order, disharmony: the particular forms sin takes after the Fall. Without the body, a creation of God and therefore good, pain has no existence. "Good may exist on its own, but evil cannot" (*CG,* 12.3). Evil thus manifests itself, as Gillian Evans puts it, by "borrowing the existence of the good in which it inheres."[29] For Satan to appear in the Garden as evil, he must borrow the form of the serpent, obscuring the substance he retains from his original form as an angel. The condition of the serpent occupied by the spirit of the devil is the prototype of the evil being. That is, the evil is not the creature itself but the will that occupies and perverts the creature. Evil is not simple nonexistence—mere void is not evil—but the loss of something it is in one's nature to have. More fundamentally, it is the active choice and the dynamic movement toward nonexistence that is evil: not death itself so much as the death wish. In that great epic of Augustinian theology, *Paradise Lost,* Satan enters the world as a mist (9.75), both insubstantial and the symbol of error. He first appears to Eve as the toad who whispers into her dream, an illusion invading a dream "to forge / Illusions as he list" (4.802–03).[30] To choose evil is to choose unreality, dream. Eve is tempted, not with substantial goods, but with fantasies of power, visions of being "universally admired" (9.542) by imaginary creatures.[31]

The first sign of Eve's propensity for evil also involves adoration of the illusory: her fascinated staring, in the moment after her birth, at her own image—a substantial creature captivated by her insubstantial reflection, "a shape within the watery gleam" (4.461). The gesture is a small, instinctive *aversio,* a turning away from God and from her material and formal cause, Adam.[32] She is here the embodiment of both the beauty of the material world and our fatal susceptibility to it. Eve and her reflection form a closed circuit of ego, the subject worshipping itself as object. The *civitas terrena,* Augustine writes, "was created by self-love reaching the point of contempt for God, the Heavenly City by the love of God carried as far as contempt for self" (*CG,* 14.28). As with Eve, evil is inherently solipsistic, a turning from community as well as creator. Eve's narcissism is corrected by her first sight of Adam. When you turn from God, you turn toward yourself, but that self is real only to the extent that it is inspirited by God and turned toward Him. To love the self for itself is to love nothing.[33] The fallen angels "would have existed in a higher degree, if they had adhered to him who exists in the highest degree; but in preferring themselves to him they chose a lower degree of existence" (*CG,* 12.6).

This argument is not so much a matter of metaphysics as of theodicy. Its overriding and explicit purpose is not to account for our experience of evil, which it does very inadequately, but to exempt God from responsibility for its creation. "All nature's substances are good" (*CG,* 12.6); evil therefore cannot be a substance. If it is not a substance, God did not create it. The substance that He did create, however, He created out of nothing. Every created thing thus contains nothingness, manifesting itself as mutability or corruptibility, a kind of entropic tendency to return to its negative source. As Gilson puts it, "a thing which comes from nothing is corruptible."[34] When Augustine, in that famous passage in the *Confessions,* tries to account for his theft of worthless pears, he concludes that "I loved the self-destruction. I loved my fall, not the object for which I had fallen but my fall itself" (2, 4, 9).[35] We are all, like Ibsen's Ulrik Brendel, "homesick for the great void."[36] The source of evil is in our will, however, not in God. If we choose not to exist, that is our responsibility. The manufacturer, in effect, does not accept responsibility for any defects in the product. The defects are held to have produced themselves.[37] For reasons that will be apparent, as Donald Cress concedes, "it is now a virtual commonplace among contemporary philosophers of religion that the privative account of evil is indefensible from both a metaphysical and a moral standpoint."[38]

Whether or not it is absurd, the doctrine of evil incorporates absurdity as a central element. Evil, in order to be damnable, must be the result of conscious choice. That choice cannot, however, be rational because it is fundamentally and obviously the choice of death over life, pain over bliss, shadow over substance. No one in his or her right mind would make the choice, therefore, it is necessary to conclude that people are not normally in their right minds. Confronted with the original mystery, Original Sin, Augustine allows himself a philosophically justified throwing up of hands. The choice of evil, he explains, is not only perverse, but also impene-

trably mysterious: "If anyone tries to discover a cause which produced" the sin of Adam and Eve "no cause suggests itself" (*CG*,
12.6). Substantive things have efficient causes; however, evil "is
not a matter of efficiency, but of deficiency" (*CG*, 12.7). God constructs; Satan deconstructs (not to mention, self-destructs). Evil's
motives, thus, have a kind of metaphysical half-life, conceivable
either as nonexistence or as the negation of real causes ("non serviam" to "serviam"). At a stroke, the second-most fundamental
and most pervasive source of human action is declared a mystery
and, a psychologist might say, relegated to that area Augustine
never quite succeeds in conceptualizing: the unconscious.[39] What
is not conceptualized, however, may still be abundantly present.
Augustine hardly imagines that his adolescent self was conscious
of stealing pears to abolish himself. That explanation is only available to the *inquisitio* of the philosopher twenty years or so after
the fact. It is not possible, within this system, to think of fallen or
falling beings as more than nominally rational. The most pervasive
fact of human mental activity, at least in its ungraced state, must
be rationalization, the processes by which we manage not to see
our motives and their consequences.

In the practice of our normal consciousness, the entropic tendency toward oblivion, which is the most basic expression of evil,
parasitically takes over the appetite for life, the root of good, and
assures that it will "naturally" be misdirected toward the wrong
objects. "I sought an object for my love," Augustine writes of his
youth in Carthage; "I was in love with love" (*Conf.*, 3, 1, 1). That
need he describes as "internal hunger," emptiness, which he tried
to fill not with "incorruptible nourishment," but with the usual
physical substitute, "the joy that enchains," producing the usual
Augustinian consequences: "I was . . . in bondage, tied with trou-
blesome chains . . . flogged with the red-hot iron rods of jealousy,
suspicion, fear, anger, and contention" (3, 1, 1). Natural (i.e., fallen)
man "naturally" tends to confuse the material with the substantial
and thus to spend his life (in two senses of that idiom) trying to
make himself more real by accumulating things less real. In that
"cauldron of illicit loves" (*Conf.*, 3, 1, 1), surrounded by the allur-
ing surfaces of the material world, the mind tends to confuse those
surfaces with reality, as Eve does with her reflection.[40] Devotion
to those material objects, of course, is reinforced by the reward of
physical pleasure, so that the mind becomes assimilated to what it
loves, confusing itself with and in the corporeal. Misdirected will
produces habit, which reinforces the misdirection. "For the specific
gravity of a body is, in a manner, its love, whether a body tends

downward by reason of its heaviness or strives upward because of its lightness" (*CG*, 11.28). As Robert Meagher puts it: A person, for Augustine, "is a creature of habit. One's own loves, whether appropriate or not to *what* one is, fashion and fit *who* one is. . . . Habit, though originating in the will, a creature of the will, becomes virtually natural."[41] In this state we are driven by what Kenneth Surin calls "an inexhaustible perversity which impels the individual to repeat, and thus to remember ever more vividly and insistently, the delight gained from every wicked deed of the past."[42] Augustine recalls that he was not merely "in bondage," but "glad to be in bondage" (3, 1, 1). The condition of sin is both absurd and perverse.[43]

It will be apparent from the aforesaid that we have been discussing the growth of the individual conceived as a system of false consciousness. "The mind goes astray through uniting itself to these images [of the external world] by a love so intense as to make it suppose its own nature to be like theirs. It becomes as it were conformed to them, not in reality but in supposition" (*De Trinitate*, 10.8.6).[44] Habit (Augustine's *consuetudo*) habitually triumphs over thought. As it does, vital energy flows out of the soul into the construction of a false identity made up of relations in this world with the mutable objects of this world; in Augustine's case, his life as ambitious *rhetor*, professor of empty words, Monica's son the doctor. The fate of the sinner is progressive alienation of the self from the soul and its divine source, the symbolic expression of which is the contract Dr. Faustus writes for himself, binding himself to Mephostophilis, making him a spirit no longer human, to become a ruler of the elements. Human beings are machines for self-deception. The power of habit over the mind is such, after all, that we do not merely choose wrongly but are compelled to repeat that choice on a daily and lifelong basis. It is not just that you commit suicide, but that you do so repeatedly, as Faustus is compelled by fear and pleasure to reaffirm his bargain again and again.

It would be difficult to overestimate the dissemination of this model of humanity as driven by irrational habit to mistake its death for its life. That is the mentality of Faustus's address to Helen, that substanceless shadow who "sucks forth" his soul when he asks her to "make [him] immortal with a kiss," and to whom he attributes all the beauties and powers of violent death, "brighter . . . than flaming Jupiter / When he appeared to hapless Semele" (*Dr. Faustus*, 5.2.99–100, 112–13).[45] The punishment toward which this mentality moves and that epitomizes it is given by Milton in the image of the devils transformed into serpents at their moment of triumph in book 10 of *Paradise Lost,* condemned to a parody of the fantasy with which Satan seduced Eve. Climbing a tree like that in Paradise,

> they fondly thinking to ally
> Their appetite with gust, instead of fruit
> Chewed bitter ashes, which the offended taste
> With spattering noise rejected: oft they assayed
> Hunger and thirst constraining, drugged as oft,
> With hatefulest disrelish writhed their jaws
> With soot and cinders filled; so oft they fell
> Into the same illusion.

(10.564–71)

The image is not directly from Augustine (though it alludes to Augustinian pears as well as Edenic apples), but it is, we might say, a digest of his definition of sinful habit: being driven by appetite to keep consuming the beautiful fruit that you know to be not even ash but the illusion of ash. On the Devil, Augustine quotes Psalm 104: "This is the dragon, whom you fashioned for him [man] to mock at" (*CG,* 11.15). "The good angels hold the others in derision" (11.34).

A literature of Augustinian evil will almost necessarily be tragicomic. Evil is tragic to the extent that it represents a choice of self-destruction, occasioned by *hamartia* in the sense of a mysterious tragic flaw very like *hubris—aversio* necessarily involves a turning to the self based on the creature's illusion of self-sufficiency from the creator—and resulting in tragic error. Sin, for Augustine, is a form of death. Every sinner's life is a little Aristotelean tragedy. At the same time, however, evil is comic to the extent that it represents a nonsensical choice in defiance of reason and experience, resulting in willful blindness and absurd, subhuman, mechanical behavior (Bergson's version of the comic). Sin, for Augustine, is a species of error. Every sinner's life is a grotesque. The fact that sin is also, as we have seen, parodic means that the grotesque will take the particular form of mock-heroic. "Pride imitates what is lofty" (*Conf.,* 2, 6, 13). Faustus, whose life is ruled by physical fear, responds to "Helen" by imagining himself as Paris before settling, more realistically given his coming fate, for Semele. Milton's Satan, retaining to the end the illusion that he is a demigod, eventually finds himself slithering through the grass trying to assure himself that a naked and unsuspecting girl represents a "foe not informidable" (*PL,* 9.486). Evil, after all, in addition to being humiliating, is invariably futile and self-punishing. From God's point of view, every fall is a fortunate fall, not least in contributing to the merriment of heaven, while ultimately and necessarily contributing to the good. Satan tempts Eve, in the long run to her salvation.

This sense of evil as, at most, seriocomic is a direct result of what is probably the most peculiar and disturbing element of Augustine's definition of sin: his tendency to see it, not as an ethical, but as an ontological problem. Sin is for him first and last an offense against being that is punished with deprivation of being, the dwindling of Satan from titan to toad, leading to the spiritual death that is damnation. The primary victim is always oneself. In the case of original sin, of course, because God by definition cannot be injured, Lucifer's crime can only be against himself. Sin is self-inflicted injury. Vice (*flagitium*), the damage that sin does to the self, comes first both in time and in priority; crime (*facinus*), the harm done to others, comes second. "When vices have emptied the soul and led it to a kind of extreme hunger, it leaps into crimes by means of which impediments to the vices may be removed or the vices themselves sustained" (*On Christian Doctrine,* 3.10.16).[46] By the same system of priorities, Augustine always privileges intention over effect in defining sin: "It is not the use of the things but the desire of the user that is culpable" (3.12.18). And the desire of the user is always at bottom the misdirected desire for being. Augustine does not steal pears for the sake of pears, but for the approval of his fellows—that is, for misdirected love—and for the theft itself, "a nothing" (*Conf.*, 2, 8, 16). Cruelty, to choose a further and more awkward example, is not an essential quality of evil but an accidental one. We injure or tyrannize others to feel powerful and thus real. Tamburlaine—in Marlowe's version, at least, a sufficiently orthodox example—does not necessarily enjoy killing people (he would save the virgins of Damascus if ritual allowed), but needs to do so to feel alive. You destroy to give yourself the pleasurable sense of not being destroyed and the consequent illusion of being indestructible. (The victim should never take it personally.)

This is an extreme form of what Stanley R. Hopper refers to as Augustine's "ontologizing of the contents of moral action."[47] Numerous objections to the contrary, Augustine does not minimize the effects of evil, as his account of Rome's cruelty and its punishment in the early books of *City of God* should remind us, but he does see them *as effects.*[48] Evil itself does not require them. The damage Faustus does to others is minimal compared with the damage he does to himself. In any case, God incorporates the effects of evil into his own benevolent plan, making evil, as Evans puts it, "irrelevant. . . . no more than a gnat-bite."[49] As Christopher Kirwan claims, given the doctrine of Original Sin, it is possible, indeed necessary, to argue that "no one is innocent," therefore, "all human suffering is punishment."[50]

Of course, the drama of salvation is inward, but the curiously indirect and predetermined shape of that drama is the product of Augustine's sense of the soul's fundamental deficiency. Leo C. Ferrari notes "an ever-increasing minimization of the role of man's free will in his own salvation, and . . . the growing importance of divine omnipotence" in the writings after *Confessions*.[51] While the vitiated soul nominally has free will, it is incapable due to the inheritance of Original Sin of exercising that freely. It is preconditioned to sin, even while it is held responsible for its sins. "Left to himself," Gilson observes, "man would have in his own right only the power of doing evil, deceit and sin."[52] To allow the soul any positive power to effect its own salvation would be to commit the heresy of the Pelagians by limiting God's omnipotence. All of Augustine's theodicy insists on God's absolute monopoly of power. The soul, created like the rest of the universe *ex nihilo,* exists apart from God, in the region of dissimilarity, but exists only as a function of God, only to the extent it is sustained by Him. "Unless you were within me, I would have no being at all" (*Conf.,* 1, 2, 2). In practice, Augustine is always liable to identify the soul with its own vitiation, and to treat it in itself as negative, save for the consciousness of its negativity. "Its life cannot be good except when God is active in it to produce what is good" (*CG,* 13.2). The condition of natural man "is rightly called death rather than life" (*CG,* 13.2) Anything good, real, alive in us is God's, everything else is ours. Vice, as we have seen, "empties" the soul, leaving that emotional hunger Augustine describes in the early books of *Confessions*. It follows, of course, that the soul cannot merit salvation; it cannot even, without the intervention of prevenient grace, effectively will its own salvation. Grace would not be grace—would not be gratuitous—if it were earned. The nearest the mind can come to earning it is to recognize its own need, to become a kind of thinking absence.

If the condition of the unaided soul is hunger, it is also enslavement. The first and defining use of freedom, as readers of *Paradise Lost* will know, was to destroy freedom. Readers of the *Confessions* will know that no complex of terms for sinfulness is more common in Augustine than enslavement, bondage, or confinement. We have freedom only in the sense that we are "free" to choose what we have been predestined to choose. If that choice is not compelled, it is also not escapable. Even within that grid, the power to choose good is not ours but the gift of God. Genuine free will, when granted, is the freedom to do God's will.

It is hard not to conclude that the soul is a kind of bystander in the process of its own salvation: officially responsible for its fate while having virtually no powers of its own, except the power to desire. God commands your love; God's grace enables your love; God supplies the energy that constitutes your love; God predestines whether you will be able to love; and, finally, God hardens your heart if you are not so predestined. Where, in all that, are "you"? The soul, in other words, exists primarily as a theoretical point through which divine love can flow back to itself. Otherwise, it is an empty house, "in ruins" (*Conf.*, 1, 5, 6). It is an object that may be worked on, but which cannot work itself. The delusion of a power of one's own over a soul with some independent existence is for Augustine, as later for Luther and Calvin, one of the surest signs of a state of sin.[53]

In terms of the self, however, that work takes more the form of demolition than of restoration. "The true latent knowledge I have of myself," as Charles Taylor puts it in summarizing Augustine's view, is "overlaid by all sorts of false images."[54] That structure of false consciousness, dead soul, what we might call *mauvaise foi*— and what Augustine himself calls his "old loves" (*Conf.* 8, 11, 26)— must be destroyed or cast off, to release whatever vital spirit remains within to genuine faith. Saul the Roman bureaucrat and Augustine the Roman rhetorician are reborn to a new system of relationships. The old Adam—and the discourse of desires that constituted him—must be killed. "I did not now seek a wife and had no ambition for success in this world" (*Conf.*, 8, 12, 30). Deconstruction of self is the necessary precondition for reconstruction.

Such a creature must, in effect, be saved in spite of itself. The first half of the *Confessions* is an elaborate (and hugely influential) exercise in the spiritual mock-heroic, in which the young Augustine, erring in every willful choice, is nonetheless brought back to salvation in the religion of his mother, "to the Christ whose sign marks him at birth."[55] The movement of the narrative, as Robert McMahon points out, is chiasmic: What appears to be escape is actually return. Going away is coming back. The rationale for the *Confessions* is, of course, Augustine's need to trace the obscure pattern of signs and promptings that have guided him through what he would like us to believe was sensual oblivion to Manichean heresy to skepticism and finally to a conversion occasioned, among other things, by Monica's dreams, Ponticianus's proleptic visit, and the voice of a child in a neighboring garden. In this pattern, every accident is providence, and every error turns out to have been a step toward truth. His conversion is the ironic fulfillment of the ambitions that prompted Patricius to invest in his son's education. It fulfills Monica's religious wish for Augustine's conversion even as it frustrates her earthly wish for grandchildren. You get what you need—even Patricius finally converts—whether you want it or not.

Augustine's God operates as a kind of Unironized Ironist, working through what Augustine called the "principle of contraries," in which "His virtues cure our vices. . . . born of a woman, He freed those deceived by a woman; . . . as a mortal He freed mortals; . . . in death He freed the dead" (*On Christian Doctrine*, I.14.13). Sin, as we have seen, is travesty, a parody of the good. God deals with evil by a further ironic inversion, an antiparody that, in its largest form, guarantees that the Fall of man is the salvation of man. Devils do God's work in spite of themselves. Within that system, God makes sin its own punishment: The lustful burn, Satan is condemned to being Satan, the nihilating are doomed to annihilation. In the system of thought that is still being elaborated by John Donne twelve hundred years later, one tree undoes another, the second Adam reverses the first, falling is rising, dying is living. Within Augustine's narrative, the theft of the pears is not only a mock-heroic replay of the original Fall, but also, as Kenneth Burke has described it, "a complete perversion, a perfect parody, of his religious motives. . . . a 'gratuitous' crime . . . motivated not by any merely worldly hope of profit [but by] a perfect parody of Brotherhood within the Church."[56] The effects of that episode are, of course, reversed by conversion under another tree. Thus the *ludus* of evil—in the sense of game, but also in the sense of theatrical play—is contained, exposed, and reversed within the *ludus* of God. Not least, it is exposed *as* theatrical, a system of illusions. Evil, after all, is parody that doesn't know it is parody: Satan thinks he is God's rival, not God's fool. "The Enemy is he who . . . by a perverted and twisted life, imitates you [i.e., God]" (*Conf.*, 10, 36, 59). Pride is the subject of comedy as well as of tragedy. Comic exposure, the humiliation of evil as absurdity, is fundamental to Augustine's cosmology.

THE AUGUSTINIAN CARNIVALESQUE

The conjunction of Augustine's ludic theology with the comic forms of carnival is a marriage made in heaven. The theology supplies the assumptions: that evil is absurd, not least in its inherent, self-regarding solemnity; that it is continually subject to the mockery of God; that human identity, especially that signified by rank, power, name, and other externals, is inherently illusory (and thus also subject to mocking exposure); that ordinary consciousness is false consciousness; and that nearly all secular life consists of avoidance activity generated by our resentment of our fallen condition of dependency and subordination. Festive activity provides that theology with the particularly appropriate comic mode—based on parodic inversion, degradation, subversive burlesque—that Bakhtin calls grotesque realism. Both deal with earthly power by denying its reality. For that matter, both deal with death in the same way. The two mentalities are linked, above all, by a shared impulse to the subversion of worldly pride and social identity in the name of undifferentiated community. Conversion, after all, saves the self by destroying the ego. God wants the same undifferentiated love from everyone. The very intertextuality of the *Confessions* subverts their egocentricity, reducing Augustine's unique experience in every case to the reenactment of universal models and greater originals, chiefly Adam and Paul.

The principle operating here is that my enemy's enemy is my friend. The carnal and the theological can make common cause against a common object of derision: the social identities that comprise the power structure of the *civitas terrena*. Hamlet-the-clown and Hamlet-the-Augustinian (each saying "the king is a thing. . . . of nothing") are both out to get the same Claudius, and both despise the same Rosencrantz and Guildenstern. That Augustinian and carnivalesque subversion operate in different keys, one toward the revelation of a spiritual core, the other toward a core of physical appetite, is entirely to my purpose. The conjunction of the two radically different definitions of man within a single process of deconstruction is precisely what complicates and enriches the process. The Wife of Bath's conscious revelation of the carnal center of her identity is also the unconscious revelation of her spiritual nonentity. The exposure of the animal core within Claudius's kingly robes is as important to Hamlet as, and inseparable from, the effort to locate the spiritual essence within his own. The latter search is, of course, conditioned by the fear that there may be nothing within himself except fear and appetite. The deconstruction of secular pretensions that Hamlet conducts in the graveyard—lawyer to skull, Alexander to earth—is both Augustinian and carnivalesque: degradation with a vengeance. And it is directly a product of the ambiguity that pervades Augustinian theology:

whether the center of the self is best described as a presence or an absence, a core that yearns or a yearning without a core. At the same time, that the two systems are antithetical as well as mirroring—one proposing to liberate the high by destroying the low, the other to liberate the low by destroying the high—means that the Augustinian carnivalesque can also be used to interrogate Augustine.[57] Clerical authority is as subject to degradation as secular authority.

Theologically inclined readers will have noticed by now that I am constructing a version of Augustine radically unlike the familiar one, "the first theorist of the Inquisition," as Peter Brown calls him.[58] It is my not entirely original belief, however, that that monologic and oppressive Augustine, the persecutor of the Donatists, the great legalist of the early Church, has obscured the subversive, questioning one: Augustine-the-Bishop, as it were, hiding Augustine-the-Skeptic. Augustine is, after all, the author of what John Cox rightly calls his great "demystifying survey of Roman history," *The City of God*.[59] The same Augustine who used the power of Empire to crush his doctrinal opponents[60] is also the man who asks what, in the absence of justice kingdoms are "but gangs of criminals on a large scale?" (*CG*, 4.4) In the same passage, he quotes with approval the pirate who, when asked by Alexander the Great what his purpose was "in infesting the sea," replied, "The same as yours in infesting the earth! But because I do it with a tiny craft, I'm called a pirate; because you have a mighty navy, you're called an emperor." "Where there is no justice," Augustine elsewhere argues, "there can be no commonwealth" (*CG*, 19.21). Now, a Christian state is, of course, a very different thing from a pagan one—its Christian status allows the possibility of justice (*CG*, 19.21)—but it is still (also) part of the *civitas terrena,* whose origin is "in self-love reaching the point of contempt for God" and "loving its own strength" (*CG*, 14.28).[61] That earthly government can be made instrumental to the Church[62] because it is necessary to the physical security of the *civitas Dei,* but it has no necessary sanctity of its own. The Christian state is a kind of usurpation of the *civitas terrena*—the double *ludus* in political action—and always liable to lapse because the earthly state's natural interests are at odds with those of the heavenly. Augustine, Markus writes, "perceived that the idea of a Christian society was a mirage" (*Sæculum,* 100). Herbert Deane concludes that "in Augustine's view . . . while this or that man who happens to be a ruler . . . may be pious and just, the state itself can never be truly just."[63] The very doctrine of general depravity that licenses coercive rule over an irremediably corrupt humanity also licenses dissent against a government that must share those vices it corrects probably because its origins are in self-love and the drive for power, in a superlative degree. The *civitas terrena* is always liable in Augustine to become—or revert to—the *civitas diaboli*.[64] In Luther's redaction of the doctrine, the world resolves simply into "two kingdoms . . . bitterly opposed to each other," one of Christ, the other of Satan, "the ruler of this world."[65]

I am certainly not arguing for a purely libertarian or purely ludic version of Augustine. I am, however, arguing for the presence of a politically skeptical and subversive strain within Augustinian theology, a way he could be read, available to those who wished to use it. Thus, John Cox cites Bartolomeo de Las Casas's resistance to slavery in the New World as inspired by Augustine (*Dramaturgy of Power*, 3–12) and analyzes the privileging of "disenfranchisement and social deprivation" (22) in the mystery cycles as evidence of "an important residual tradition" (11) of Augustinian social criticism, pitting *potentia humilitatis* against the *libido dominandi* typically represented by Herod. Thus, Alasdair MacIntyre cites the proliferation of *quaestiones* in the margins of medieval manuscripts—creating dialogic texts—as well as the dissent of Abelard as demonstrating "the large possibilities of radical intellectual dissension even within the constraints imposed by an Augustinian framework."[66] Romand Coles distinguishes, as I wish to do, between the "polyphonous" Augustine, "who views the world [as] the infinitely rich incarnation of God's Word"; and the intolerant founder of an "imperialist church"; between the open, dialectical enquirer and the restrictive legalist.[67] Markus, who analyzes Augustine's authoritarianism in authoritative detail, can also write that "'political Augustinianism' is, of its nature, politically radical" because it assesses all human values "in eschatalogical terms," measuring lower versus infinitely higher, temporary versus final (*Sæculum*, 168).

Augustine's theology necessarily views the *civitas terrena* from an alienated position: "God's City lives in this world's city, as far as its human element is concerned; but it lives there as an alien sojourner" (*CG*, 18.1.761), a *civitas peregrina*. As resident expatriates, of course, you owe gratitude to the city's protection and obedience to its laws, but not reverence to its leaders. You make use of "earthly and temporal things like a pilgrim in a foreign land, who does not let himself be taken in by them or distracted." However comfortable the Christian community's accommodation, "it leads a life of captivity in this earthly city" (*CG*, 19.17). You must live in it without being of it. You must not take part in its self-mystification.

This combination of alienation and obligation licenses carnival as well as dissent because it mirrors the political position of the humble in a hierarchic society. Both parties—who may in practice be the same party—are liable to see the unreality as well as the injustice of their earthly rulers. The point at which those rulers lose the protective legitimacy of their status as divine agents—the point, say, at which Claudius replaces Hamlet's father—is the point at which they can be seen as merely "criminals on a large scale," kings of nothing. In such a situation, we might say, theology looks down on their bald heads while carnival looks up their regal robes. Demystification necessarily precedes defenestration. At the very end of the *Institutes,* Calvin, whose Augustinian doctrine of depravity and grace has led him to just the authoritarian conclusions it did Augustine, suddenly turns from preaching the absolute submission of private citizens to the unjust rulers they are invited to consider as God's scourges, to preaching the equally absolute duty of magistrates to rebel against the same scourges (4.20.30–31). To convey the full vehemence of this passage, the editors of the standard English edition cite Calvin's commentary on Daniel (Lect., 30, on Daniel 6:22), where citizens faced with such rulers are advised "to spit on their heads" [Latin: *conspuere in ipsorum capita*]: an example, if ever there was one, of the Augustinian and the carnivalesque coming together with a rhetorical bang.[68]

To recognize that the submissive and the skeptical, the authoritarian and the ludic coexist in Augustine is to rescue him from the monolithic form imposed on him by Robertsonian criticism, with its habitual pursuit of a totalized version of "medieval attitudes and opinions which . . . account in part for the peculiar character of medieval literature."[69] As medievalists will know, that single body of opinions, producing a single "peculiar character" uniting a vast and apparently disparate literature—uniting, say, *Troilus and Criseyde,* Andreas Capellanus, and *The Miller's Tale*—nearly always turns out to be Augustine or Augustine as translated into legislative authority by Robertson's version of "the" medieval church. This formulation, of course, ironically mirrors Bakhtin's rigidly monologic version of official medieval religion. Augustine, however, spoke with many voices and could be read in many ways for many purposes. "Complete uniformity of opinion," as he himself realized, "was a privilege only of angels."[70] One of those voices gave rise to the tradition of destabilizing skepticism I call the Augustinian carnivalesque.

In the prototype I am constructing, the Augustinian carnivalesque enacts the subversion of a world that is apparently ordered, unitary, hierarchic, and explicitly known, as well as the type of personality defined by and dependent on that order (for example, Ophelia). Both the state and the self are revealed to be disordered, multiplex, indefinite, unknown. Ordering authority is subverted along with the security of an apparently stable world. Hyperion is displaced by the satyr; the mad Ophelia displaces the sane.

One way of figuring that process is through the loss or subversion of figures of idealized stability, coherence, and authority: the young Hamlet who was "the rose of the fair state"; Gawain the Knight of the Pentangle; Faustus the idealized public scholar, the master of all the fundamental disciplines; Hieronimo the chief justice; even perhaps St. Jerome the figure of clerical authority invoked when Jankyn, the mercenary defrocked priest, reads Jerome's works to Alisoun. Such individual cases reflect larger, social processes of loss: the transition from the quasi-Edenic Denmark of the past to the disordered masque-world of the present; from the unchallenged Camelot at the beginning of *Sir Gawain and the Green Knight* to the diminished one at the end; from the communitarian past represented by the approved Canterbury pilgrims (Parson, Plowman, Knight, Clerk) to the world of predatory specialization represented by the rest; from the (ferociously unreal) hierarchies of military aristocracy—the world of Bajazeth—to the world of Tamburlaine; or from the apparently restored Spain at the beginning of *The Spanish Tragedy* to the bloodbath at the end. Indicative of that change are the figures of diminished, ironized authority who preside over the endings: Fortinbras, Callapine, Jankyn the conquered husband and scholar, Wagner the inheritor of Faustus or the scholars who find his remains, an Arthur who has been measured against Bertilak and Morgan.

These figures register a change from Authority to "authority." Within the text, carnival release is permanently subversive. When a character steps outside the conventional discourse he or she comes to see it as not a world, but only a discourse, though she or he may later come to see that discourse as a logocentric necessity. Gawain cannot restore the identity he brought into the games and tests of Hautdesert because that rigid identity depended on a fundamental unawareness of his own deficiency. To enter the world of carnival subversion is to become aware of your "self" as mask or role, something detachable from and at odds with the fluidity within you. The inheritance of Augustine guarantees a concern with subjectivity and with the complex relation of the protean self to its external masks that cuts across the customary separation of "medieval" and "Renaissance." When Augustine imagines the contents of the mind in book 10 of *Confessions,* he imagines wandering in "the fields and vast palaces of memory" (10, 8, 12). "I myself cannot grasp the totality of what I am" (10, 8, 15). Public identity, let alone public authority, depends on the illusion that one can grasp the approximate totality of what one is and at least the general outline of what others are. That belief in boundaries and definitions will not survive the experience of carnival, any more than it will survive an Augustinian interrogation.

Augustinian carnival does not lead where C. L. Barber thought festivity customarily did, through release to clarification, but through release to a clearer sense of uncertainty.[71] The texts I deal with in the chapters that follow present different forms of chiasmic narrative or ironic quest: confined, circular, self-reversing movement. A chiasmus is, of course, a rhetorical figure in which the order of the second term reverses that of the first. There are few larger examples of this figure than the relation of *Tamburlaine, part 1* (the hero's ascent to the illusion of freedom) to *part 2* (his descent into futility). Like Alisoun he moves by outer enrichment to inner impoverishment. In these texts the pursuit of the truth of the self customarily leads to dissolution of the self as the pursuit of certainty leads to skepticism. That, of course, is the movement of Augustine up to the point before his conversion. That the next stage of that process—the stage reached in books 7 and 8 of *Confessions*—is not reached in any of these texts, except in the parodic form of Alisoun's conversion to love or in the subverted form of Hamlet's discovery of providential faith, may indicate that skepticism toward Augustine himself is also a constant that cuts across the separation between medieval and Renaissance. Augustine, for example, writes necessarily from the standpoint of the saved addressing the savable. The comic structure of the *Confessions* depends on its assertion of a vast machinery of benevolence dedicated to saving Augustine (and Monica, Patricius, Ponticianus, Alypius, et al.) regardless of desert. Genuinely gratuitous grace must seem to human reason as absurdly arbitrary as evil appears to Augustine. It is possible, as Marlowe demonstrates in *Dr. Faustus* to write a strictly Augustinian play from the standpoint of the damned: a textbook illustration of the anti-Pelagian argument that natural man is unable to will his own salvation without prevenient grace. The absurdity of evil looks both very different and eerily familiar when seen from within.

In the chapters that follow, I look at a sequence of texts that reproduce the kind of deconstructive and political tension that we see in *Dr. Faustus* between interrogation and reinforcement: a carnivalesque mentality that sees through official order but still, like Augustine-the-Bishop, affirms the need for what it subverts. I have intentionally selected works from different formal genres because, if I am correct, the patterns of the Augustinian carnivalesque should be apparent in a romance like *Sir Gawain and the Green Knight* and a mock-romance like *The Wife of Bath's Prologue and Tale,* in Shakespearian tragedy, in Marlovian tragicomedy, and in Miltonic epic. I have also selected my texts with a conscious intention of smudging the lines that at least used to be drawn between medieval and Renaissance. The questions Augustine asks (and the carnivalesque implies) about identity, authority, knowledge, and self-knowledge are neither soluble nor temporary. The Gawain-Poet and Chaucer interrogate, for example, the relationship between subjectivity and social identity, or the social and artistic construction of the self, in terms very similar to those employed by Shakespeare and Marlowe. The privative definition of evil underlies the Pardoner and the Wife just as it does Barabas and Claudius or Milton's Satan. The Reformation did not, after all, get rid of Augustine so much as reinstate him. On grace and privation and politics, Luther and Calvin are explicitly rewriting the anti-Pelagian Augustine.[72] As any reader of the *Confessions* knows and as critics like Lee Patterson and David Aers have recently argued, subjection is not a discovery of the Renaissance but the necessary inheritance of a thousand years of Augustinian discourse.[73]

At no point, however, do I wish to say that all Elizabethan discourse was "Augustinian" or that all Ricardian literature was necessarily preoccupied with the tension between fluid subjectivity and rigid social identity. I am identifying a tradition that runs through these periods; I am not attempting to reduce them to that tradition. I am, in short, constructing out of the available material a genre of my own defining that crosses barriers of period and genre. If the scope of this work and my wit allowed, I would extend this line to include, among others, *The Dunciad, Clarissa* and *Mansfield Park, Peer Gynt,* and *The Waste Land.* I suggest in occasional asides and digressions how these extensions might work. My intention is to create a paradigm, however, not to provide a comprehensive history, and so I should make clear now that this project is not primarily historicist, whether new or old. I am looking at certain major texts and the way they cross and flout barriers of genre and period. I am concerned to show what Augustine says about earthly selves and powers and to indicate that this body of thought was at least residually present in the culture of fourteenth- to seventeenth-century England. My concern, however, is to reveal a pattern that recurs in these texts, rather than to create, in the manner of Cox or Greenblatt, a detailed picture of that culture as a whole. Formally, if not politically, therefore, my project is closer to that of Jonathan Dollimore in *Radical Tragedy* than it is to Cox's.

Like Cox, however, I sugggest that theologically the Renaissance represents less a radical break than a modification of an Augustin- ian discourse. While the assertion of a fundamental ideological continuity is implicit in my choice of texts, I have chosen to empha- size different aspects of the carnivalesque in different works: two significantly variant cases of the subversion of social identity in *The Wife of Bath's* text and *Sir Gawain and the Green Knight;* the comedy of appetite and power lust in Marlowe; the use of carnival as a weapon of political subversion in revenge tragedy; and the commercial aspects of the carnivalesque in *Antony and Cleopatra.* I do not, in short, regard this tradition as preaching the same mes- sage—say, the preferability of *caritas* to *cupiditas*—over and over, but as applying a certain body of comic practice in light of a certain (large, complex) body of theological assumptions.

When Bakhtin describes the character of woman in Gallic carni- val he might be—in a sense, he is—describing the Wife of Bath:

> Womanhood is shown in contrast to the limitations of her partner (hus- band, lover, or suitor); she is a foil to his avarice, jealousy, stupidity, hypocrisy, bigotry, sterile senility, false heroism, and abstract idealism. The woman of the Gallic tradition is the bodily grave of man. She represents in person the undoing of pretentiousness, of all that is fin- ished, completed, and exhausted.
>
> (240)[74]

It is not merely that Alisoun's five husbands neatly share among them the adjectives describing the male or that the Wife makes herself fairly literally their "bodily grave." Her text is a remarkable conflation of the varieties of carnival inversion: female lecturing and dominating male, both in her narrative and in her dealings with the pilgrim audience; the *illiterata* triumphing over the doctors, the laity over the clergy; flesh impeaching spirit; the female mock- bishop displacing St. Jerome; and Chaucer's particular addition: the character impugning her authors.[75] Since those authors are predominantly clerical—Jerome and Paul chief among them—Ali- soun's rebellion inevitably figures a larger one: the creature interrogating the Author of creation. The first auctoritee she questions in her *Prologue* is Christ (2.10–25).

The fact that Alisoun is apparently sterile, not "the inexhaustible vessel of conception" Bakhtin goes on to describe after the passage above, leads to Augustine by a different route. The same pattern that interrogates official authority can be used to interrogate the carnivalesque identification of life with the bodily and instinctive. Both the *Prologue* and *Tale* use a multilayered version of the chiasmic *ludus,* in which the pursuit of life (carnal) is the pursuit of death (carnal and spiritual); in which the accumulation of material wealth produces spiritual impoverishment; in which the pursuit of earthly freedom through power and wealth is itself a form of enslavement (it is what produces the "wo that is in mariage"). The same narratives will yield other, nearly opposite readings, however. As critics have been noting for years, the Wife's pursuit of power can be seen as an unconscious pursuit of love, rewarded in spite of itself in both *Prologue* and *Tale,* a sexualized, grotesque version of heavenly reward. In both happy endings, Alisoun and her Hag become grotesque parodies of grace, bestowing unearned love, to which Jankyn's love provides a parody of the Church's blessing. As usual, the Augustinian carnivalesque can be read in opposing ways: Misdirected love is still, of course, love; a perverted sign of the survival of the soul, but a sign nonetheless. Typically, I believe, the carnivalesque works as carnival—to validate the physical—but also as anticarnival. As I try to show in the following chapters, that simple ambivalence can produce texts of notorious complexity.

2

"Vanysshed Was This Daunce, He Nyste Where": Alisoun's Absence in the *Wife of Bath's Prologue and Tale*

THE carnivality of the occasion of the *Canterbury Tales*—the holiday tale-telling game, festive activity presided over by a mock-king and leading to a promised feast—creates a complex game of category subversion and assertion that is the primary cause of the notorious and presumably endless critical debate about the character and the ontological status of the pilgrim narrators.[1] The pilgrims are at once present as their professional selves (a Monk, a Prioress) and on holiday from those selves ("Huberd," "Eglantyne"). Each is present to the others as a professional type, but also—potentially, at least—as an unknown individual who happens to occupy that type or play that part. Even when you insist absolutely on your identity with the part—as the Parson does—your insistence is necessarily a theatricalization of the category. In the Parson's case, the ostentatiously impersonal preaching manner of the "Tale" is clearly at odds with the colloquial vehemence of the speaker's prologue. The sermon is what you offer as an alternative to "'rum, ram, ruf,' by lettre" (10, 43).[2]

A pilgrim's estate is, obviously, present to us and to the pilgrim audience primarily as performance, something that is, to one degree or another, put on. You may hide behind it, as the Reeve does when insisting that the Miller has attacked him for being a carpenter; you may flaunt it, as the Miller does his churlishness; you may distance yourself from it, as the Pardoner does by creating a comic performance around his customary performance; you may reassert it, as the Monk tries to do with his catalogue of tragedies. In the case of the Prioress, you may shore it against your pretty ruins, offering theatricalized feminine piety in the face of the other pilgrims' (Harry's, Chaucer-the-pilgrim's) insistence on treating you as a glamorous lady, and still more in the face of the fragmentation evident in your portrait, with its mixture of affectations, vanities, misplaced details (local French in place of Latin), and problematical pieties (a passion for small animals). The performance offers a semblance of coherence at least as obviously as it does a semblance of piety.

Although the Prioress's motives are unknown, she seems to be reacting, also, to a general subversion of authority marked, for example, by the displacement of priest by publican as spiritual guide and by the substitution of tavern for shrine as the ultimate object of pilgrimage. Within the carnival game of tale telling, role-based authority is regularly renounced by those who ought to have it—most vividly, by the Pardoner—and assumed by those who do not. Wives preach, Franklins discourse on nobility (as, for that matter, do hags). As any reader of the *Tales* knows, these performances and assumptions regularly hint at unrevealed motives and relationships: What is the private relation of Pardoner and Summoner? Or the personal history, if any, of Reeve and Miller? What is the "story behind" the story of the Merchant's marriage or the Wife's missing fifth husband? As with the question of the Pardoner's true anatomy, however, these mysteries are invoked in order *not* to be solved. The regularity with which these lacunae occur is what primarily drives critics like C. David Benson to try to escape the whole fiction of the pilgrim tellers into an impersonal "drama of style."[3]

Rather than destroy the structure Chaucer has so elaborately created, I offer a more conservative suggestion: that carnival in the *Canterbury Tales* functions precisely to enigmatize character, to open a gap between performer and performance, between private subject and public role. Generally speaking, each pilgrim exists not only as category, but also as principle of resistance to (and subversion of) that category, one that manifests itself as a failure to sustain role (the Merchant, for example), as fragmentation into multiple roles (the Monk as hunter, sensualist, outrider, contemplative), or as a refusal to accept categorization (the Franklin or, more aggressively, the Wife). As has long been recognized, the illusion of "personal" drama in the *Tales* is a function of this conflict: the tendency of each pilgrim's performance to separate "I" from what "I play." Thus, the Clerk puts on the conventions of his Petrarchan text while also insisting on his role as a dialogic glossator who fills its margins with *quæstiones,* at once enacting the Tale and resisting it. The Franklin insists that he is *not* the sort of person who understands the rhetoric he then uses. The Pardoner claims to be the negation of the preacher he plays, the non-presence who performs only by rote. The "I" that remains can be imagined simultaneously as plenitude of energy (the carnivalesque sense) or absence of *ens* (the Augustinian sense).

This dynamic is nowhere more evident than in the performance of that most carnivalesque of pilgrims, the Wife of Bath. I want to concentrate on her performance for the rest of this chapter, trusting that the implications of the paradigm I am constructing for other performances in the *Tales* will be apparent or at least implied. To cover them all would require another and different book from this one.[4]

There Is No Single Key

Anyone who has studied the criticism on the *Wife of Bath's Prologue and Tale* will know the sinking sensation that attends the appearance of yet another version of the one true Alisoun followed, at the requisite two paces, by the one true Chaucer. Thus, Alisoun the heretical exegete is shadowed by Chaucer the Pauline moralist (for D. W. Robertson), just as Alisoun the battered wife is attended by Chaucer the sympathetic humanist (for Robert Burlin). For Kenneth Oberembt, Alisoun the "temperate" social critic is followed by a Chaucer who is likewise, while for Sheila Delany an antifeminist Alisoun is followed by a rapist Chaucer. In recent criticism, Alisoun-as-feminist-spokeswoman has tended to appear with a Chaucer who is the precursor either of John Stuart Mill (Long) or Luce Irigaray (Barrie Strauss), not to mention Lacan (Louise Fradenburg, of course).[5] John Alford is being only marginally less modest than the norm by announcing that when the Wife is seen as Rhetoric and the Clerk as Logic, "the two characters immediately become coherent *in every detail*."[6] The details this reading fails to explain include, by the way, the name Alisoun and the place Bath.

You can group these readings in several ways: profeminist versus antifeminist (Marjorie Malvern versus Bernard Huppe), for example; or psychological (Burlin) versus archetypal (Robertson).[7] You can divide the Wife's critics usefully into those who wish to remove her from history into the realm of permanent types, as Alford does, and those who wish to put her back again: Mary Carruthers, Dorothy Colmer, David Aers.[8] Even feminist critics can be separated into those who think Chaucer is on their side (e.g., Peggy Knapp) and those who think he isn't (Sheila Delany).[9]

All of these approaches, valuable as they are, share a tendency to reduce one of the most ambiguous, "dialogic" texts in our literature to a monologic "right" reading. She's good or she's bad, she's smart or she's dumb, Chaucer's for her or against her. The text is constructed as either . . . or, not both . . . and. Thus Robertson, for example, announces that "Alisoun is not a 'character' at all . . . but an elaborate iconographic figure."[10] I call this the fallacy of the single key (one to which Robertson's version of Augustinian criticism is particularly prone: using the allegory to "solve" the text), which says that Alisoun must hail either from Scripture or from Bath, when, manifestly, she hails from both.[11] Rhetorically at least, she is the Wife of Both. Given the enormous critical controversy surrounding this text, it is remarkable how few critics acknowledge its full complexity. With the honorable exceptions of Lee Patterson, Peggy Knapp, and Barrie Strauss, critics usually approach it in the hope of finding a single, simplifying answer.[12] The uncertainties of the text need to be confronted, however, not eliminated. Reductive answers are precisely what it rules out of play. One of the dangers of a single key, of course, is locking yourself in (or out). Once we have recognized, for example, that the hag is obviously a projection of the Wife, we then have to notice that—as someone who denounces property, covetousness, and social privilege—she is also *not* the Wife's representative. What appears to be identity is also opposition. Alisoun's advocate is also her accuser.

To make some comprehensive sense of this text, we have to recognize that Chaucer has provided an extraordinary number of keys for an extraordinary number of wicket gates: Jerome and Walter Map, the wool trade, the Samaritan woman, birthmarks and horoscopes, an analogue in Gower, Pauline doctrines of marriage, and the very different marital customs of the land-holding classes of fourteenth-century England, not to mention enough hints of a murder mystery to entertain Beryl Rowland and D. J. Wurtele.[13] If Chaucer meant to create a single key for all these references (and many more), he has been remarkably unsuccessful. We should remember that when the knight of Alisoun's *Tale* asks his simple question, he gets any number of more or less right answers before the hag gives him one general enough to encompass all the rest. We might also remember Susan Crane's warning that "when we make the Wife of Bath coherent, she becomes too easy to dismiss."[14] We should not deal with category subversion by restoring the categories.

We also have to recognize that as a character the Wife is remarkably incomplete. Virtually, no part of her story is whole or trustworthy. Is Jankyn alive? How many Jankyns were and are there?

Was there ever a second Alisoun? Who was the first one's "dame"? The list is too long and familiar to need repeating. Far more of Alisoun is absent than is present. I think we have to take seriously Marshall Leicester's proposition that "there is no Wife of Bath," and not use that as a modish way of saying that she is a fictional character, so that we can get back to the business of discovering her motives and rhetorical purposes (as even Leicester himself does).[15] Alisoun is a text whose salient feature is incompleteness. If that text can be said to be "about" any single thing, that would be absence: the absence of other characters (husbands, children, parents); the absence of the class of people for whom Alisoun seems to speak, other women; the absence of Alisoun herself. As Patterson reminds us—in the best single essay on the *Wife of Bath's Prologue and Tale*—Midas's wife (3.951–82) was once, in Alisoun's Ovidian source, his barber.[16] We have to look for the man who isn't there in order to understand the ambiguity of an apparently simple reference. The barber is not the only one who disappears. Alisoun's knight, at the point where his life is about to be settled, has a ludicrously perfunctory and apparently pointless vision: "He saugh upon a daunce go / Of ladyes foure and twenty, and yet mo" (991–92), who disappear, leaving the hag, who is herself an afterimage of a vanished Lady Ragnell and who in turn will vanish, leaving the beauty who is the solution to (or figment of) the knight's desires. This text is about who and what isn't there at least as much as it is about what is. "Vanysshed was this daunce, he nyste where" (996). We would do well to ask why disappearance—whether of dancing ladies, hags, or Jankyns—is so central a feature of Alisoun's performance. The absence of a real woman in or behind this text, I argue, is the single most significant fact about it.

THERE IS NO ALISOUN

Alisoun's peculiar status as a metafictional puzzle has been widely, if only recently, recognized. Carolyn Dinshaw puts the basic problem as simply as I could wish: "The Wife . . . presents in herself a perfect image of a text"; her "fantasy of the perfect marriage [being] analogous, in her *Prologue* and *Tale,* to the perfect glossing of a text."[17] Susan Crane calls her "a fiction who tells a fiction."[18] Dinshaw's observation, especially when it comes near the head of an essay titled "Eunuch Hermeneutics," may sound slightly more original and impressive than it is. The burden of Jill Mann's argument in *Chaucer and Medieval Estates Satire* (1973) is that the Canterbury pilgrims have their sources less in literal reality than in satiric types, not in Millers but in texts about Millers.[19] More specifically, P. M. Kean has traced the originals of both the Pardoner and the Wife of Bath to the allegorical figures of Faux Semblant and La Vieille in Jean de Meun's sections of the *Roman de la Rose*.[20] Fourteen years ago, Robert Burlin located Alisoun's exact textual source: "when [she] describes in detail the contents of Jankyn's treasured volume, we have reconstructed the genesis of her *Prologue*. . . . When she attacks its three pages, it is as if she were trying to extinguish the reality of which she is made."[21] In my own metaphor, the Wife is a kind of Moebius strip: a fictional character originating in an imaginary book (made nevertheless from real authors: Jerome, Theophrastus, Walter Map, Matheolus) that is also an object within her own narrative, against which she can launch an attack that amounts to the attempt to refute her own existence: what we might call a postemptive strike.[22]

What Burlin fails to address, however, is why, of all the pilgrims, this one should so pointedly and Pirandellianly signal her textuality, her status as one character in search of six authors. What has the puzzle of the Wife's reality to do with the politics of her *Prologue*, her notoriously ambiguous relationship to the priestly antifeminism that she seems at once to parody, attack, and embody? The solution to this puzzle lies, I think, in the solution to a relatively simple paradox: Alisoun is a *lusus naturae* of a common literary kind: a woman born of man, conspicuously without a mother or daughters, but with many fathers, nearly all of them—from St. Jerome to Jean de Meun—priests. She is the summation of a tradition of men writing through—at, about, and especially over—women, condensed and dramatized by another man (Chaucer) who must, literally or figuratively, have performed her. In the tradition of carnival transvestism, she is a drag act, a female impersonation, a "creature of the male imagination."[23] That is one reason why so much about her—the spurs, the hat like a "targe" (I.471), the Martian/Venerian horoscope—suggests androgyny. She is what men produce when they think about women. As Thomas Hahn puts it, "the discourse of 'speaking Woman,' as it unravels in the Wife's Prologue, is, like Woman itself, a masculine fabrication."[24] As a woman, however, she does not exist. It is therefore beside the point to treat her as a real woman, no matter whether you try to make a case for her as a feminist heroine (Strauss, Malvern, or the 1989 version of Peggy Knapp[25]), a battered wife (Burlin), or a *momento mori* (William Blake).

It is, in fact, a mistake to try to treat Alisoun as either a consistent emblem or a consistent character, since "she" is an unstable projection of male fear and desire. To alter Crane's formulation, she is a fantasy who tells a fantasy, the characteristic mode of which is dreamlike exaggeration linked to dreamlike transitions (maiden turning into hag turning into maiden). The *Wife of Bath's Prologue and Tale* is one of the last and greatest of Chaucer's dream-vision poems. The subject of that dream is not woman, but male sexual obsession and the anxieties, guilts, and fears that attend them. Consistently throughout the text, appeal gives way without transition to threat, seduction to repulsion, advertisement to consumer warning. That process continues to the end of the *Tale,* where the assertion of mutual submission and harmony is followed immediately by the *Playgirl* fantasy of "housbondes meeke, yonge, and fresshe abedde" (3.1259), and the murderous curse against "nygardes" (1263–64). The *vagina dentata,* of which Alisoun is literature's most famous example, is not a fact of nature but of male fantasy. The Pauline version of that fantasy is the subject and source of Chaucer's text. The women, as Conrad's Marlow says in a related case, are out of it.

As a character, Alisoun presents us not so much with a psychology as a table of contents.[26] A glance through the notes in Robinson will remind you of what I mean: an opening imitated from the *Roman de la Rose* (12802ff.), followed by an argument with male authority and Pauline Christianity imitated from Jerome *Adversus Jovinianum* but incorporating extensive quotation from John 2:1 (3.11) and 4:6 (14), and from 1 Corinthians 7:9 (46), 7:39 (47), and 7:2 (51).[27] As most readers will already know, Alisoun's description of life with her three old husbands is a pastiche of Eustace Deschamps's *Miroir de Mariage* (e.g., at 3.198–202, 233, 235–47, etc.) and his source, the *Lamentations of Matheolus* (the source of 129–30),[28] plus Theophrastus's *Liber Aureolus de Nuptiis* (e.g., at 235–47 again, 248–75, 282–92, 293–302, etc.), topped with lashings of the *Roman* (227–28, 229, etc.). The Wife's sexual history draws heavily on that of La Vieille in the *Roman* (e.g., 503–14), but, according to Robinson, may also derive from the history of "la mere" in the *Miroir.* By the time we reach Jankyn's "book of wikked wyves" at 3.685, Chaucer is ready to name his sources because Alisoun is about to burn them. The character, having found her authors and found them not to her liking, tries to destroy them, an attempt whose futility is measured by her continuing dialogue with them through Jankyn or with Jankyn through them.

At least one part of her complaint is, of course, famously cogent:

> if wommen hadde writen stories,
> As clerkes han withinne hire oratories,
> They wold han writen of men moore wikkednesse
> Than al the mark of Adam may redresse.
>
> 3.693–96

That women have not written—and, even in this case, are not writing—the stories is precisely the point of Chaucer's own version of the book of wicked wives.

The apparent exception to this rule actually confirms it. Jankyn's book of wicked wives does include "Helowys / That was abbesse nat far from Parys" (3.677–78), and Jill Mann has recently argued for Heloise's *dissuasio*—"the only other case in medieval literature where anti-feminist satire is uttered by a woman"—as a major source for Alisoun's text.[29] The *dissuasio* was in fact incorporated into chapter 7 of Abelard's *Historia calamitatum* because it is addressed to him and later incorporated into the *Roman de la Rose* (lines 8729–8801).[30] Like Alisoun's, Heloise's text is a tissue of paraphrases from masculine anti-feminism: Paul, Jerome, Theophrastus, Cicero cited by Jerome, Seneca. To teach her teacher, an inversion very like the one Alisoun attempts, Heloise has to borrow masculine authority. Heloise, in other words, is a striking example of the way actual women are incorporated into this discourse in a way that deprives them of a voice while seeming to give them one. Jerome, we might say, programs her text; Abelard processes (not to mention, glosses) it; Jankyn reads the printout. Alisoun doesn't read it because she can't. Jankyn owns the book that encompasses the discourse and thus takes, literally and figuratively, the voice of the only woman in it. The most Heloise can do is to inflect Jerome by repeating him in a context that puts pointedly ironic quotation marks around his text. We might well assume, as Mann argues (54) that many medieval readers did, that the mere fact of a woman selflessly using his arguments against herself undermines those arguments. In subverting the authorities that comprise them, both Heloise's text and Alisoun's are proof well before the fact of Irigaray's argument that women are compelled to mimic and alter male discourse (not to mention Bakhtin's argument for the superiority of dialogic texts to monologic).

Like Jerome's antagonist Jovinian, Alisoun represents a conquered and silenced enemy: in her case, women, who are the subject of a debate from which they are generally excluded, present not as text but pretext.[31] Alisoun, in turn, imitates—in suitably grotesque, carnivalesque form—the authoritarianism of male authority, its ability to exclude other voices. Her husbands are dead, thus silenced and incorporated into her discourse, as Jovinian has been incorporated into Jerome's. She not only speaks for them, with the ambiguous power of mimicry to annihilate the subject even while insisting on its prior existence, but also reenacts the annihilation. She hasn't killed them so much as displaced them because that is what mimicry does. She eats their words. As the antifeminist clerics have appropriated the voices of women (and Chaucer singles out those, like Jean and Theophrastus, who mimic women), so Alisoun appropriates theirs in a kind of verbal trans-vestism. Her elaborately repeated "seistow" (270, 273, 292 et al.) conflates a whole world of male discourse, neatly blending her "olde dotard shrewe[s]" (291) of husbands with the old dotard clerks who are the source of their purported opinions. At the same time, of course, what "thou" sayest is literally nothing becaue Ali-soun says it for you. The old husbands become by-standers at their own marriages. Of all her husbands only Jankyn, briefly, gets to speak in his own voice.

This Text Is Not about Women

In the process of what Knapp calls reappropriation, however, Alisoun necessarily speaks for her clerical enemies as well as for herself.[32] Both the accuser and defender of women, she creates a closed circuit of discourse that effectively excludes other voices, including those of the women for whom she claims to speak. She silences the Prioress and the Second Nun even more thoroughly than she does the Friar and the Pardoner. She is large, she contains multitudes, but only at the cost of turning them all into versions of herself. There is no woman in her *Prologue* who is not named Alisoun; no woman in her *Tale* has a name at all. The "dame" who taught her to invent dreams (576) might be her otherwise unmentioned mother, but could equally well be La Vieille, Ali-soun's literary mother.[33] Throughout her monologue, in fact, there is a remarkable tendency for characters to flow together: the three old husbands with one another; Jankyn with the other clerks from whom he derives his opinions; the fourth husband, who makes Alisoun jealous, with Alisoun, who makes him jealous; Alisoun with her "gossib" Alisoun. The two women, if there are two, talk exclusively about (the first) Alisoun: The other exists only as a mirror of the self. The Wife's purchasing of love when she is old mirrors the husbands of her youth; the behavior of her last two husbands mirrors her own youthful behavior. She sells her "bele chose" when young; she buys Jankyn's "sely instrument" when old. The two sexes are economically and psychologically interchangeable, however much Alisoun's version of reality may seem to insist on their essential opposition. Like other carnivalesque depictions of woman, Alisoun-the-act seems to reinforce sexual difference by exaggeration even as she, more fundamentally, subverts it by reducing it to ostentatiously self-ironizing performance. Trust the (Lacanian) tale, not the teller.[34]

Other people exist as mirrors or instruments for the entertainment of the self. Most usefully, perhaps, they exist as audience. The pilgrims, like the old husbands, sit quietly, serving as the pretext for Alisoun to talk to Alisoun about Alisoun. Those who attempt to become participants, like the Friar and the Pardoner, are ruthlessly put down. The other Alisoun knew the Wife's "privetee / Bet than oure parisshe preest" (531–32). Only your mirror-image knows your secrets; the male authority is out of the loop.

Alisoun's argument with auctoritee thus becomes remarkably self-canceling: two mirroring examples of Keats's egotistical sublime. She talks to herself about the truth of her own discourse and denies the existence of other truths. Twenty-four ladies vanish, leaving one hag. The one swallows the many. The multitude of answers women give to the question of what they want is displaced by the one answer given by the hag, who may not be human herself. Alisoun, a digest of male authority, silences women by the simple tactic of claiming to speak for them. In the process, she confirms what men say about women because she *is* what men say about women. Because she is herself a text, there is no experience in her history with which she could refute authority that is not itself derived from authority. Manifestly, her experience can neither affirm nor deny what the books say because, being the product of those books, she can have only the "experience" in them. The loop is closed. Authority, at least when it is male authority ruling on female experience, is an autoclarificatory system (as Anne Elliot points out to Captain Harville). Texts confirm other texts, whose authors in turn have become authorities by generalizing from their own (asserted, unverifiable, lost) experience, a process Alisoun and the Merchant will both enact. My marriages are— of course!—all marriages. But her marriages are, also of course, fictions; they exist only in her assertions, which are, as she makes clear, the confessions of a liar.

Sympathetic as the attempts of Knapp, Long, Malvern, Oberembt, and others to turn Alisoun into a feminist heroine may be, they miss the point. To try to save the text for humanism by defending Alisoun involves at least three fallacies: (1) confusing her point with Chaucer's, (2) confusing her with womankind, and (3) confusing her with a real person. She is none of the above. It is no good theorizing, for example, about the psychological history of someone who exists only as a discourse, even if that discourse were not both internally contradictory and explicitly derived from other texts. Alisoun is absent. The very fact of her performance creates a complex kind of absence: the performer separating herself from the group to present herself to it through a confession that is also a screen. This text is not her; this is her act. Aside from that act, there are no available "facts" except those of her physical appearance. The history given in her *General Prologue* portrait turns out to be proleptic paraphrase of the version given in her own *Prologue*. Unlike the Guildsmen or the Merchant and Franklin, she travels alone; unlike the Miller, Reeve, and Summoner, she is known to no other pilgrim; unlike Roger Ware or Harry Bailley, she has no known sources in actual people.

For all its apparent confessionality, Alisoun's *Prologue* insists on its own secretiveness. She parades her hiddenness, speaking "after [her] fantasye" (190). Her professed, carnivalesque "entente nys but for to pleye" (192). Alisoun's "play" is, however, at once a deadly serious defensive tactic and a demonstration of how solipsism can be used as a weapon. Her way of controlling her old husbands, for example, is to use the power of her secrecy against them: She invents plausible charges against herself—"Thou seydest this, that I was lyk a cat" (348ff.)—puts them into the husband's mouth, then refuses to affirm or deny them, while denouncing his right to think what she has coached him to think. The torment is not betrayal but uncertainty. Killing the fourth husband by creating what she insists was only the illusion of adultery is just a refinement of the tactic. To keep your secret is to hold your power. To withhold your self is to resist being possessed. Alisoun the entrepreneur, of course, offers her sexuality as a substitute for herself, just as she offers the mask of the carnival grotesque as a substitute for a personality: "Ye shul have queynte right ynogh at eve . . . I shrew yow, but ye love it [not 'me'] wel" (332, 446). Alisoun, meanwhile, makes herself "a feyned appetit" (417).[35] Her husbands "know" Alisoun in just the way that we and the pilgrims do: as an impenetrable performance that also signals its unreliability at every turn. At what point(s) in her climactic confrontation with Jankyn is she acting? "I lay as I were deed," she says (796), but not so dead that she can't watch him reacting to her.

We have to resist the temptation to complete the text precisely because the temptation is so blatant. It is, after all, the one Alisoun uses so successfully on her husbands: I am/am not/am planning to/ never intend having an affair with Jankyn our clerk [check one]. It is deceptively easy to invent a story to account for the demise of the fourth husband that the text will not necessarily deny. He could have died of jealousy, natural causes, or murder. He could even have died of natural causes at the time he was about to be murdered![36] The multiplicity of possible stories allows us to read in the one we want, but it also prevents us from designating one of those as the "true" story.

On a more sophisticated level, the Wife's rapid shifts of pose should prevent us from trying to decide which pose is the face and which is the mask. It should, in other words, prevent us from doing what Kenneth Oberembt does when he announces that "behind all that persiflage in her monologue is a temperate woman espousing a cogent marital theology."[37] Behind all that persiflage is more persiflage. God knows, it would solve a lot of problems if we could treat the "wys womman" pose—as Malvern and Long also try to do—as only a parodic mask meant to seduce the male-chauvinist auditor. If that were the tactic, however, you would expect the mask to be dropped in time for sweet, non-sexist reason to triumph (as Oberembt, 300, thinks it has). In fact, in both the *Prologue* and the *Tale,* the combative, virulent Wife gets the last—for now— word. The Alisoun who blesses Jankyn's soul (and probably his memory) at the end of the *Prologue* gives way immediately to the router of the Friar and the propounder of the *Tale,* which is announced as another demonstration of the necessity of female sovereignty. At the end of the *Tale* itself, the blessing of marital harmony gives way to the cursing of husbands. Both blessing and curse are part of a performance directed, literally at least, to an automatically estranged audience of twenty-eight men and two nuns. She treats them as the official, noncarnivalesque world, pretending to include them in her "play" while rigorously excluding them. The case hardly allows for the possibility of full, let alone objective, disclosure.

This text does not allow you to choose whether the blessing or the curse is "real" or which one has priority over the other. The *Tale,* after all, doesn't prove any simple case. The hag isn't necessarily the Wife's mouthpiece. The parting curse *can* be seen as a joke already discounted by the happy ending. Rather than trying to find the real Alisoun in this haystack of contradictions, we should see that the contradictions are the point. It solves many problems to pretend that the Wife is really heretical carnality or, as Walter Long calls her, "an equalitarian moral revolutionary" (282). It solves many more, however, to assume that her secrets are indeed secret. On one level of the fiction, then, she is unknowable because her discourse is a screen; her life, like her birthmark, is referred to but never shown. As with the Great Soviet Encyclopedia, one assumes that the contradictory assertions must refer to some facts, but those are almost certainly not the ones being stated. Her life, we might say, is a closed book; part of the point being, of course, that male authority *cannot* know the privetee of female experience.

On another level, however, the facts of her discourse do not refer to any actual events, only to the events of other discourses. What she has actually "followed" are not her lusts but her sources. If her performance is not consistent with the psychology of a single, coherent woman, it is consistent with the fears and obsessions of men writing about women. Her words are about other words, those of clerical antifeminism, about which she demonstrates the only truth available in that tautological system: It says what it says. She does, necessarily, what the *Roman* says she does. The text "proves" what it is programmed to prove. It invents its object—however startlingly lifelike that object may seem to be—just as Alisoun invents herself and her world. If she is what clerks say women are, then her husbands, the beasts, are what women say men are. Not surprisingly, the "beasts" of both fantasies are much alike, governed by the same desire to possess without being possessed. Alisoun is most like her clerkly inventors in wishing to define the other while exempting herself from counterdefinition.

The clerkly author possesses his subject by "glosyng" it, as Jankyn does, both verbally and sexually, to that animated text, Alisoun (3.509). Alisoun is Jankyn's book in the double sense of having been made out of it and being contained (defined, interpreted) in it. Like it, she is also his property, the thing he acquired along with "al the lond and fee" (630) when Jankyn the would-be cleric became Jankyn the merchant and marital adventurer. He uses the book, of course, as an instrument of control through definition. Their marital conversation consists of his reading her identity to her, very much as she has earlier lectured her first three husbands. Sexual glossing gets Jankyn his property by the same means that Alisoun got it before giving it to him. Textual glossing gives him the illusion of authority over it. The common thread linking clerks, wives, and merchants is, of course, acquisitiveness.[38]

It is important to see just how much Jankyn and Alisoun are the same person, aside from a minor difference in their "sely instruments." One problem with Robertson's antifeminist reading of Alisoun, which privileges the authority of clerks over women and blames Alisoun for a constitutional unwillingness to heed that authority, is that it is a blow from a clerk—defrocked but still claiming scholarly authority and striking in defense of authority—that has made Alisoun deaf.[39] Her inability to hear is not inherent but induced by clerks as much as by her own sinfulness. "I was beten for a book, pardee!" (712). You cannot talk about that book, as Robertson (with his usual drive toward the monologic) tends to, as if its authority were abstract and beyond scrutiny; you have to talk about the use to which it is put. Jankyn, that conjunction of clerkly, commercial, and male sexual acquisitiveness, does three things to Alisoun: he beats her "on every bon" (511), he "glosses" her (509), and he reads to her (669–85). All three are methods of control. The violence of the blow is simply reading carried on by other means. "Who wolde suppose / The wo that in my herte was, and pyne," says Alisoun, referring at this point only to the reading (786–87).

Like Alisoun, however, Jankyn is also constructed by his book. He speaks through it, it speaks for him. We never hear him use his own words until after she takes it away from him. It gives his personal complaints the appearance of universality and objectivity; it makes him (inter alia, a fortune hunter and a wife beater) into the victim of his wife; and it allows him to go on claiming the authority of the orders he has renounced. Jankyn and his book form a closed circle of mutual reinforcement: His experience confirms its authority; its authority confirms his interpretation of that experience. *The Wife of Bath's Prologue and Tale* is notoriously a monologue full of other monologues, each of which requires the presence of a silenced other. Alisoun's harangue, the hag's sermon on gentilesse, and Jankyn's reading are all monologues pretending to be dialogue. In each case, the speaker pronounces on the nature of the other while the other listens and groans. In each case, the voiced one tells the unvoiced that it is so because we, the authorities, say so. In this text, habitually, people do not talk to each other but to themselves, reflecting the kind of separation and self-absorption habitually mocked in carnivalesque texts.

As Jankyn reads, the book stands literally between himself and Alisoun, a physical as well as mental intermission. Naturally enough, her rebellion consists of attacking the book and her final possession of Jankyn necessarily involves burning it: the would-be "code user" literally breaking the code.[40] As Alisoun tells it, of course, getting the book out of the way produces—after a spasm of inarticulate rage—the magical transformation of both parties in part, perhaps, because the rage takes a carnival form of mutual leveling: He flattens her, she flattens him. Like the marriage of Dame Ragnell in the analogue, it breaks a spell, here releasing a loving husband and a devoted, solicitous wife. Neither of these creatures is ever seen, however, because they are absent from the clerical texts out of which Alisoun has been made. There is no counterbook to "Valerie and Theophraste," save perhaps for the one the Wife tries to make out of the story of Gawain and Ragnell in her *Tale*. And now, of course, Jankyn is gone, and the Wife has returned to being what clerical authority says she must be. Through the gap Chaucer has induced in the discourse of antifeminism, we are allowed to glimpse the possibility of a sexual relationship outside the logic of control and subjugation. Not surprisingly, perhaps, the tale Alisoun tells turns on the ability of women to evade control by evading definition.

ALISOUN'S TEXT

The most striking thing about the women in *The Wife of Bath's Tale* is their combination of power and insubstantiality. The king abdicates the power of life and death to the queen who passes it along to the hag. Both women are nameless, however—no longer Guenevere and Ragnell—like all the other women in the *Tale*. The nameless women show a remarkable tendency to flow into one another: the maiden who is the victim of the knight is displaced by the queen who is his judge; she in turn is displaced by the hag on whom the queen's power devolves; the hag becomes the knight's bride and, when assured of his submission, becomes a ravishable maiden.[41] As we have seen, twenty-four dancing ladies—women plural—are liable to turn into one hag—woman singular—who in turn speaks for all women. The court ladies mirror the queen's response both to the crime and the answer. The many individual replies to the knight's question merge into the one general reply. We cannot avoid seeing the women as aspects of one personality, avatars of one goddess, nor seeing that all the aspects are "defined" by their relation to the knight. They are his victim, his judge, his salvation, his desire.

"Defined," in this case, does not mean controlled because the women remain impenetrably mysterious even while playing their roles to (with? upon?) the knight. The knight rapes the maiden "maugree hir heed" (887), but what her "heed" is remains undefined, except perhaps through the actions of the hag who displaces her. But why does this hag want this knight, especially since, in the Wife's carnivalesque mock-romance, he has been stripped of the name he bears in the analogues—he is *not* Gawain—as well as all the qualities that made his original desirable? The answer is available neither to him nor to us. Along with her name, the loathly lady has lost all external signs of identity: She no longer has relations (a brother who is a giant) nor location (in Gower's version, she is the Princess of Sicily), and her choice no longer has an explicit logic. She wants him because she wants him. We do not even know whether she is enchanter or enchanted. She is mysterious precisely because she is entirely self-contained. In the analogue what happens in the bed is self-revelation: The lady tells her name and her story, then she turns back into her real self. In the Wife's version, she turns into somebody else. It is seldom noticed that the chief function of the hag's curtain lecture is to deflect personal questions into general statements about nobility and old age, even as the hag avoids exactly identifying herself with the categories. She will be noble "whan that I bigynne / To lyven vertuously" (1175–76): not quite yet, not quite certainly. As the knight is about to find out, she is not necessarily old. Her speech is not self-revelation; it displaces self-revelation, just as the general question of what women want displaces the particular question of what the maiden wants. Everyone recognizes that the knight's quest is for a non-answer to a nonquestion.[42] It is not often seen, however, that the nonquestion displaces real questions: It is a way that women avoid talking to men while pretending to explain themselves. What is the hag doing for all that long sermon? She is protecting her privacy, preserving her absence.

The knight's question is not, of course, his. A woman asks a question about women (in response to a crime against a woman) and another woman answers it, using the knight as a kind of ventriloquist's dummy. Simply because he is a man, he cannot know the answer. (This is, in every sense, a fool's errand.) He can only know what women tell him. As many critics have noted, the answer he receives is a public one, what the queen and her ladies will accept, not necessarily what they believe.[43] None "dar seye nay" (1019), which is not the same as saying yes, even if public affirmation (in the presence of men) could be trusted. The knight is left with little choice except to take it on faith: It is so because they seem to say so. And, of course, the "right" answer is partly belied by the plethora of other answers, all partially endorsed by Alisoun, that the knight has previously received. It is most obviously belied by the hag's own submission—"she obeyed hym in every thyng" (1255)—when she has obtained his.[44] The answer functions as a declaration of solidarity and exclusion. Women close ranks behind it, safe from having to reveal their individual answers. It is a means of securing absence.

Alisoun's *Tale,* I think, suggests that a woman's real connection is with other women, even if her overall performance questions that suggestion. The hag knows what the queen will accept. After all, they are aspects of the same personality. Women in the Wife's tale operate in the same way she conceives of clerics doing: They form a closed circle of discourse from within which they pronounce on themselves and on the other.[45] The knight, standing outside the circle, is compelled to accept their auctoritee: "he / Constreyned was" (1070–71). The women who accept the answer compel him to marry the woman who gives the answer. They are a conspiracy— oddly enough, considering their source—of silence. As we should have learned from Alisoun's *Prologue,* the more she speaks the less she reveals.

The knight learns nothing from his experience except blind sub- mission, though even a critic as astute as Susan Crane can talk of his being guided "to change for the better."[46] He learns to parrot the hag's answer without even seeing that it has any application to himself. He surrenders to her curtain lecture as silently as Pertel- ote submits to Chauntecleer's. He gives up the sovereignty be- cause he is unable to choose: "I do no fors the wheither of the two" (1234). His earlier reference to "youre wise governance" (1231) is no more than the customary language of surrender. It doesn't even directly acknowledge that she has promised to "fulfille youre worldly appetit" (1218). To the end of the story, he has no idea whom or even what he has married. He knows what he wants, beauty and submission, but not who has given them to him. He fails to learn partly because he is manifestly stupid, but also because he is male, and this text invites the most serious doubts about whether either sex can understand the other, except as a reflection of itself. In both the *Prologue* and *Tale,* the sexes can be reconciled by magic, not by education.

Women, in this text, are absent because, after all, a man wrote it, using texts by other men, which are necessarily about men's experience of women. The reality is elsewhere. With a nice dou- bleness, Chaucer shows us the two sexes as at once mirroring and mutually mysterious: ultimately not knowing one another and probably incapable of doing so, but longing to know because being imprisoned in one's sexual identity is only a larger form of being imprisoned in one's self. Even Alisoun dreams of mutuality.

ALISOUN'S NONENTITY

Let us not whitewash, however. Stalin too, we must suppose, dreamed of being loved, like Milton's God. The most important fact about Jankyn is that he too is not there. Whatever the quality of the love she gave him, he did not survive it. Like virtually every other external thing in her life, he is absent. "Vanysshed was this daunce, she nyste where." However much Alisoun may be imprisoned by the discourse of male authority, she is still more imprisoned by her own isolation and cupidity. Her motto might well be that of Marlowe's Barabas, her fellow protean entrepreneur: "*Ego mihimet sum semper proximus*" (*The Jew of Malta*, 1.1.192): roughly, "I am always closest to myself."[47]

The parallel with Barabas, not so great an associative leap as it might seem, reminds us of something more theologically serious than the sexual paranoia of celibate clerks: that the Wife's unreality—the dissolution of her past into fictions and her present into poses—also identifies her with privative evil. We do, in fact, arrive back where Robertson assures us we always do: at the doctrine of *caritas*. By a typical indirection, Chaucer leads us through the false problem of the "evil" of women to the true problem of the evil of *cupiditas*. Like all the great Satans, including the Pardoner as well as Barabas or Iago, Alisoun is not so much an actor as an act, a mask without a face. As we have seen, in the great paradox that descends from Augustine and Origen into the orthodoxy of medieval Christianity, *malum est non ens:* evil is not-being; that is, it exists phenomenally without existing essentially because it represents a turning away from not only the source of good, but also the source of reality, God as absolute being. Evil is privation, absence. Satan's first satanic act, as in Milton's version (*Paradise Lost*, 5.852 ff.), is to deny his own birth, just as the first authority Alisoun rejects is Christ (3.9–23).[48] Satan's act of autonomy is the first step toward becoming the father of lies, the self-made creature of unreality. Having negated your essential being, you can exist in the world only through appearances as a protean shadow taking on the form and voice of others. As always in the tradition, evil is linked with acting and mimicry. Carnival performance accurately, if grotesquely, mirrors the performative unreality of the secular world.

If your performance is your existence, you must keep talking, as Alisoun does, or you will vanish, as the Pardoner (symbolically, at least, in being silenced) does.

In this doctrine, Alisoun is a figure of evil precisely because she represents personality detached from any essential core, language detached from substantial referents: carnival fluidity without either underlying or containing stability. She's a balloon filled without air. All her waxing amounts to the multiplying of zero. *Amor* converted to the uses of *cupiditas* is, of course, necessarily barren, productive neither of love nor of life. When we define Alisoun in the present, we must speak almost entirely in terms of absence: no love, no friends, no children, no future. "I have had my world as in my tyme" (473): The tense is past. As is widely recognized, the mode of the *Prologue* is elegy. Alisoun's world is defined by what is missing, dead, or unborn. The carnival of her sexual life is measured against the Lenten imminence of old age, celibacy, and death.

Unreality longs for reality and builds itself fantastic substitutes, as Pandemonium substitutes for Heaven. (The creation of substitutes for unsatisfactory reality is the underlying activity of both halves of the text.) An undercurrent of self-rejection pervades Alisoun's discourse. The woman of wealth, via the hag (1177–1206), praises virtuous poverty. "Whan that I bigynne to lyven vertuously," then I will be noble, then I will be something. The more Alisoun denies love, the more, in the cell of herself, she dreams of it. The implicit fairy tale of her life with Jankyn transforms itself into the explicit fairy tale of the hag and the knight (a fiction that will in turn breed other fictions in the *Tales:* January and May, Chauntecleer and Pertelote). Her tale is a parable not only of man's inability to know woman, except carnally, but also of the most aggressive forms of *cupiditas*—the knight's rape of the maiden, the hag's purchase of the knight—converting magically to love, just as the hag's flesh acquires the self-renewing power of spirit.

The hag's transformation only compounds the sense of unreality that goes with her being the alter ego, the distorted rewriting, of Alisoun.[49] In this text, the logic of devotion to the flesh and the material world ends in the attempt to deny their reality. *The Wife of Bath's Tale* is a sustained figuration of the unreality of the material world, which, like the Wife herself, is a kind of grotesque mask over a void. What *has* the knight married: a beautiful young woman who appeared to be a crone or a crone who appears to be a beautiful woman? Whatever, it is a blessing without substance. When the knight grants the hag the right to choose what she will be, she chooses to be what he wishes, to fulfill *his* worldly appetite. She makes herself the insubstantial shadow of someone else's desire.[50] She chooses unreality. What is presented as self-determination is actually a choice determined by the "worldly appetit" (1218) of the other. To control him by his desire she must be controlled, literally shaped, by that desire.[51] A woman, the hag's magic trick implies, is best defined as something in a mask. Her visible social identity is not her, but her adaptation to the needs, demands, and fantasies of others. The subject is not the object.

D. W. Robertson reminds us that Alisoun and the hag, faced with the problems of aging and death, choose "'renewal' through the desires of the flesh [which] must necessarily prove to be illusory."[52] That, I would say, is almost exactly half the point. The *Prologue* and *Tale* taken together force us to think in two apparently opposed forms of nonbeing: the imposed unreality of woman glossed and defined by the desires, words, and authority of men (what we can call Alisoun's political absence, the withholding of her self); but also the more fundamental unreality of privative evil, which chooses the world of illusion and thus generates its own unbeing (Alisoun's existential absence, the diminishment of her soul). The hag is presented by Alisoun, deceptively, as a woman speaking for other women, but she is also an elf-queen, a succubus, offering in place of woman a ghostly substitute: the shadow of men's desire and women's desire to be desired.[53] The *Tale*, like the *Prologue*, is at once sinister and wistful, embodying both the action of *cupiditas* and the dream that it will, somehow, transform itself into *caritas*, from foul and loathsome to fair and loving. The chiasmic movement of both her narratives carries her protagonists toward peace and reciprocity in spite of themselves. These "confessions," like Augustine's, can remind us that people are not saved by their conscious efforts. In the *Tale*, certainly, the acquisition of beauty is inseparable from the renunciation of sovereignty. It marks, in fact, the acceptance of the hierarchic order that the text has previously carnivalized. If the hag still chooses the renewal of the flesh, she at least chooses it in a form—renewal through the gaining and granting of love—that can easily figure the desired renewal of the spirit. As always, the text is multiple not single.

It is not, I repeat, necessary to defend Alisoun in order to defend women. The true case against her is not sexually linked. She is not "right" because her husbands are wrong, any more than she is fertile because her enemies are celibate. As her five husbands together demonstrate, lust and cupidity are human sins, not female ones. The Jankyn who marries an old wife for her money is, obviously, the moral equivalent of the young Alisoun. Like Becky

Sharp, she is a sucker for the bargains of this world. Like Barabas, she is an embodiment of the curiously innocent wickedness of privative evil at play in its toy shop of the flesh. The absence of her *ens,* her essence, the evanescence of her goods, the loss up to which her life adds are qualities that apply to nearly all the pilgrims regardless of sex. The emptiness of economic man and woman, for whom all relationships are those of ownership, debt, and thralldom, is a property of the unstable world of material transaction. Her solitude and absence convey a fundamental comment on the values of the class of pilgrims to which she belongs, not least her chief accuser, that man of insubstantial substance, the Merchant.[54]

The Wife of Bath's Prologue and Tale are about woman, but also about more than woman. They remind us of the illusory evil of women as imagined by clerical authority to remind us of what evil (in the Augustinian sense) really is. They parody an official interpretation of woman to remind us that interpretation creates the thing it pretends to describe. In doing so, they remind us of that fundamental problem of the *Canterbury Tales:* that of knowing the Other who lies behind the other's performance. Alisoun's absence reminds us that Alisoun is in the eye of the beholder and that her sins—especially the desire to control and define others— are also the sins of those who imagined her. When we think of Alisoun as a text, we are reminded that no woman has taken part in the creation of this "woman." That I take to be Chaucer's intricately ironized protest at the silencing of women in the official culture of which he was a part. But it is something more. Far from being what Wayne Shumaker once called him, "a docile scholar," Chaucer is magisterially subversive.[55] This text is an authoritative warning about the dangers of authority. It is a sustained demonstration of the incompleteness of all texts and of the dangers of that necessary imaginative act we perform to complete them. We create the Alisoun we see, Chaucer's Alisoun is an absence.

3

"Ther He Watz Dispoyled, with Spechez of Myerthe": Carnival and the Undoing of Sir Gawain

F EW characters project a categorical view of human nature more strongly than the Wife of Bath or subvert it more thoroughly. In her world of discourse everyone is first, last, and always male or female. Those categories are ever and always separate and opposed, not only as black to white, but also as official to carnival. Either men are on top or women are. As we have seen, however, both her "real" and "fictional" narratives dissolve those categories and their alternative hierarchies. "I am woman," roars the androgynous grotesque. Seen as an individual, that grotesque is the construction of false consciousness that is the characteristic expression of Augustine's version of natural man: a worldly self excreted by, but now controlling and imprisoning, a vitiated being whose salvation must be an escape from that self. Seen as text, that false consciousness is the discourse of sexual fear and alienation that prevents community and imprisons individuals within genders.

The Wife's *Tale* is a parable of such imprisonment and release. A nameless, categorical "knight" is sent in search of a category: to learn what woman is by learning what woman wants. His reward is to get an individual being whose public shape is transformed in private intercourse. That being remains nameless, undefined, unknown, except to the extent that we know her desire cannot, in any direct or literal way, accord with the categorical definition of feminine desire for which she is the source because she seeks freedom only to relinquish it and exercises sovereignty only to obtain (or coerce) mutual submission. She exists as a protean object of desire projected by a mysterious, inaccessible subjectivity. Like her wifely maker, she subverts the categorical definition of gender that she projects.

Sir Gawain and the Green Knight enacts a process of category subversion similar enough to remind us that Alisoun's knight is a nameless, de-individualized version of Gawain. In testing the *sourquydrye* of Camelot, Morgan and the Green Knight test the correlation between the collective and the individual as well as between outward and inward, reputation and substance, sign and signified. In particular, of course, the narrative tests Gawain's relation to his *conysaunce,* that by which he is known, the pentangle, a public and categorical form of identity signifying the court that bestows it as well as the individual who receives it. As we shall see, the testing both reaffirms the category and decisively separates, as it was clearly designed to do, that individual from the category his behavior has upheld. It would be easy enough to test the group as a group: that is what the Green Knight first appears to be doing. The actual test, as has long been recognized, removes the individual Gawain from his social context and requires him to define himself in terms of what he has internalized. A predominantly male world of hierarchies and closed boundary definitions, Arthur's court, is tested by a carnival, female world of indeterminacy and narrative possibility, Morgan's court and the Lady's. Gawain's initiation into that world of subjection is to be stripped of the armor and emblem that represent his external, categorical identity: to be "dispoyled, with spechez of myerthe" (860).[1]

THE PEER AS DISAPPOINTED BRIDGE

Back in 1969 John Halverson applied the term *template criticism* to readings of *Sir Gawain and the Green Knight* in which "a ready-made pattern [is] superimposed on the text that allows only the design you wish to see appear and screens out the rest."[2] Twenty-seven years later we can see that the templates change but the mentality lingers on. Criticism of the poem, to a remarkable extent, is dominated by two closely related fallacies: the pursuit of definition and the pursuit of closure. One fallacy attempts to find a center, the other an outline; both try to contain the multiplicity of the text. In Larry Benson's classic account, the poem is centrally about renown, courtesy, and the testing of those qualities.[3] In John Burrow's equally classic account, it is centrally about the testing of *trawthe.*[4] In more recent versions, Geraldine Heng centers the poem on the problems of feminine and linguistic indeterminacy, whereas R. A. Shoaf locates it in the display of a world of transactions, religious and otherwise.[5] Ivo Kamps, with the confidence of one who sees all his dogmas coming true at once, offers to find "the real challenges" to the values of Camelot in "female autonomy, incest, and magic."[6]

All these readings involve a staircase approach: giving one set of signs within the text priority over other sets of signs. If one assumes that the poem has *a* point, after all, one will nearly always assume that the other person has missed it. Otherwise, what is the point of one's own article? If my challenges are real, yours are less so. When you have accepted Derek Brewer's Freudian contention that the poem "is focussed on the family drama, whose latent drives control the story," you have also accepted that theological or political issues do not.[7] To argue that they do, you have to deny Brewer's major premise and declare his "latent content" out of play, as A. V. C. Schmidt proceeds to do.[8] What we have here is a skirmish in the War of the Templates.

A template, of course, imposes an outline, and template critics tend to seek monologous closure as avidly as they do centering. When Gawain is tested, he will be shown to be proud or not proud, courteous or not courteous. If he is being taught the meaning of penitence, he will either learn or not learn it. If he is undergoing a rite of passage, he will either pass, as he does for Brewer and Stephen Manning, or fail, as he does for Virginia Carmichael.[9]

The massive irresolution that results from this pursuit of exclusionary readings mirrors the teasing, carnivalesque irresolution of the text, which ends, as we know, in a series of abortive gestures toward explanation and reconciliation. When Gawain attempts a definitive exposition of his experience, the court refuses (or seems to refuse) his interpretation, as he has refused Bertilak's. The two parties might negotiate their differences, but they do not. That should be a warning to those of us who are tempted, as we all are, to negotiate it for them. If it is impossible to agree on something as basic as whether Gawain's sin is mortal (D. F. Hills) or venial (P. J. C. Field), then perhaps the critics' version of the Summoner's question—*questio quid iuris*—is the wrong one.[10] The point might be precisely that Gawain cannot know how seriously his fault will be judged in a higher court than Camelot, in which case we might want to view his insistence on its seriousness less as an assertion of truth than an application for insurance. More generally, we might want to distinguish the patterns of the poem from our explanations of them.

It is not merely that critics cannot agree on the meaning of the facts, they cannot agree on the facts. As anyone who has read the criticism knows, there is a silent controversy over whether to call the figure who explains things to Gawain "Bertilak" or "The Green Knight." That is because he calls himself the former but rides out of the poem as the latter, "þe knyʒt in þe enker-grene" (2477). Because Gawain declines to go with him, we do not learn if his story is true. There is no reason to suppose he is lying, but there is equally no reason to suppose he is telling the truth, save that we, like Gawain, are expecting a revelation or at least an explanation. Of course, having been told that Gawain's aunt has been behind his testing, we might also reasonably expect him to confront her when Bertilak gives him the opportunity. The text offers not closure but an ironic, frustrated gesture toward it, like Magritte's famous vanishing bridge. The poem begins in "certainties" of the kind signified by the pentangle and ends in uncertainties, not only of truth, but also of fact.

Template criticism is a function of the lingering belief in a definitive text that can be subjected to a right reading. This is a sympathetic but, as most readers will know, widely discredited approach. *Gawain,* like most of the texts I discuss in this study, is one of the classic cases that demonstrates the fallacy of this approach, for example, by an ending that converts Gawain's monologic vision of the significance of his story into a dialogic contestation with the court's version. The processes I am identifying as carnivalesque serve primarily to destabilize terms, as we have just seen with *The Wife of Bath's* text. For that reason, carnivalesque texts are liable to be significantly, even ostentatiously, indeterminate. Nearly all the important recent studies of the poem, regardless of critical school, assume, as I do, that the poem's indeterminacy is the point from which useful readings of it are likely to begin. Those I have found most useful include the works of Kent Hieatt, Robert Hanning, R. A. Shoaf, and Geraldine Heng.[11]

Like those critics, we should avoid rushing across a bridge that ends in midair. We should assume that the poem means what it explicitly does not say. The failures of resolution and communication with which it ends are part of its meaning. Gawain, who rides into the wilderness bearing the meaning and honor of Camelot on his shield and who rides home to tell the court—with manifest unsuccess—the results its testing, is himself (to borrow Stephen Daedalus's definition of a pier) a disappointed bridge: a failed messenger, an interpreter doomed to uncertainty.[12] If the poem denies us the information necessary to decide the meaning of the court's laughter or the degree of acquiescence in Gawain's final silence, perhaps it leaves us in something very like Gawain's dilemma.[13]

BOBBAUNCE AND ITS DISCONTENTS

In the course of the poem, Gawain loses an illuded view of the world as heraldry; that is, a system of decodable symbolism and apparently firm definition in which Camelot is first among courts, and he is first among its knights. As a moment's reflection will remind us, the most persistent action of the poem is the penetration and dissolution of defining boundaries, beginning in the first stanza with those between victory and defeat, destruction and foundation, "blysse and blunder" (18).[14] Then is now: Primeval Hautdesert is a modern fourteenth-century castle, rich in chimneys and with drawing rooms, as our ancestor Gawain is a thoroughly fashionable young man. There is here: Wild, black-magical Hautdesert and civilized Camelot are siblings under the skin. Gawain rides out into the wilderness to arrive back at a mirror-image of "home." The excluded is the included: your sinister, unrecognized persecutor "is euen þyn aunt" (2464). We meet the enemy and he is us. "He" is also "they" or perhaps "she," Bertilak being the Green Knight but also Morgan's proxy, just as his wife is his proxy. To kiss one, Gawain finds out, is to kiss all three. At the denouement, of course, Bertilak "explains" twice: In the first version he takes responsibility ("I sende hir to asay þe" (2362); in the second he assigns it to Morgan ("Ho wayned me . . . to assay þe surquidre," 2456–57). What exactly "it" is, of course, remains notoriously uncertain and ambiguous. In the poem's famous shorthand, Gawain moves from the rigid clarity and explicitness of the pentangle to the shifty entanglements of the lace.

That movement—from daylight to dark, official to unofficial (the world of the king to that of the witch), ordered and hierarchical to disordered and mingled—is the movement of carnival, the pattern of action Bakhtin designates by terms like *degradation* and *uncrowning*.[15] *Sir Gawain and the Green Knight is* "The uncrowning of Gawain," a pervasively carnivalesque text in a way that goes far beyond the sporadic elements of horseplay, "grotesque realism" in the service of an orthodox Christian vision, cited by Robert Levine, the only critic to have noted the presence of the carnivalesque.[16] The elements of literal carnival are, of course, everywhere in the text. King Arthur is confronted, as a seasonal "enterlude" (472), by a boastful and insulting mock-king inviting him to a Christmas *gomen*.[17] Wenore is bawdily impersonated by Bertilak's Lady. As so often in carnival, sexual roles are reversed, the predatory woman pursuing the chaste and blushing man. The

Lord and Lady, rustic enough to fool Larry Benson into equating them with churls, outwit and tease the courtly Gawain. Games, "handselles," "ferlyes," feasts, masking, and laughter abound. Even a severed head is liable to turn into a football. For that matter, as A. V. C. Schmidt has pointed out, the story of a handsome stranger, a beautiful young wife, and a middle-aged, frequently absent husband is the familiar stuff of *fabliau*.[18]

I do not mean that the poem becomes "low" comedy, only that it includes that "lowering" potential. My primary concern as well as the text's is with carnival as a trope, specifically a trope for deconstruction and parodic subversion. The most fundamental way in which Morgan's plot tests the "surquidrye" of Camelot is by refiguring the world *sub specie ludi*. To confront the king with a mock-king is, obviously, to test the idea of kingship. Carnival prototypically creates a world of masks in which "king" is a role available to any number of actors. High is low and vice versa. As Bakhtin argues, carnival degradation dissolves artificial social identity to reconnect us with the natural and universal. To do so, however, is to interrogate the whole idea of identity: What we are at the "lower bodily level" is, of course, interchangeable. The Lady can thus be Guenevere's opposite, the sexually untouchable replaced by the sexually unavoidable, and the proleptic shadow of Guenevere's future, even while being interchangeable with Morgan. By inviting Gawain to enact his desires, by drawing him from a world of romance toward a world of fabliau, by showing him his potential multiplicity as well as by questioning his right to his name, she subverts his identity and the system of hierarchies and exclusions, the official order, on which it depends. Hautdesert offers, as carnival usually does, the possibility of liberation and the threat of dissolution. If the rules of courtesy by which Gawain shapes himself are arbitrary or multiple, as liable to signify licensed adultery as mariolatrous sublimation, who then is Gawain? If the official order is simply one game among many, what then does Gawain, the embodiment of Camelot, represent? Why is your uncle more "real" or authoritative than your aunt?

Carnival, I will argue, does not lead, as C. L. Barber would have it, "through release to clarification," but to a chaotic dissolution the only solution to which is the reimposition of order for the sake of order: Gawain's elaborate and patently inadequate attempt to expound his story by naming his sin, separating his antagonists into enemies (the lady), friends (Bertilak) and unmentionables (Morgan), and resymbolizing himself as the knight of the green "bende."[19] In the process, Gawain loses a world of discourse in which his identity, his relation to truth and to others seemed certain, exchanging it for a world of (necessary but jerry built) fictions. That is what I would like to call the tragicarnivalesque mode: an inclusive frame rather than an exclusive template.

Gawain's shield, as we all know, carries two images: the pentangle facing outward and the image of Mary facing inward. The former, for public consumption, asserts the bearer's perfection and self-sufficiency even as it (paradoxically) incorporates the idea of dependency ("alle his forsnes he feng at the fyue joyez" of the Virgin, 646). The latter, for Gawain's own consumption, implies that his dependence on higher powers is decisive. Similarly Camelot presents an outward image of perfection—the "most kyd knyȝtez" guarding the "louelokest ladies" (51–52)—that it notably fails to manifest when challenged from within. We are looking here at two closely related instances of the "bobbaunce" bequeathed at founding to the kingdoms of stanza one, the common inheritance of Arthur's court and the poem's audience. The business of carnival is the subversion of bobbaunce, of all claims to dignity, self-sufficiency, and hierarchic elevation. To see that this business is at the center of the poem is to see how it coheres: how a poem about the testing of Gawain's individual "trawthe" is also a poem about testing the "surquidrye" of the court; how that testing can at once be directed toward the masculine epistemology of the courtly world and toward its class base; how a deeply internalized, dreamlike rite of passage can also be an Augustinian demonstration of human dependency on grace. Concentrating our attention on this basic pattern rather than on a line of interpretation will also warn us against privileging any one reading of that pattern. This is a poem, in the most multiple senses of the term, about bobbaunce and its discontents.

THE LIFE YE LIE NEXTE

Gawain's pentangle stands, of course, not just for the individual, but for the culture that supports him and for the epistemology that supports that culture.[20] Significantly, it is not so much claimed by him as presented to him: When they have dressed him in armor "Then þay shewed hym þe schelde" (619). The "pentangel nwe" (636), it is often forgotten, represents a social judgment: Gawain as a reflection of the values of those around him. (For who else's delectation is the golden armor intended?) Rather than springing organically from him, it is "happed" (655) upon him. Like the armor, the pentangle signifies enclosure: an "endless knot," pointed but impenetrable; its outline more containing Gawain than contained by him. As Stephanie Hollis says, "he appears to wear his distinguishing identity . . . as an extraneous ornament."[21] A figure of rigid lines, it exists, in fact, as pure outline. The points of the figure signify, the space it contains does not. On the shield, of course, that space is *gules,* indistinguishable from the surrounding ground. The figure is presented to us, however deceptively, as if its meaning were entirely explicit: five points, each one five ways significant, as overdetermined a figure as one could find. It designates a man wholly conscious, controlled, self-known, and knowable. And a fully knowable hero implies a fully knowable world, just as Arthur's dinnertime custom implies a world where wonders are domesticated, and as Gawain's mariolatry and "luf-talkyng" imply that sex is. A pentangle—one point facing upward, two outward, two downward—is a geometrically abstracted version of a man. This is not Gawain, who never actively claims the figure as his (let alone as "him"), but a form for Gawain: the hero as billboard. Where a knightly title or emblem customarily works by metonymic suggestion—"Agravain of the Hard Hand," "The Knight of the Green Chapel"—this one works by exhaustive definition. One effect of any such list is to prompt readers to start searching for anomalies. It inspires almost instant disbelief. "What, never?" say the critics, like the chorus in *Pinafore.*[22]

While seeming to expound the figure with numbing explicitness, the text leaves its provenance remarkably obscure. *Has* Gawain ever worn the pentangle before? What was it before it was "nwe"? Are we supposed to remember its blackmagical associations?[23] If so, are we meant to connect its excluded history with that of Gawain: his other-textual life as a seducer, which shapes the Lady's version of him? The fact that it is a "syngne þat Salamon set" (625) is more explicitly booby-trapped, referring in the end to the biblical hero's dereliction as much as to his wisdom, a sign of *untrawthe* presented to us initially as a sign of *trawthe.* That, in turn, suggests another way in which the figure misrepresents Gawain. It is, of course, a figure of unity, an endless knot. Each of its five points signifies something different but each is identical and interchangeable. Gawain is not unified in this way and could not be. He has a human body—the one revealed when he is "dispoyled" by Bertilak's servants (860)—inside the figure of his armor. Similarly, "Gawain" signifies a controlling but separate intelligence manipulating the social forms visible to others. That "Gawain" habitually distinguishes himself from his deferential gestures. No one, certainly not the Green Knight, assumes that Gawain accepts the challenge either because he is unworthy or because he thinks he is. Bertilak's liegemen expect to see an exhibition of "luf-talkyng" as they might expect tennis tips if their guest were Boris Becker. As the Lady seems to do, they recognize "Gawain" as a performance as well as a partly detached performer.

Here and elsewhere, the innocence of Camelot—not to mention its *hubris*—is epistemological, not moral. In figuring Gawain, the court figures its own imagined perfection, unity, and stability, and it maps a fully explored world of discourse. Gawain's doubleness is obscured, for us as well as for him, by its very transparency. The performance is, or seems to be, immediately readable to what we might call Gawain's interpretive community.[24] Modesty is, after all, the most familiar of heroic tropes. The appearance of interpretive consensus, however, allows him to mistake its judgments for absolutes. If everyone agrees on his perfection, for example, why should he regard it as a fiction? And Gawain, without claiming the virtues of the pentangle, persistently acts as if he possessed them as his outrage at the loss of his perceived perfection famously indicates. The presence of an audience apparently at one with him spares Gawain, in other words, from acknowledging his own theatricality, the extent to which his social identity exists in performance and in the reception of that performance. An embodiment, like the court he represents, of Bakhtin's "official feast," Gawain figures his present condition as unchanging and inevitable. Perfection does not evolve, after all; a pentangle does not change shape. Performance, on the other hand, is inherently unstable, responding to circumstances and audience expectations. In Camelot, however, there is only one audience, whose expectations of Gawain remain constant, arguably even in the face of his final confession. They know him, he knows them. He knows himself as what they "shew" him.

The most fundamental of the Lady's tactics for subverting Gawain's pentangularity is to foreground the theatricality and textuality of courtly behavior. By invoking his public reputation, engaging him to "expoun / Of druryes greme and grace" (1506–7), and requesting that he teach her "of your witte" (1533), she emphasizes that she regards—or pretends to regard—the courtesy Gawain sees as essential to his character as a set of sporting rules and literary conventions.[25] "I com hider sengel, and sitte / To lerne at yow sum game" (1531–32). She does not offer to be his lover so much as to play his lover, to use or occupy the role for some hidden purpose of her own (or, it turns out, Bertilak's own or Morgan's own), which could be lust or true love or boredom or a mistaken idea of courtesy or an exaggerated form of literary imitativeness or a desire to kill or "what-so scho thoʒt ellez" (1550). As usual in games, she is not in the role but behind it. Even "ʒe ar welcum to my cors" carries, inter alia, the bizarre suggestion of a diligent hostess with a slightly exaggerated idea of what is due to a guest. More obviously, as a striking shift of tone and register, this apparent dropping of the style of courtly indirection is a reminder of the very gaming it seems to renounce. Her habitually sudden shifts of role, for example, from teacher to student and back, make clear that all her behavior is play. The point, for Gawain and for us, is not to find out her secret, but to recognize that it and she *are* secret, unknown, and ultimately unknowable. Hautdesert, as we all know, is literally off the map. Mentally as well as geographically, it is uncharted territory.

It looks, of course, familiar. So does the Lady, "wener þen Wenore" (945), with Wenore's grey eyes, sitting in Wenore's place in a court that exists as a funhouse mirror of Camelot. Moreover, the Lady invites Gawain to the same games of "luf-talkyng" that he engages in with the queen-his-aunt (as opposed to the goddess-his-aunt). Wenore, however, is a figure of the official feast: static, silent, and out of physical reach, a hierarchic and disembodied emblem, who can be described by cataloguing her clothes and jewels (74–80). The Lady, active, vocal, sexually predatory, seminude, and seemingly frank, is Wenore's carnivalesque counterpart. (Gawain is, of course, dressed as the knight of one lady and undressed, "dispoyled" as the knight of the other.) As such, she embodies desires that are usually repressed; she doesn't just act, she acts out. Sexual role reversal—"women on top," Alisoun's and Cleopatra's position of choice—is, of course, as basic an aspect of carnival inversion as the suspension of taboo. When Gawain kisses the Lady, he does not merely kiss Wenore's shadow, but also the Lady's husband (to whom the kisses, like the lace, must be returned), and he kisses his aunt, who literally or figuratively operates through the Lady. Carnival figures a world of masks in which identities are interchangeable. It is strikingly difficult, to be sure which of the castle's three ruling inhabitants is tempting Gawain at any particular point, a confusion acknowledged indirectly by Gawain's later eagerness to separate his antagonists into two evil temptresses and one male bystander. The games of Hautdesert are polymorphous as well as perverse.

As Camelot contains "gamnez" (1319, 1894), Hautdesert seems contained by them. The very fish are transformed by "sawes so sleȝe" from penance into feast (893).[26] The most important game, however, is playing house. Hautdesert at least seems to be a parodic shadow of Camelot in which each of the figures of Gawain's daytime world is reproduced in distorted form. Bertilak shadows Arthur as the Lady does Wenore, but Morgan, Arthur's sister, shadows both the King and Merlin, whose magic she has taken, as well as the nearly invisible Bawdewyn, Camelot's spiritual supervisor. In each case, however, the figure at Hautdesert is more vigorous, active, and substantial than its counterpart, so Camelot inevitably seems the shadow of Hautdesert. Merlin has vanished; Morgan has not. The magic castle is detailed and substantial; the real one virtually undescribed. The id, as we know, contains the vital energy. The ego constructs itself by denial, as Camelot denies its links to Morgan's realm (even to the omission of Morgan from Gawain's confession at the end). The pentangular Gawain is, of course, a creature of denial, a courtly lover devoted above all to sublimation: the servant of Wenore and Mary who can "defeat" the Lady by denying that he loves anyone, "ne non wil welde þe quile" (1791). A post-Freudian reader might be tempted to paraphrase the lady's invitation as "welcum to your id."

As we have seen, the deconstruction through caricature and ridicule of ego-based social identity is perhaps the most basic process of carnival.[27] The first thing the residents of Hautdesert do to welcome Gawain is to strip him—in the friendliest possible manner, of course—of the armor put on, or assembled around, him at Camelot: "þer he watz dispoyled, with spechez of myerthe, / þe burn of his bruny and of his bryȝt wedez" (860–61), lines that usher him into a world of puns and linguistic subversion as well as of deceptive creature comforts. To *dispoyle* means literally "to strip (sb.) of his clothes" [*MED, despoilen*, 1b]; but also "to plunder or ravage" [2a]; "to take away or ruin (the mind, etc.)" [3a], and "to deprive (sb. or sth. of honor, security, beauty, etc.)" [3b]. "Dispoyling" in the first sense is prologue to dispoyling in the other senses. Forewarned, in this case, is disarmed. As usual when this text deals with Hautdesert, the secondary meanings of words contradict and subvert the primary, springing a series of verbal traps on hero and reader. Here also, an image of Gawain is undone, then another, distinctly feminized, is constructed: a Gawain who sleeps in furs and soft robes rather than in his irons.

Camelot, as we have seen, figures a world of singular and explicit definitions organized into distinct hierarchies, which assert its own preeminence. It is, above all, this claim of primacy that Morgan tests. Hierarchies depend on singularities; things cannot be definitely ranked unless they are definitely known, the "most kyd kny-ʒtez" (51) also the hardiest "here on hille" (59). From her first audible address to him ("ʒe ar a sleper vnslyʒe," 1209), the Lady sets about undoing Gawain's heroic singularity by confronting him with other "Gawains," separating what is from what is "known."[28]

As scholarly readers have long known, this poem's Gawain is not so much created from previous versions of the character as in opposition to them. *He* is a "pentangel nwe," a chastened version. The other Gawains enter the poem only through Hautdesert's knowledge of them. Because the Lady and her courtiers have (apparently) read the Gawain-books while Gawain has not, they have the effect of making him suddenly aware of himself not merely as a text, but as a different text. He is required to become, that is, his own resisting reader: "I be not now he þat þe of speken" (1242). But, of course, he is, in some important sense. The ladies of Camelot, to judge by the "vrysoun" they have made him, "entayled" with "tortors and trulofez" (612), share the Lady of Hautdesert's version, whether they derive it from literature or not. That "vrysoun" opens on a disturbing possibility: that "Gawain" is not so much a free-standing individual as a locus of competing fictions, among which the pentangle-fiction is privileged only in the sense of being the one the man himself prefers to believe.[29] Different audiences, however, have different preferences. Gawain as a preeminently social being—defined by what he offers service to: Mary, Wenore, Arthur, but also Bertilak (see especially 1964), the Lady, and ladies generally—can no more avoid belonging to his audiences than any other performer can. As an object of spectation, definition, and desire, he cannot avoid existing in others' reception of him. The Lady's temptation draws out possibilities previously foreclosed by Gawain's choice of his own fiction. It invokes a Gawain who is "hende" (the epithet used of him at 405, 940, 1633, 1731, 1813 et al.) like Nicholas instead of like Arthur (or Mary at 647). There is, he finds, a life he lies next to, less a saint's life than a Shipman's Tale.

"Blame ʒe disserue," the Lady tells him, in her usual densely encoded and blithely suggestive style, "ʒif ʒe luf not þat lyf ʒe lye nexte" (1779–80). The "lyf" is her, of course, though it is also more generally any lover. In a more figurative, but also more important, sense, however, it is the life that lies at hand, the alternative existence she has been offering him for the past three days, the chance to slide into a different identity in a different, more carnivalesque genre. That "lyf" is inevitably the product of a discourse in which "lives" proliferate and Gawain's name becomes a negotiable commodity capable of denoting a whole series of narrative possibilities. Famously, of course, the Lady's challenge centers on her denial of Gawain's right to his own name: "Bot þat ȝe be Gawan, hit gotz in mynde" (1293). In her speech Gawain's identity habitually slips into the conditional: "so god as Gawayn gaynly is halden . . ." (1297). Here the reputation is real, the man's reality will be confirmed or denied only by his subsequent actions; the real Gawain, she assures him with Alisounian bawdiness, would always seek a kiss at "sum talez ende" (1301). That Gawain accepts his own conditionality is given away in the line I quoted earlier: "I be not *now* him þat ȝe of speken," a phrase that leaves open the question of who "I" am in other times and texts. What is lost here is Gawain's pentangular stability; what is seemingly gained is the freedom of carnivalesque indeterminacy, the freedom gained by treating "Gawain" as a mask. In terms familiar to critics of the poem, it is the freedom gained by substituting the loose, endlessly retie-able lace for the endless knot of the pentangle.[30]

That the apparent offer of a more richly physical life is, we will quickly discover, an offer of death reminds us of the biblical echo also encoded in her speech. "ȝe lufed your lyf" (2368) is, of course, the grounds on which the Green Knight both charges and acquits Gawain. If Gawain loves this life, he will lose it. The logic of that connection, I want to suggest, is intimately connected with the Lady's role as embodiment of the duplicity of language, indeed, as virtually a figure for language itself.[31]

Both characters exploit the duplicity of language; courtly speakers could hardly do otherwise. Gawain, however, goes on believing in his own transparency. The Lady gives him lessons in opacity, paradoxically enough because of the way signification proliferates in her speech. The more rich a phrase may be in possibilities, the poorer it is in certainties. The concept of courtesy, the subject of so much of their discussion, dissolves in her definition of it: the "lel layk of luf" (1513). A glance at the *MED* and a moment's consideration will remind the reader that *layk* means: (1a) "amusement, diversion . . . a game," which covers Bertilak's hunting and Morgan's entire scheme; (1b) "amorous dalliance," which is the Lady's most obvious meaning; (1c) "an amusing adventure," which is one way of describing what Gawain is having; (1d) "holiday, festival," which includes the season when the action takes place; and (1e) "place of joy, heaven," which is what is promised by the season and may be lost by yielding to the Lady's offer of 1b. At the same time, *layk* signifies (2a) "a fight, contest, battle" and (2b) "an assault, attack," both of which refer fairly literally to the Green

Knight's actions and metaphorically to the Lady's. More neutrally, the term also means "a deed, act, action" (3a); "conduct, behavior" (3b); and "sin, vice" (3c). The relevant meanings of *lel* include "loyal" (1a); "loyal to God, virtuous" (1b); "Christian" (1c); "of a class or action: proper, just" (1d); "truthful, veracious, reliable, trustworthy" (1e); "full of prowess" (2a); "fair, beautiful" (2b); "excellent" (2d); and "legally valid" (3). *Luf,* of course, carries roughly its modern range of meanings from lechery to *agape* with intervening stops at loyalty, friendship, and true love. As a concise demonstration of the duplicity of language, this is Wittgenstein condensed by Henny Youngman. The Lady's phrase opens out like a particularly ambitious Chinese menu: Pick one (or more) from column a, ditto from column b and column c. I invite you, as the Lady is doing to Gawain, to play with the full range of combinations. I remind you, however, that a "lel layk of luf" will describe what the Lady asks from Gawain, but also what he owes to Bertilak, what he performed by taking on the challenge, and what Mary expects from him. To consider the relation of those four "layks" is to see something of the contradictions of Gawain's situation. At the same time, the phrase reflexively echoes the "lel lettres loken" (35) in which the story is to be found, echoed also by the second half of 1513, the Lady's punning reference to the "lettrure of armes." That echo folds the Lady's deconstructive puzzle neatly into the poem's. I remind you also that the phrase combines, in order to subvert, three of the most fundamental terms of Gawain's courtly world and of his self-definition.[32] One sense of the Lady's use of *lel* is echoed in the Guide's offer to Gawain the next morning: "I schal lelly yow layne" (2124). Lying is loyalty, as an "amusement" is also an "attack."

Any attempt to find the Lady's true meaning or even to prioritize the available meanings, a la Ross Arthur, will miss not only the sense of the phrase, but also the point, which is precisely the impenetrable duplicity of words. The Lady is not a puzzle to be solved; she is other; therefore, she is radically unknowable. In this sense, both she and her language hold the mirror up to Gawain, showing him what the interpretive consensus of his community normally hides. For three days, of course, Gawain has been evading the Lady by hiding behind the various senses of *luf,* which enable him to refuse her request for love, in the sense of sexual attention, by professing love, in the sense of chaste respect, even while invoking love (loyalty, friendship) for her husband, and glancing at (religious, quasi-monastic) love for the Virgin. In the end, as we have seen, he will deny that he loves (is emotionally committed to) anyone. All the while, Gawain thinks of himself as "trwe," and will continue to do so a moment later when he accepts the lace and agrees to hide the gift. If the other is unknown, so, belike, is the self. Both pentangular self-knowledge and conscious control are illusions.

THER HE WATZ DISPOYLED

To subvert the illusion that the other is knowable is to dissolve the heraldic world, which requires at least the illusion of a stable sign system. That is why shape-shifters and disguised figures, as in *Caradoc* and *The Wedding of Sir Gawain,* are so important to it. They are, of course, customarily recognized and disenchanted, thereby restoring the stability of the system. If a *conysaunce* does not enable you to recognize (*connaitre*) the person in front of you, what good is it? In the mental realm of Hautdesert, however, you might as well wear a Magritte on your shield. (One of the "Lost Jockey" series would be appropriate in Gawain's case, signifying The Knight of the Epistemological Dilemma.) Signs here signify in the multiplex way of the girdle, which represents in rapid succession magic, safety, feminine power, "falssyng," "surfet," shame, honor, and sin. Of course, when Gawain returns to Camelot and finds that his interpretive community now insists on readings opposite to his own, taking the girdle (as the Green Knight does) to represent honor, he is reminded, yet again, that there is here, and others indeed other.

As R. A. Shoaf has suggested, what most clearly marks the state of being that Hautdesert represents is an enormous proliferation of (apparent) significance and an almost total absence of meaning.[33] Gawain can hardly sit down without forming an emblematic picture: "bitwene two so dyngne dame" (1316), one (unspecified) on the left, one on the right, both, we suspect, making a wish. Flagrantly heraldic animals, kisses, chapels, private chambers and canopied beds, disguised fish, days of the Christmas season, summer warmth in the midst of winter cold: Everything says, "read me!" "Peter," says the Porter (813) on first sight of a man who, like St. Peter, will prove remarkable both for loyalty and disloyalty. We do not know, however, whether the Porter means anything. The text itself takes no explicit note of the connection.[34]

Signs abound, but guarantors of meaning have gone missing. The Lady is not in her game; she is a player, displaced rather than represented by the game.[35] "What-so scho þoȝt ellez" (1550) remains hidden from Gawain and from us. Like a Barthesian (or Alisounian) text, her game signifies her absence, the more so because, if we can trust Bertilak's word, she is at best only its co-author: "þe wowyng of my wyf: I wroȝt hit myseluen" (2361). Bertilak, in turn, is "wayned" by Morgan, who remains silent behind her larger game, "what-so scho þoȝt" expressed only by surrogates. The markers that might lead Gawain through this wilderness of signs have been erased.

Not content with being unknown, the figures in that wilderness show a remarkable tendency to flow into one another. "Hit is my wede þat þou werez," the Green Knight/Bertilak tells Gawain (2358). As the Lady's sexual object, Gawain has taken her lord's place. At the same time, however, her lord woos him through her and, inevitably, his aunt woos him through both of them. "Know I wel þy cosses," the Green Knight adds, rubbing it in (2360). The poem does not regender power, as Sheila Fisher and (more subtly) Geraldine Heng have argued.[36] Life would be much simpler for Gawain if it did; instead it ungenders power. The lace (feminine) entwines the axe (masculine), literally (at 216 and 2226) as well as figuratively. Morgan's magic is Merlin's; it expresses itself equally through Knight and Lady. What *is* the gender of whatever is tempting Gawain? The Lady's power, as we have seen, is essentially the entropic power within language to rename and unname. The most essential thing about power, as Stephen Greenblatt has taught us, is that it circulates.[37] If Gawain could locate it anywhere short of God, he would be able to remap his world with more confidence than he does. Morgan's castle, if it is Morgan's, appears, remember, in response to a prayer to Mary.

Gawain is dispoyled in yet another fundamental way, however, since the radical instability of the world is matched by the instability of the self, whose theatricality is (or should be) revealed to him by every move the Lord and Lady make. When they make him consciously play "Gawain," they make him eventually aware of the gap between the actor and his performance. Gawain's striking lack of introspection is the result of his being committed both to a highly theatrical mode of existence and to the denial of any element of falsification. He cares for the "fourme of his castes" (1295); he seldom asks what motives lie behind the forms. What pride lurks behind his professions of modesty? With what degree of sincerity does he offer himself as "on of yourez [Bertilak's]" (1964)? To honor the form of interchangeable devotion is to avoid considering the possibilities for betrayal in that offer. Gawain's punishment is, of course, to have his falsification seen and made visible to himself.

The sense of being a performer does not interfere with your sense of identity as long as your performance is confined to a single role. When that role opens out into a life of improvisation, the illusion of an inherent self vanishes. Whatever the motive of Bertilak's final offer, it is an invitation to return to the world of unstable transaction, where your "enmy kene" (2406) will become your friend. Whatever the impiety of Gawain's permanent penance, it is a refusal of instability. Wounds heal, he decides, but sin endures: "for þer hit onez is tachched twynne wil hit neuer" (2512). Permanent guilt is at least permanent identity. Otherwise, what are you when you have stopped atoning?

Instead of accepting a world of "relativity and relationship" in which "authentic exchange replaces prideful insistence of static absolutes," as Shoaf argues, Gawain spends the latter stanzas of the poem reinstating those absolutes, redoing what has been dispoyled.[38] From the moment he receives his wound and the knowledge of the falsity of his perception of things, he is preoccupied with naming and categorizing, redrawing the lines that have been erased: in short, de-carnivalizing his world. "Trwe mon trwe restore" (2354)! Gawain's final moves cohere if we see them not merely as what Hollis calls an "attempt to maintain a limited conception of himself," but as a sustained attempt to restore the official hierarchy, not to mention literary dignity, that has been subverted by the carnival at Hautdesert.[39] The so-called antifeminist outburst serves the important purpose of locating an enemy safely outside oneself and timeless. (The Lady alone could well turn into your friend and may already be.) Continuing courtesy to Bertilak draws a line between them and us, while reasserting a hierarchy in which men love and protect women without trusting them. In the process, as we all know, Gawain enrolls himself in the ranks of biblical heroes, reclaiming not just self-respect, but also tragic status; refusing the comic role usually reserved for misguided kissers, like Absolon of *The Miller's Tale,* to reclaim, with a difference, his link to Salamon (2417), doomed, like Samson and Gawain, by the "faut . . . of þe flesche" (2435) and the wiles of women. Gawain's sin can be named, with suitable grandeur of generality, as "cowarddyse and couetyse" (2374). The girdle, after a few false starts, can be pinned down as "þe token of untrawþe" (2509), replacement for and analogue of the sign of "trawþe" the pentangle.

This process of variously crude and subtle misnaming is richly comic and not to be dismissed. Of course he is blaming the Lady after Bertilak has told him that "I sende hir to asay þe" (2362). Of course "cowarddyse and couetyse" are right in kind while wrong in degree. Logocentrism, however, *is* what we do to survive. Unchecked carnival release is customarily fatal—as it is, for example, to Ophelia—and Gawain is saving more than just his vanity. He's imposing a form of order on the carnivalized world.[40]

Thus we have a model of the carnivalesque hero's progress, in the first phase of which (roughly up to his "dispoyling" at line 860) Gawain is a controlling user of courtly language: It speaks through him, but he appears to control its duplicity. In the second phase, however, Gawain is a victim of the duplicity of courtly terms now controlled, and subverted, by the Lady. He is outside the discourse he and we thought his own: an innocent reader (mis)led by her. She demonstrates the play of signification while tantalizing him with the possibility of a key which would determine the meaning behind the play. In fact, the play *is* the meaning. She exploits and embodies the entropic, carnivalesque element in language. In the third, post-*nirt,* phase, Gawain uses the syntactic power of language to reconstruct orders of meaning and reimpose definition, however objectively inadequate those meanings may be. Here, for the first time in the poem, Gawain is the originator rather than the recipient of signification. The Lady, the Green Knight, his own first impulses have all offered him definitions of the lace. Gawain rejects those in order to construct his own symbol for his own purposes.

It is important, if seldom noted, that the *lace* does not remain a lace; nor is it the delicate, insubstantial thing the modern word suggests. It is a "blykkande belt" (2485), shining, ornamented; and Gawain wears it as a "bende" (2506).[41] That word means "an ornamental lace" (*MED,* 3a), all right, but it also means "a fetter" or "hoop" (1a, 1b) and thus figuratively "captivity, imprisonment" (2a). Gawain wears it in the sense and probably in the literal form of its heraldic meaning: "a broad diagonal band or stripe placed on a coat of arms, banner, shield" (4). It is no longer fluid or amorphous, but a rigid figure that represents a loose cloth, but no longer is one. In its emblematic form it represents not fluidity but definition imposed on fluidity, as, we now know, the pentangle also did. A diagonal stripe, however, as any set designer knows, is dynamic; it implies movement without moving itself. It is rigid like the pentangle, but not self-contained and self-referential; it points. The "bende," now both signifying privation and pointing beyond it, is an appropriately Augustinian symbol because it defines Gawain not by his fullness but by his lack. He reorganizes his identity around the recognition of his dereliction.

This "bende" is a new *conysaunce:* a device by which you recognize yourself, an emblem you put on to be recognizable. Since, however, it also represents a radical and distorting simplification—indeed an explicit denial—of Gawain's complexity and the (relative) purity the Green Knight finds in him (see 2394), it is also a *meconysaunce*, a device of misrecognition, a sign that signifies the arbitrariness of the signs by which we signify ourselves. Gawain now, I hardly need add, constitutes an interpretive community of one. He, not the narrator, expounds this new sign. The court rejects his exposition in favor of their own.

Gawain's reordering of the world is thus essentially a private matter. The Gawain of the beginning of the poem has been constituted by his social world; the Gawain of the end reconstitutes his mental world as a way of reconstituting himself. The "bende" hoops, contains his disorder. In the world at large, however, carnival is not contained, it contains. The Green Knight, having never quite returned to being Bertilak, rides out of the poem "whiderwarde so-euer he wolde" (2478), what force he represents still undefined and thus uncontrolled. The order of the world which Gawain might once have taken as natural and given, he may now see as constructed, though the need to believe in that order requires that he assert it as given. Carnival subversion is, in an important sense, always permanent because what has been demystified cannot be remystified. The court can, indeed, go on behaving as if there had been no demystification, though neither we nor Gawain, being outside that community, can say confidently what they know. The poem, however, as a game about games, shows us a world structured by necessarily arbitrary rules—Camelot rules, but also Hautdesert rules (okay?)—which operate in place of absolutes. C. L. Barber's well-known formula for festive action needs to be revised: not "through release to clarification," but through the danger of release to the illusion of clarification. Gawain chooses a new emblem because he has to. A willed fiction of identity or truth will save you, as he has found at Hautdesert. The larger fiction of the heraldic world, however, remains deconstructed. The poem directs us to its final blessing by an epistemological *via negativa:* In the wilderness of signs we must all pray for the guidance of an authority beyond our fallen discourse: "He bryng vus to his blysse."

4

The Unbeing of the Overreacher: Privative Evil, Protean Carnival, and the Marlovian Hero

THIS is not, appearances perhaps to the contrary, the place to rehearse the discontinuities that separate the Elizabethan period from the Ricardian. Those changes in economic and political structure, in theology, in demographics, and even in vowel pronunciation are the stuff of introductory lectures in every undergraduate course in Renaissance literature. I do not mean to disregard or minimize, let alone deny, them, either in their traditional forms (feudal to early capitalist, as in L. C. Knights, or scholastic to Baconian) or in more recent varieties, such as Jonathan Dollimore's contention that Renaissance drama is marked by the pervasive subversion of medieval essentialism and Francis Barker's claim that it reflects new, post-*Hamlet* forms of subjection.[1]

Instead, I want to concentrate on certain lines of continuity that link two phases of the carnivalesque and that are perhaps obscured by the common tendency, especially among Renaissance scholars, to set the two periods in opposition. One line, which I have mentioned in chapter 1, is the continuity of certain basic doctrines from Augustinian Catholicism to Lutheran and Calvinist Protestantism. As I have earlier argued, both Luther and Calvin see themselves as reinstating the rigors of late-Augustinian religion in the face of semi-Pelagian laxity and compromise.[2] They reemphasize Augustine's belief in inherited depravity, in the unfreedom of the will (Luther's *servum arbitrium*) and in man's consequent dependence on grace; in predestination; in the unknowability of God; in the privative nature of evil and the consequent gravitation of the fallen soul toward nothingness.[3] If anything, what Walzer calls Calvin's "theology anti-theological" puts God (and thus the grounds of certainty) even further beyond the reach of logic and explanation than Augustine's does.[4] Calvin, for example, warns against the grave sin of trying "to break into the inner recesses of divine wisdom, in order to find out what decision has been made" concerning us; such "stupidity" will be "punished with dreadful ruin" (*Institutes,* 3.24.4). Like Augustine, Calvin condemns the worshipper to epistemological and ontological uncertainty. Both Luther and Calvin restate the doctrine of the two cities in even more extreme terms than Augustine does, Luther because he sees the two perpetually at war, Calvin because he foresees the *civitas Dei* conquering and absorbing the earthly city through the process of reformation. Each, in short, foregrounds the alienation of *civitas peregrina* from *terrena.*

These are, however, changes of degree and are generally represented not as revolution but as conservative reform. They thus account for my second line of continuity. Because there is a body of doctrine (*malum est non ens,* for example) so basic as to lie beneath the turbulence of Reformation debate, Augustinian literature of the fourteenth century and of the late sixteenth century is liable to reflect similar concerns.[5] As we have seen, the "Renaissance" concern with subjectivity, with the conflict between inner and outer identity, is elaborately anticipated in both Chaucer and the Gawain-Poet, as is an extreme skepticism about the reliability of earthly authorities and the reality of earthly powers. As we shall see in looking at Marlowe and Shakespeare, there is also a continuity of carnivalesque means for dealing with these problems. Characters as different as Gawain, Tamburlaine, Hamlet, and Antony share what we might call the fallacy of self-sufficiency: the belief that they can or ought to be able to control and stabilize their essential characters by the exercise of their will. If the devil were not, as D. J. Enright tells us, the father of alliteration, I would call the resulting pattern—which leads from pentangle to lace, from "plated Mars" to dragonish cloud—the Punishment of Pelagian Presumption. The pattern in all four works is given shape by the subversion of stable ego and its attempts to stabilize the world around it. As we have seen in chapter 1, whoever attempts to exercise that kind of control builds on ruins.

The soul, as Augustine conceives it, is at once a form of being and of nonbeing, defined not only by its substance but also by its vitiation. Until fulfilled by God, it is characterized, above all, by absence, need, and hunger. To analyze the self is to discover the emptiness and dependency that is hidden by the appearance of power, coherence, self-sufficiency. The analysis of character, whether in medieval or Renaissance literature, is primarily the revelation of its theatricality. The Augustinian soul in the absence of God—an absence that can be read as literal non-existence, as the effect of Calvinist preterition or as the Augustinian alienation of God from the fallen creature, and which is all the more threatening for this very uncertainty—is Marlowe's particular subject. The activity of that soul—the expense of appetite in a waste of death, the generation of protean role-play around an inner void—is his particular variation on the Augustinian carnivalesque.

AUGUSTINIAN PRIVATION AND MARLOVIAN INSTABILITY

Students, we all grudgingly admit, are useful people, not least because they have not quite learned not to ask naive questions or to have naive—unstructured, "humanistic"—responses. When you teach them Marlowe, for example, they tend to observe something that we specialists train ourselves not to observe: that his characters are obnoxious to an astonishing degree and with astonishing frequency. Nearly all of them—Theridamas as much as Tamburlaine, Mortimer as much as Edward, Wagner as much as Faustus, Ithamore even more than Barabas—combine villainy and folly in equal and remarkable parts. Those who do not (Dido and Zenocrate, for instance) are almost always in love with those who do. Even Abigail loves her father, the sole sign that she actually belongs on Malta. Her death in the arms of a lecherous friar seems designed, like so much in Marlowe, to leave us poised between outrage and dismissive laughter. He is an extraordinarily discomforting writer.

I should like to start with this calculatedly naive response because it reminds us of things commonly ignored or minimized in the critical literature. As anyone who has addressed a Marlowe conference is liable to know, there is a remarkable (if slowly declining) reluctance among specialists to acknowledge, for example, that Faustus is an idiot and that the play relentlessly exposes his idiocy from line one onward. The sticking point, of course, is that he is a "tragic hero." But Marlowe nearly always uses the word *tragedy* provocatively, as when Machevill promises us "the tragedy of a Jew / Who smiles to see how full his bags are cramm'd" (*The Jew of Malta,* Prologue, 2.30–31).[6] We need to retain a sense of the disorientation—the carnivalesque category subversion—that such phrasing is calculated to produce. At the same time, the naive response leads fairly directly to issues that can be phrased in more respectable terms: Why, for example, do these plays and their protagonists so elaborately invite sympathy—soliloquy after solilo-

quy, each one crammed with every conceivable rhetorical appeal—
and so violently discourage it, distancing irony piled upon distancing irony? A correlative problem, endemic to the Augustinian carnivalesque, is the notorious difficulty of classifying the plays. If
Faustus *is* a twit, what then is *Dr. Faustus?* One answer, of course,
is *slapstick tragedy,* a term not always treated with the seriousness
it deserves.

A tragic plot, Marlowe knew as well as Hamlet, is a joke with
the safety catch off. That is why Barabas's tragic fall is also a
pratfall, the last of many he takes in the play. As actors know,
there is a certain precise pitch at which you can play Tamburlaine
straight. One decibel above or below and you topple into farce.
Indeed, you often seem directed to do so, as when the character
concludes thirty lines of much-anthologized praise for Zenocrate
by turning to an incredulous aide, shrugging and saying, "Techel-
les, women must be flattered" (*Tamburlaine, Part 1:* 1.2.107); only,
apparently, to reassert his love in the next line.[7] We are, of course,
looking at a comic pattern. We all secretly know that the parts in
Faustus's pre-contract arguments with Mephostophilis should be
played by Laurel and Hardy, respectively. These manic-depressive
swings-and-roundabouts—the shortest of which is "my girl! my
gold!"—are not only a favored Marlovian device, but also small
models of how the plays themselves work: inflation of the protagonist, followed by immediate deflation, followed by immediate refla-
tion. This is the essential Marlovian rhythm of action; it is also the
rhythm of *Waiting for Godot.* "We have kept our appointment,"
says Vladimir in act 2. "How many can boast as much?" "Billions,"
replies Estragon. The parallel, I suggest, is not coincidental, but
reflects a fundamental similarity of vision and purpose rooted in
Beckett's and Marlowe's common, if gloomy, inheritance of Augustinianism, including a common delight in carnivalesque subversion of worldly pretensions.[8]

This pattern of rapidly alternating seduction and repulsion of
the audience can be explained in several ways. Constance Kuriyama, for example, explains it psychologically in terms of the fundamental conflicts of an unresolved, ambivalent, homosexual author
whose protagonists act out an obsessive pattern of extravagant
adolescent rebellion and retributive parental humiliation.[9] This
reading has the unfortunate side effect of turning Ferneze into
Barabas's father, to the dismay of both parties. More important, it
subordinates a conscious perception of the external world into an
unconscious internal drive. I want to offer a less Freudian, possibly
less contentious version, one that begins with the fact that each of

Marlowe's "heroes" is based on a well-established, immediately recognizable stock type of villainy (which is also usually a stock type of the grotesque): the Jew, the Machiavel, the pagan tyrant descended from Herod of the mysteries, the diabolical conjurer, the homosexual, the misruler, or of course the academic. Even Dido has her more than tangential relation to the Temptress, and Aeneas carries remnants of his medieval reputation as one of the types of the Betrayer. As most readers will have noted, the protagonists of the mature plays tend to combine at least two of these stock types, even while the plays subvert our moral responses to these types. If Tamburlaine is Herod, he is also Miles Gloriosus. In the simplest instance, "Barabas" is juxtaposed not with Christ but with Ferneze. The villainy is there, but the evaluative context has been removed.

As may already be clear, I view Marlowe as a grand obsessive, continually circling the same set of related problems. These can be and have been described in a variety of ways: as problems of unresolved Oedipal rebellion (Kuriyama), as conflicts between imagination and reality (Altman), or even as a struggle between Renaissance self-assertion and Christian submission (Ellis-Fermor and many others).[10] I would call them The Perils of Protean Personality and see them as another aspect of the Augustinian tradition of defining the self in terms of hunger for being. Under whatever label, they remain constants: The frustrated aspirations made explicit in *Faustus* are implicit in *Tamburlaine, Part 1* or in *Dido and Aeneas*.

Thus, in what follows, I have deliberately suppressed chronology. Interpretations that depend on finding a radical change somewhere in Marlowe's career—a religious conversion, for instance—seem to me a matter of finding a story in the carpet where there is only a figure. Moreover, they depend on our pretending to know that we do not know: the order of composition of the plays. We do not know, for example, whether *Tamburlaine, Part 2* was composed as a hasty sequel after the success of *Part 1* or whether Marlowe wrote the two together and sprang the second on his audience after they had fallen for the first. The latter possibility strikes me as an eminently Marlovian device, but I cannot prove it occurred, so I let it pass. In the same way, I prefer not to choose between Greg's order and Steane's, on the grounds that both are necessarily conjectural.[11]

I have chosen instead to view the pattern as one would the figures in a carpet, walking slowly around them. If this involves some element of repetition, of viewing the same conformation from different angles, I can only plead that that is dictated by the product. The problem of creating a self *is* inseparable from the creating of a world: Neither Faustus nor Tamburlaine (nor Edward, for that matter) can do one without doing the other. Defining the nature of one's desires is inseparable from verifying the existence of a reality external to the self. In what follows, then, I talk first about the conflicting traditions—Augustine's prominent among them—which Marlowe combines in unstable synthesis; then about the prevalence of Proteanism as a figure of evil in the English Renaissance; about the subversion of heroic rhetoric in Marlowe; about the subversion of the heroic quest; and finally about the quasi absurdity of Marlowe's world. These topics necessarily overlap: Problems of personality with the rhetoric that expresses it with the purposes that define it. That, however, is a linkage that Marlowe, operating within the tradition of carnivalesque destabilization, imposes. His vision, for all its focus on contradictions, is remarkably of a piece.

It is a fundamental and characteristic Marlovian tactic, for example, to foreground simultaneously two opposing tendencies in the Augustinian view of privative evil: the sense of evil as tragic potency—the self undoing the self—and the sense of it as comic impotency. This combination of hierarchic and grotesque gives us Faustus, universal genius and abject fool; Barabas, persecuted victim and monster; Tamburlaine, scourge of God and victim of a fever. Faustus's desire to "be on earth as God is in the heavens," to reign over the elements, is the desire to be a lord of unreality, closely comparable with Volpone's willful substitution of gold for God. In both cases, evil is dramatized as folly; that is, it is carnivalized. Volpone's materialism, like Iago's malice, is not merely a perversion but the expression of a fundamental lack: the absence of spirit that expresses itself as a lack of imagination (paradoxically combined with a superabundance of fantasy). Like his uncle Barabas, Volpone can imagine endless permutations of himself (and those most like himself, his victims), while being totally unable to imagine, or "realize" in the Lawrentian sense, Celia. Volpone, like Barabas, is both prolifically and aggressively *there* and metaphysically absent at the same time. That is why his vitality expresses itself in playing dead. That is why the plot turns on his ability to declare himself legally nonexistent. Similarly, Aquinas in the *Summa Theologiæ* (Q. 48, art. 3), adopting a familiar Augustinian trope, compares the absence of good with the absence of sight. Abigail learns to "see the difference of things" (3.3.68); her father cannot.

Privative evil, as we have seen, exists both negatively and paradoxically. It is real phenomenally, in the sense of having effects, while being unreal essentially. If you prick it, it will bleed. But it is matter turned away from life, being in motion toward nonbeing, unconsciousness, mere materiality. Marlowe is particularly aware of this gravitational drift of natural man toward nothingness, the tendency of vitiation to operate as what we would call a death wish, producing a chiasmic movement of seeming expansion as real diminishment. Augustine's theft of the pears is the great proto-type of Marlovian action: the rapt pursuit of worthless objects, each of which is discarded as soon as it is obtained. Faustus's provision of grapes for the Duchess of Vanholt repeats the Au-gustinian prototype in particularly literal terms. In Marlowe as in Augustine, the fallen soul habitually attempts to realize itself through the consumption of the unreal, becoming assimilated to the unliving objects it loves.[12] "I loved my fall" expresses the con-trolling drives of Edward and Barabas as well as the young Au-gustine. Privative evil is first and last a crime of the self against the self, whatever external actions may be by-products of that crime. Evil is primarily reflexive: Faustus can do nothing to others remotely comparable with what he does to himself. (The way in which Lightborn contrives that a parody of Edward's vice will be his death is a particularly savage illustration of the principle.) La-tent in the doctrine, available for Marlowe's subversive exploita-tion, is a kind of demoralization of evil: The essence of the crime is internalized and separated from external consequences.

Evil, then, becomes a form of suicide. In terms of privative evil denial of self and denial of God are essentially the same act, but only the self can be the victim of that act, one that derealizes both it and its world. When Faustus chooses to be a spirit and not a man, he acquires protean powers only at the cost of trapping himself in a world of shadows. Privative evil is necessarily protean *because* it lacks essence. It can exist only through appearances, and those appearances are bound to no essential core. Thus, privative evil is almost always comic: Its acts rebound upon itself, although para-doxically, there is no self there to be hurt. The Vice figure, the most famous manifestation of privative evil, is polymorphous not only in his mimicry of human fellowship and of his would-be vic-tim, but also in his degenerate, blurred form (human overlaid with animal elements: tail, horns, hooves) and in his ontologically am-biguous status. Is he external and "real" or internal and "subjec-tive"? Like Faustus, he is a spirit who only looks like a man. Like Faustus, the Vice, a figure of impairment, represents man derealizing himself, in an intermediate state between being and nonbeing. Degraded at once toward material reality and spiritual nullity, he is an emblematic figure of the ambiguity of the Augustinian carnivalesque.

AUGUSTINIAN AND MARLOVIAN THEATRICALITY

At the same time, the Vice embodies in his protean action a perception essential to the behavior of Marlowe's protagonists: that mimicry (as Hamlet also knows) is a form of aggression. When I play before you, I play upon you. My aim—whether I am Gaveston working on Edward or Faustus working his various audiences—is to charm, to deceive, to ravish; in short, to take you over while appearing to serve you. The power of protean, privative evil is its ability to embody imagination and desire. Fascinated by the "lovely boy in Dian's shape" (*Edward II*, 1.1.61), Edward will become the Actaeon he is to watch in Gaveston's imaginary show. Acting is thus both hostile and parasitic, the generation of shadows not only of fact, but also of the fantasies of others. (Alexander and his paramour, typically, embody both historical fact and the Emperor's fantasy.) Privative evil is necessarily protean; protean being—that focal figure of evil from Barabas and Iago to Milton's Satan and Richardson's Lovelace—manifests itself through acting.[13] Small wonder that "to entertain," as Gaveston means to do with Edward or Barabas with Calymath, should have so sinister a meaning in Marlowe's plays. Small wonder that the plays themselves should so explicitly set out to play upon and puzzle their audiences.

Playing upon an audience to prey upon it is, of course, the Vice's particular, ambiguous function. From the firecrackers on up, the Vice offers his victims and the spectators threat disguised as entertainment. Like the Marlovian protagonist, he entertains through mimicry to a sinister purpose. Lacking essential reality, he must manifest himself phenomenally through performance, playing, for example, the friendly adviser, as Mephostophilis disguises himself as a friar, Faustus's confessor; and as Milton's Satan manifests himself to Eve by playing a serpent, who in turn plays a courtly lover. When Faustus asks the meaning of Mephostophilis' first show, the devil replies, "Nothing . . . but to delight thy mind" (*Dr. Faustus*, 1.5.83). It is, in the most literal sense, a distraction—a theatricalized version of Augustine's *consuetudo*—drawing Faustus away from his real concerns toward shadows of wealth. What Lucifer offers Eve, as we have seen in chapter 1, are dreams, shadows of power and gratification, and images of her desire, which draw her away from the real power and satisfaction she already has. The Vice literally has nothing to offer, but that nothing is the embodiment of appetite and emptiness. "Nought" is the name of one of the devils in *Mankind*. To be evil, in a trope derived from this tradition, is to be "naughty," a thing of nothing, as Hamlet calls Claudius.

Fundamentally, the Vice appears to his human victim as evil imitating good, the subhuman imitating the human, the unreal the real. Because his power to create anything is as unreal as that of Mephostophilis', he appears to be powerful and is revealed to be impotent (but only after impressing other characters and the audience with the "reality" of his illusory power). Titivillus enters roaring and scattering fireworks, only to depart beaten and humiliated. The Vice is comic to the extent that he is vain and impotent, a painted devil, but he is comic also because, lacking humanity, he is immune to genuine suffering. (It is a characteristic Marlovian reversal to make the pain of Mephostophilis the most real thing in *Dr. Faustus*.) An exposer of human weakness who is ultimately exposed himself—in the characteristic double *ludus* of this tradition—the Vice operates as both *eiron* and *bomolochos*. At the same time, his protean role-playing, his prankishness, his habit of establishing ironic rapport with his audience at the expense of a victim who none the less represents them, and his lack of explainable motive—the Vice's "motive" for viciousness is, of course, his name—all contribute to the characteristically English manifestation of the Machiavel. The situation of the audience of the moralities, asked to identify with both victim and practicer while detaching itself from both, is very close to the situation Marlowe constructs for his audience. English Machiavels are experts in self-defeat, *bomolochoi* who imagine themselves to be *eirons,* embodying pride while deflating it in others. D'Amville brains himself with his own axe; Barabas cooks in his own pot. The same combination of qualities is readily apparent in Gaveston and in the later career of Mortimer as well as in Kyd's Lorenzo and the most resolutely opaque, "unmotivated" of Shakespeare's villains, Edmund and Iago. The glee with which Edmund tosses us the red herring of his bastardy in lieu of a motive, Lady Mabeth's discarding of her sexual identity, the final and impenetrable silences of Iago and Goneril, all reflect the tradition of privative evil. They manifest the presence, that is to say, of absence, as does the shiftiness of motive, that habit of reversing what had appeared to be fundamental biases of character which is apparent, for example, in virtually all the characters of *Edward II:* in Gaveston, in Kent, or in Isabella, the devoted victim who turns abruptly into blood-stained adulteress.

The radical instability of such characters has been seized upon by Jonathan Dollimore and Simon Shepherd as evidence of Marlowe's proto-Marxian disbelief in humanist conceptions of a stable, essential soul.[14] It might be wiser, I am arguing, to trace the quality backward to an inherited tradition of residual Augustinianism that defines evil in terms of role-playing and disguise, in which spiritual essence is not so much an illusion as something that can be abrogated or renounced. The devil is, after all, the father of lies and thus, naturally enough, of theater, especially carnivalesque theater.

However, Marlowe also inherits an alternative tradition in which proteanism signifies power rather than impotence, creativity rather than nullity. In Pico della Mirandola's *De hominis dignitate* man's protean nature, far from being a sign of his sinfulness, is potential glory. In the Oration, God tells Adam that "constrained by no limits, in accordance with thine own free will . . . thou shalt ordain for thyself the limits of thy nature. Thou shalt have the power to degenerate into the lower forms of life. . . . Thou shalt have the power, out of thy soul's judgement, to be reborn into higher forms, which are divine."[15] Man in this definition is radically self-determined, equally capable of rutting like a beast or reasoning like an angel. The human essence expresses its divinity in its fluidity, in process. Humanist idealism, in this case, mirrors carnival, both insisting that category destabilization *is* our category. Man alone is outside the stable hierarchy of creation: a "fourth circle," outside but partaking of the vegetable, animal, and spiritual worlds. Man is not merely multiplex, as Augustine argued, but protean: a congeries of potential selves directed by a will radically free to select its own form or forms in the process Greenblatt has taught us to call "Renaissance self-fashioning," Pico's version is, in short, the protean Faustus we are told of at the beginning of the play—now physician, now legalist, now demigod, now fool—but without the presumption of guilt. "Who," concludes Pico, "would not admire this chameleon?"[16]

Aversio and *conversio* both involve a breaking away from former identity. Loss of self is the way up as well as down. It is equally possible to respond to formlessness as void, emptiness, and evil or as capacity, fullness, and potential good. In fact, it is possible to respond to it in both ways at once. Pico does so in the Oration; Hamlet does it all the time, most notably in "what a piece of work is man," where the two responses are linked, Marlowe-fashion, by a single "but." This ambivalence is one of the most pervasive in major Elizabethan writing. For Donne in the *Songs and Sonnets,* man's (or, more to the point, woman's) inconstancy is virtually the definition of sinfulness; even in the *Holy Sonnets* the most terrifying of psychological states is the paralyzed fixity of the sinful soul unable, like Faustus's in his final scene, to transform itself. This is the state, common to Augustinian theology and its Lutheran and Calvinist descendants, in which the soul can lose itself in distraction but is powerless, in the absence of grace, to move toward its own salvation. To impose a radical, Marlovian simplification on material more properly treated at book length by John Carey, one could say that for Donne (and Marlowe), protean fluidity is what gets you damned, but inescapable fixity is the punishment for being damned. Faustus, that most Marlovian of Marlovian protagonists, displays this very doubleness: the apparent freedom of the man who has "legally" transformed himself into a spirit and the unavoidable confinement of slavery and despair. Seemingly at the other pole, Tamburlaine maintains his identity by the maniacal pursuit of a single self-image to the exclusion of all temptations to become human. While he does so, however, the terms that define that self-image dissolve into ambiguity. In what sense is he the "scourge of" (for? against?) what god (Jove? Allah? Jehovah?)? The two protagonists are united, of course, in the desire to make themselves lords of the elements, to create identity out of a blind commitment to the illusory and insubstantial. The fools of unbeing, they are the natural protagonists of slapstick tragedy.

"The God Thou Servest"

Marlowe, I am suggesting, subverts his heroic characters in the act of creating them, a method Shakespeare amplifies in the case of Antony. It is customary to talk of these Marlovian heroes in terms of their aspirations. This has the effect of saying that their identities are fundamentally negative: each is defined, in classically Augustinian terms, by desire, by that which he does not have. The Marlovian hero is a kind of subatomic particle: energy moving swiftly enough to create the illusion of substantiality. Faustus's aspirations—to godhead, immortality, untrammeled freedom—do not merely reflect the qualities most lacking in himself; they are also the very opposites of what he obtains in pursuit of them. Tamburlaine's enormous material power coexists with his constant, obsessive sense of that ever-retreating power that lies beyond it. In Part 2, he carries about with him the corpse of Zenocrate, the emblem of his ultimate inability to control the physical world. The Guise speaks for the all: "That like I best that flies beyond my reach" (*The Massacre at Paris,* 1.2.42). Tamburlaine keeps discovering, always to his outrage, that to be "the scourge of god" is merely to be the instrument of something larger than yourself. It humiliates you even as it glorifies you. When he is an outlaw, he dreams of being a king; when he is a king, he dreams of being an emperor; when he is emperor, he dreams of being a god. In his dying moments, he is preoccupied not only with storming the heavens but also, more practically, with that map which shows, more clearly and finally than anything else, what he has *not* conquered. "Give me a map; then let me see how much / Is left . . . / That these, my boys, may finish all my wants" (*Tamburlaine, Part 2,* 5.3.124–26). I am that I lack.

The Marlovian hero tries to absorb the material world, the not-I. He wants, like Tamburlaine, to reduce it to a map with his name on it. If he can incorporate it into his imaginative order, impose his will upon it, he will have acquired a substantial reality; he will have made himself tangible. (Thus, the snake of imagination swallows the pig of fact.) He will be "on earth as Jove is in the heavens." The literal-mindedness of Tamburlaine and Faustus, their obsession with grapes and crowns and gold, is a function of their need to make fantasy materially real so that others must see and acknowledge it. They are engaged in the continuous creation of emblems that will force others to endorse the reality of what the emblems imply (a quintessentially literary activity, of course). One gains identity by affirmation. This is to say that Tamburlaine does not exist without an audience, but by the same token he does not exist *with* an audience. The theatrical self-consciousness of the performance (costuming himself and setting his own stage to meet Theridamas; serving constantly as his own presenter; arranging his power in tableaux) is all a constant reminder of the actor within the role. The reflexiveness of the presentation reminds us of the unreality of what is being asserted as real. This, the play keeps saying, is Alleyn imitating Tamburlaine, just as a famous advertising slogan once told us that "Dustin Hoffman *is* Tootsie," a similar example of simultaneous affirmation and denial of the actor's presence. Even more than Alleyn, it is the Scythian shepherd who imitates "Tamburlaine." Who and what is Tamburlaine? A part playing a part: an illusion pursuing an illusion by means of illusion. Such a being clearly needs help. Thus Tamburlaine's rule becomes a perpetual process of demonstration and reaffirmation: see, I'm divine (aren't I driving this chariot pulled by kings?); yes, you're divine (aren't you driving this chariot . . . ?), and so on. Tamburlaine needs Theridamas to tell him he is there, just as he needs to kill to know he is alive. In effect, he needs to have every speech countersigned by witnesses. Early in Part 2 he reminds his sons that he is "the scourge and terror of the world"; Amyras and Celebinus solemnly announce that they, too, want to be "the scourge and terror of the world." "Be all a scourge and terror of the world," their father replies, "Or else you are not sons of Tamburlaine" (1.4.58–64). Repeat the magic formula enough times and it will come true. The moment Calyphas refuses to repeat the formula, he induces murderous panic focused obsessively on the fear that Calyphas is "not my son" (4.1.91). If your son is not your son, then your essence is not your essence (and your wife may not be your wife). Everything begins to slip back into otherness.

In this curiously infantile system, other people become accessories or reflections of the self. Lacking essential identity, the heroic self continually seeks phenomenal manifestations, as Tamburlaine tries to manifest himself through endless ceremonial. As he becomes further involved in ceremonial, he increasingly becomes a travesty of the kind of imperial power he originally has mocked.[17] If all these people are followers, the shows imply, there must be a leader. Every day is coronation day (lest we forget, lest we forget). In other words, Tamburlaine is his army, as Faustus is his shows, Barabas his wealth (his "substance," as in 1.2.89), and Edward his crown. "But what *are* kings when regiment is gone / But perfect shadows on a sunshine day?" (*Edward II*, 5.1.26–27; my italics). "Perfect" here carries its literal sense of "complete"; perfect shadows amount to a complete absence or privation. A moment later, Edward is playing with giving away the crown and in 5.5.92–93 is asking: "Where is my crown? / Gone, gone! And do I remain alive?" The answer, to be given in a moment, is "No." Without the symbol how shall we find the thing symbolized? Like evil in the Augustinian formulation, you are real phenomenally—you have effects—but you are not (or conceive yourself as not being) real essentially. You may exercise Pico's freedom to ascend or descend the hierarchy of forms, but, as Faustus finds, the more richly your forms proliferate, the more starved becomes the will that directs them, the harder it becomes to find the soul within the show. Freedom is conceived as exhilarating (each act a ravishment, a little death), as illusory to the extent that apparently free will is governed by obsession, and finally, as annihilating: an investment of life in the acquisition of dead matter. This is essentially the process of *consuetudo* in which the vitiated soul becomes assimilated to the material things it loves and with which it confuses itself. My crown is real, Edward assumes, but I am not; *it* confers reality on *me;* it confers life, as gold seem to do for Volpone.

As Marlowe subverts the reality of his heroes, he does something very similar to their apparent goals. The Marlovian protagonist continually reinvents the tangible object of his aspiration, without necessarily realizing that he is doing so. "Nature," as we all know,

> that fram'd us of four elements
> Warring within our breasts for regiment,
> Doth teach us all to have aspiring minds.
> Our souls, whose faculties can comprehend
> The wondrous architecture of the world,
> And measure every wandering planet's course,
> Still climbing after knowledge infinite,
> And always moving as the restless spheres,
> Wills us to wear ourselves and never rest
> Until we reach the ripest fruit of all,
> That perfect bliss and sole felicity,
> The sweet fruition of an earthly crown.
> *(Tamburlaine, Part 2,* 2.7.18)

The tendency in trying to come to terms with this is to note the thunderingly positive tone and summary sweep of the speech and to assume that it must therefore be an authoritative and final statement of what Tamburlaine is. But, of course, everything he says is thunderingly positive, and this speech, also of course, is a tissue of fallacies. Each element in nature, according to the Tamburlaine version, wars against every other element. The appearance of *natura naturans* is only an illusion created by a stalemate in the strife of *natura naturata.* The war of all against all is presented as a permanent condition expressed by present participles like *climbing* and *moving,* a matter of struggle without closure, strife as its own reward, and thus as something radically different from Tamburlaine's own ostensibly purposive struggle. We are "to wear ourselves and never rest / *Until we reach* the ripest fruit." Not atypically, he approaches a logical conclusion only to swerve away in the next line. If this version of the state of nature teaches us anything, it is "to war," not to seek a specific goal and then stop.

The entire argument is based on a fallacy of personification that becomes a fallacy of circularity: I behave like the elements because they behave like me. If we for a moment ignore the fallacy, we are led to a still less tenable position. As Tamburlaine's own death from an overdose of choler will prove, the war of the elements must be a perpetual stalemate, otherwise nature destroys itself. What *do* the elements strive for? A victory that is indistinguishable from death. They strive for their own defeat.

Thus, far from subverting Elizabethan (or Christian) orthodoxy, as Shepherd and Dollimore might wish, the illogic of the speech leads directly back to it. The movement of the "restless spheres," as Faustus finds out, is in fact regulated and in the long run stable. It is ordered, fixed movement, not rebellious energy. Again, it suggests the opposite of the lesson Tamburlaine attempts to draw. And the attainment of a crown, as he should know, having just overthrown Mycetes and Cosroe, brings nothing like rest. Tamburlaine's own kingship is a continual war of aggression-as-defense; even his "truce with all the world" is an interval filled with the campaigns of his lieutenants. At this moment, Tamburlaine himself, having attained his first crown, has no intention of rest. He is instead psyching up the troops for the next campaign. That, more than disinterested metaphysical speculation, is what the speech is really about.

SELF-FASHIONING AND ITS DISCONTENTS

Like the goals of Marlowe's other heroes, in fact, "the sweet fruition of an earthly crown" is a nonce symbol. It provides the illusion of an attainable end, the usual false comfort of the obsessive. It is the warrior's version of the compulsive gambler's big win that will allow him to quit. In very short order, crowns will become so devalued that they can be distributed as party favors. It tells us something about the value of an earthly crown—and the carnivalesque terms of its reduction—that we cannot be sure whether Tamburlaine's "course of crowns" are real or pastry. Typical of Marlowe's heroes, he confuses symbol and substance, just as Mycetes does when he tries to preserve his kingship by hiding his crown. Like Faustus, Tamburlaine tries to place heavenly satisfaction, "perfect bliss and sole felicity," in an earthly, material, easily transferable object, his own version of "infinite riches in a little room." The Marlovian protagonist obsessively seeks the infinite in the finite, the absolute through the relative. Thus, as each nonce symbol is attained, it turns out not to be the real thing but a kind of material parody and is devalued and discarded as the imagination reinvents its object. The Helen who is to make Faustus immortal with a kiss is forgotten entirely once he or she or it has been enjoyed and is never mentioned again. As Greenblatt puts it, the "one critical link" between Marlowe's protagonists is that "they are *using up* experience" (*Renaissance Self-Fashioning,* 198). The tangible goals experience can provide are valuable because they stand for something beyond themselves, but contemptible and disposable because they cannot *be* that something. The true end, the thing these nonce symbols are meant to stand for, remains both ineffable and unattainable, beyond not merely the treacheries of possession but those of expression: "one grace, one wonder . . . / Which into words no virtue can digest" (*Tamburlaine, Part 1,* 5.2.109–10). You can, briefly, have Zenocrate; you can not have Beauty. When you have the (mere) woman, you alternate between deifying her and regarding her as a source of effeminate pollution: the "amorous" looks that remind you that your sons are not exclusively yours (*Tamburlaine, Part 2,* 1.4.21).

The analogue to Tamburlaine's subtly nebulous quest is Barabas's pursuit of "vengeance": another ever-expanding, evereluding, imaginary goal.[18] If a convent full of nuns is not enough, how many would be? Both Tamburlaine and Barabas achieve the the appearance of sanity by substituting a finite object for an infinite: "vengeance," a temporal misnomer for an eternal negative, a literally unquenchable hostility that turns eventually to the destruction of one's own progeny. Whereas Shakespearian villains (Goneril, Regan, Iago, Macbeth) seem to have been born sterile, Marlovian heroes achieve sterility through the process of selfassertion.[19]

If the reality of the goal is subverted, so is that of the quest for it. In a typically chiasmic movement, the temporal goal of the Marlovian hero, while seeming to lead to the essential one, actually leads away from it. Every step Edward tries to take toward freedom and sanctuary with Gaveston leads toward prison and death. Every step Faustus takes to gain freedom and power is a further confinement, as the pursuit of absolute being leads him to absolute destruction. Tamburlaine's own quest becomes a similarly rigid confinement disguised as freedom. Trapped in the role of a man playing "Tamburlaine," he cannot spare the Virgins of Damascus because the tents are black. If he makes a free choice, he violates the order of his ritual and thus destroys the construct of his own identity. At the same time, he cannot stop fighting because his enemies will not stop "managing arms against him." Every victory creates new enemies, yielding a war that is ultimately as inconclusive as that between the elements. What first appears to be a barely qualified power fantasy turns out to be something close to actualized paranoia. As in the myth, Proteus can be trapped in a form

from which there is no escape. Not surprisingly, much of Tamburlaine's rhetorical energy is devoted to foreclosing choice while
seeming to assert it. If you *are* sons of Tamburlaine, you *must* be
"the scourge and terror of the world"; otherwise, you must not
exist. He does not choose to love Zenocrate. Given the fact of that
love, he devotes the famous soliloquy on beauty to disguising his
enslavement as mastery, reducing her from an unreachable muse
to a glorified cheerleader paying the tribute of her "just applause"
to his *virtu*. Given the domination of his nature by the element of
fire, he must assert simultaneously that his nature is the result of
free choice and that it is a natural inevitability. In the end, that
element, chosen or not, destroys him. The warring Nature that
teaches "us all to have aspiring minds" must in fact virtually compel us to have them. If all nature is at war, how can we as objects
in nature be at peace? The intellectual problem is how to make
that destructive compulsion appear as freedom, even as the plays
subvert the notion of freedom.

Clearly, every Marlowe play from *Dido and Aeneas* to *The Massacre at Paris* focuses on the self-destruction of its protagonist.
Douglas Cole, in a once widely accepted formulation, argues that
tragedy in Marlowe is something personal to the protagonists; "it
is not cataclysmic," and it is not primarily social.[20] But this implies
a moral distinction between hero and onlookers that the plays consistently obviate. Heroic appetite is, after all, only appetite writ
large. Theridamas admires kingship, but he "can live without it"
(*Tamburlaine, Part 2*, 2.5.66). Charles the Emperor is entranced
with Faustus's shows, but only as a diversion (which is also how
Aeneas is entranced with Dido). The Scholars are awed by Helen,
but, again, can live without her. Where others accept more or less
arbitrary limitations on their desires, the protagonist does not because the maintenance of desire is essential to his sense of identity.
Figuring carnival appetite and refusing the return of Lenten re-
striction, he needs to have his cake and go hungry too. While the
infinite degree of his desire separates him from those around him,
the kind of his desire links him to them. He acts on their wish.
Thus Marlowe at least partially subverts the apparent difference
between heroic and unheroic. The Marlovian protagonist is a summer lord who imagines himself a real lord.

The correlative of this is that the Marlovian hero is both more
and less imaginative than his fellows. Like other fantasists he is
remarkably attuned to the worlds generated by his own mind while
being remarkably insensitive to a world of fact we are finally never
allowed to think is unreal. Marlowe's is a world of rock, not a world

of dew. It does not yield, it does not vanish, and it does not respond. Except in the minds of men, poetry makes nothing happen. Callipine's army will retreat at the mere sight of Tamburlaine, but Death will not. Indeed, Death's action, first retreating from Tamburlaine's glance and then sneaking back again (*Tamburlaine, Part 2,* 5.3.67–71) mocks both the hero who imagines it and his human enemies. Here and elsewhere, Marlowe insists on strict, literal, earthbound limitations: Twenty-four years is twenty-four years, to the minute: "The clock will strike, / The devil will come" (*Dr. Faustus,* 5.2.153–54). Death, we might say, is regular as clockwork. The dying Faustus's eloquent attempt to talk Time into stopping is the prototype of all Marlovian rhetorizing. Zenocrate's depressing commonplaces come depressingly true: One *does* grow old, get sick, and die. She fares "as other empresses" (*Tamburlaine, Part 2,* 2.4.42).

A process that necessarily accompanies the other carnivalesque subversions I have described in each play is the ritual destruction of poetry. While Tamburlaine talks (and talks) Zenocrate dies. Repeatedly, the crucial lines are thuddingly, deflatingly literal and prosaic: "Ah, good my lord, be patient! She is dead," which is Theridamas's response to Tamburlaine's wounding the earth and threatening Jove (*Tamburlaine, Part 2,* 2.4.119). "Nothing prevails," he adds helpfully. "I think hell's a fable," blusters Faustus, and we all know Mephostophilis' puncturing response. "I view'd your urine," says the Physician (*Tamburlaine, Part 2,* 5.3.82) and proceeds to reduce the hero's fiery spirit to the enflamed bowels from which it springs. If the proleptic shadow of Swift's "mechanical operation of the spirit" hangs over Tamburlaine's career, so does the shadow of carnival degradation and Augustinian *perversio.*

With remarkable consistency imaginative rhetoric is shown to be not a way of penetrating reality, but a way of evading or reshaping it. When Mephostophilis gives Faustus the facts of cosmography, Faustus is comically outraged. "These are freshman's suppositions," he complains (2.1.54–55). Despite having renounced the only book capable of offering miracles, he still innocently expects truth to be fantastic, exotic: "Strange philosophy, / . . . the secrets of all foreign kings" (1.1.85–86). When he asks for the secrets of nature, Mephostophilis hands him three textbooks containing the sort of knowledge he has just renounced. At a minimum, Tamburlaine expects a bolt from the heavens; he gets a fever.

It cannot be said too strongly: The reality of Marlowe's world is prose. The lies about it are in verse.[21] You ask for color, you are given black-and-white. Poetic imagination deceives precisely because it heightens and colors the facts, transmutes them into myth; inflates the self; reshapes neutral events (the defeat of Sigismund) into "meaningful" patterns (the divine intervention Orcanes decides he would like to believe in to account for the defeat).[22] The facts of *Tamburlaine* are that the cosmic revenge tragedy demanded and predicted by character after character for ten acts never, in any verifiable form, comes. Poetic justice does not obtain, though Marlowe practices upon us to make us think it does. Tamburlaine burns the Koran, Tamburlaine falls sick and dies: *post hoc, propter hoc*. Then the Physician enters, talking of urine. Typically, the Marlovian swing carries us toward a meaningful pattern, so that the roundabout can carry us away from it. Slapstick tragedy operates at the expense of its audience and their theocratic assumptions as well as the hero and his. (He is not the only one subverted.) Here, unlike *The Spanish Tragedy*, there is no prologue in hell; unlike *The Revenger's Tragedy*, there is no monitory thunder. Tamburlaine's god, unlike Antony's, is never heard to leave him because he has never been heard at all, except in Tamburlaine's assertions.

The tongue, Marlowe constantly suggests, was given to man so that he could tell lies with it. If language is power in Marlowe, it is primarily the power to deceive. That is why "poet" is another of his comic and sinister words. "I must have wanton poets," says Gaveston, "to draw the pliant king which way I please" (*Edward II*, 1.1.51, 53). The masque that Gaveston, a wanton poet himself, proceeds to conjure leads to the destruction of Actaeon, Edward's own archetype, and Gaveston's bland comment that "such things as these best please his majesty" (71). "Sweet speeches . . . pleasing shows" (56) mask death as pastoral, warning as entertainment. Where they present truth at all it is in a form that will not be read or accepted. Indeed, Marlowe's plays can be seen as a virtual catalog of the abuses of art: as deception or distraction or narcotic, the enactment of privative evil's world of shadows. Poetry and theatricality are the arts by which the art of self-fashioning constitutes itself. Gaveston, Barabas, Faustus, even Tamburlaine, are examples of the showman as Vice, playing upon himself while playing upon his various audiences.

The fundamental drive of his poet heroes is to turn reality into a manipulable fiction. For example, love in Marlowe is always involved with domination; it occurs between master and "slave" (Edward and Gaveston, Jupiter and Ganymede, Faustus and Mephostophilis, Tamburlaine and his captive Zenocrate), but it reverses the social domination. As usual in the carnivalesque, instinct levels what the will erects. The master falls in love with slavery as well as with the slave. Thus, finding himself abased by love for Zenocrate, Tamburlaine must cast the relationship into a form more suitable to his fiction of himself. He does this, in his great soliloquy on beauty (*Tamburlaine, Part 1:* 5.2.72–127), by drawing a firm distinction between essential Beauty, which is heavenly, ineffable, and unreachable, and its representatives on earth, who are not only reachable, but also disposable. He has, after all, just had a hundred of them put to death. He can then conflate the two, beginning at the point where the earthly Zenocrate gives "instructions" to the heavenly Beauty (83) and proceeding through the lines about poets, where Beauty is at once transcendent and subsumed (it "hover[s] *in* their restless heads" [108; my italics]), until he arrives at the point where beauty is reduced to passive and applauding spectatorship at *his* glory (115–19).

Simply put, the speech is not about Zenocrate or about Beauty; it is about Tamburlaine, as what speech of his is not? (Self-love, as Augustine would say, is always admiring the image of its own strength.) Its function is to restore him to a position of centrality in his own mind, to convert beauty from a source of pain to a source of applause and to declare his own virtue (not hers or the poets') "the sum of glory" (126). The notorious grammatical confusion about "conceiving and subduing both" is an enactment of his confused effort to assert mastery over whatever in the speech (beauty, thought, self, other) threatens to escape his control. He has, after all, just admitted a kind of defeat, neatly transferred from himself to poets, whose brains (not his own exactly) finally cannot "digest" essential beauty into words. He can then push that failure further away by reminding himself of "the terror of [his] name" (113)—an assertion of the power of a word following upon an admission of a failure of words—and going on to reassure himself that even stooping to love is proof of his Jupiter-like divinity (121–25). At the point where he has finally assured himself that submission (love) is really assertion (conquest), that he will "march in cottages" (124) as if he were sacking them, he can afford to turn his attention to whether Bajazeth has been fed. Once again, an effort toward the sublime and transcendent collapses into the literal and grotesque. What Tamburlaine does to his enemies is nothing compared with what he does to logic.

The misuses of rhetoric are, in a way, the subject of all three of Tamburlaine's great set speeches about Zenocrate. The first (*Part 1,* 1.2.82–105) is undercut by the addition of "women must be flattered"; the second ("what is beauty") covers the massacre of the

Virgins with a show of concern for that other virgin, Zenocrate; the third (*Part 2*, 2.4.1–38) attempts to deny the reality of her death, which follows hard upon it. In all three, the rhetoric creates its own reality in opposition to what the scene shows. Tamburlaine escapes from the scene of Zenocrate's death into a fantasy of her entrance into heaven, in a speech addressed to no one on stage and thus clearly designed to comfort himself, not her. While he gives orders to heaven, the skies remain as silent as ever. The heaven invoked is a mishmash of Christian and pagan, without internal consistency even as fantasy. The woman deified is the boy actor about to "die" before us. The seductive rhetoric draws us into the fantasy while virtually every literal aspect of the stage picture, including Tamburlaine's unpersuaded auditors, pushes us away. The hero cheers himself up as nature goes about its own (deadly) business. As Faustus acknowledges, all the Marlovian hero's frantic and poetic activity is, in effect, a remedy against despair and suicide: "Long ere this I should have done the deed, / Had not sweet pleasure conquered deep despair" (2.1.24–25). The reality of the Marlovian world is death. Everything else, literally and figuratively, is distraction and thus subject to subversion.

In the process of self-distraction, the Marlovian protagonist— out-heroding Herod—is liable to look singularly foolish, as when Tamburlaine bellows challenges at his two surviving sons, and the little piping voices answer. Being unwilling to accept the limitations of the physical world, the hero is remarkably prone to be tripped up by what is obvious to everyone around him. Thus the Guise imagines himself as Caesar without remembering the most caution- ary fact about Caesar: He went to the Forum. At the same time, because the hero's appetite is self-generating and because its ob- jects are inherently substitutes of about equal (non) value, the hero is also apt to resemble a child in a sweet shop, spying out a new obsessional object as fast as the previous one is exhausted. Ed- ward, who has believed that he cannot live without Gaveston, re- places him with Spenser, hardly even pausing for the requisite anguish. And surely no character, not even Fanny Hill, was ever ravished quite so often as Faustus and by quite so little. As the Evil Angel has learned, you do not even need to give him wealth; saying the word will suffice (as it does at 1.5.23–24).

Finally, Marlowe half subverts the very passions that seem to be the most real thing in his world. Quite simply, in terms of the world of fact and in terms of his ability to focus on or sustain interest in other people, the Marlovian hero is astonishingly and infantilely fickle: Given the essential insubstantiality of the objects of desire, he could hardly be otherwise. Famously, Tamburlaine reacts to Zenocrate's death by swearing (à la Edward) that he cannot live without her, wrapping the body in gold, massacring the usual victims, proclaiming (again) his eternal devotion, and passing without a blink into a lecture on fortification. This is not to say that the grief is not "there," but only that it has no duration. Grief is coterminous with the rhetorical performance that seems, inevitably, to have created it. The impression is of intensity without extent. But if passion for a particular object is radically foreshortened, passion per se is radically extended. This is a lesson in what Augustine calls the distension of the self in time: Need is constant, relationship is fragmented. While one minion replaces another, the desire for a minion remains constant. "The God thou servest is thine own appetite" (*Dr. Faustus,* 1.5.11). Faustus's crucial formulation divorces appetite from its objects, making it curiously self-sufficient and solipsistic. Like those other servants Gaveston, Mephostophilis, and Cupid, it is actually a master. When Ferneze asks the Basso what brings him to Malta, the latter replies, "the wind that bloweth all the world besides, / Desire of gold" (*Jew of Malta,* 3.5.3–4), a phrase that turns "all the world" into human dust. It makes all these greedy strivers oddly passive, things blown by an impersonal force. The desire does not belong to you, you belong to it. It is a wind that bloweth where it listeth, anywhere and nowhere, and it blows all the world together: Jew, Christian, and Turk without distinction.

The effect of each of these plays is to reduce what appear to be essential distinctions to mere labels, arbitrarily distinguishing people whose behavior is fundamentally the same: Jews, Turks, and Christians in *The Jew of Malta;* legitimate and illegitimate rulers in *Tamburlaine;* homosexual tyrant and heterosexual in *Edward II;* "heroic" and "unheroic" in all the plays. The furious obsession with self-definition that afflicts nearly all Marlowe's characters—they are united, if by nothing else, in their desire to be separate—coexists with structures that obviate difference, much as *Waiting for Godot* obviates distinctions between traveling and waiting. The more the characters proclaim their differences, the more they are the same thing.[23]

A similarly reductive confusion operates within each one, pulling him down to the lower bodily level. Faustus's own language relentlessly reduces his most idealistic posturing to *cupiditas* and *cupiditas* itself to brute physical appetite. His imagination feeds, "gluts," "surfeits" him. The language of consumption and thus of carnival degradation pervades the play from "how am I glutted with conceit of this" (1.1.77) to the "surfeit of deadly sin that hath damned both body and soul" (5.2.39–40). Naturally, the appearance of the Seven Deadly Sins "feeds my soul" (2.1.177), and Helen will "glut the longing of my heart's desire" (5.1.89). But even this reduction is a metaphor for something else: the desire, which is the natural correlative of privative evil, to fill up one's emptiness. The most significant point about Faustus's power fantasies is not that they all reduce to a norm defined by the most material element, but that they are so hopelessly incoherent. Typically, fame, freedom, silk, secrets, and tropical fruit all jumble together in shapeless reveries that do not end, but are interrupted, as they are by Valdes and Cornelius in scene 2.

Anything will serve so long as it creates the illusion of commitment. Inconstant as he is, Faustus clings to the idea of having made an unbreakable contract: "Now, Faustus, must thou needs be damned. . . . What boots it then to think on God or heaven?" (1.5.1–3; that is, before he has signed the contract). Manifestly, while instructing himself to despair, he takes comfort in despair because it conveys not merely identity but quasi-heroic identity, from the height of which he can instruct Mephostophilis in "manly fortitude" (1.3.85). While appearing to seek freedom and expansion, the Marlovian protagonist in fact seeks limitation in a form he can disguise as aggrandizement; in the roles of damned sinner or mechanically inflexible conqueror, of malevolent "Jew" or homosexual outcast. Each role leads to what Kuriyama calls "this peculiarly Marlovian theme of being imprisoned in a personality bent toward self-destruction."[24] Each character turns himself into a caricature, a suicidal travesty of a free self.

Of course, Marlowe's heroes are remarkably unheroic. The most basic enterprise of each play is the deconstruction of the concept of heroism, revealing it as the half-comic and half-pathetic expression of a desire for grandeur, uniqueness, and meaning. His subject is the egoistic imagination at desperate play in an apparently silent world. Tamburlaine creates gods and nature in his own image; Faustus disguises his bondage and cowardice as freedom and heroism; Edward, a moment before his death, reinvents his lost kingship in the chivalric image of running at tilt in France for Isabella's sake, an image that momentarily expunges virtually every fact of his present situation, from puddle water to cuckoldry. Barabas and the Guise invest themselves with a myth of Machiavellian omnicompetence that fatally obscures the dangers around them. The tragicomic death of each is a typically savage Marlovian uncrowning.

What is Marlovian "heroism," then, but a capacity for believing one's own propaganda, the better to impose it on others? The only thing defeated in Marlowe more often than heroic aspiration is common sense. Theridamas and Zenocrate are always capable of deflating Tamburlaine's fantasies, but never capable of shaking off their own addiction to them. The more serenely mad you are, the more likely it is that you will carry all others with you. Blindness is power. Intermittently and very much against his will, Faustus sees more than Tamburlaine, sees something beyond, above, inimical to his myth of an all-powerful self. (That is one reason why he has fewer followers.) Similarly, the weakness but also the dignity of Edward is his final ability to see, dimly, the difference between self and myth: "What are kings when regiment is gone"—in the process of denying his specious glory, he also denies his own existence. The sun king redefines himself as a shadow king. The reality he discovers is his own privation. After Dido, however, no Marlovian protagonist is granted even the heroism of Hedda Gabler or Miss Julie: to act on the discovery of one's own nullity.

A correlative of this process is that no Marlovian protagonist has any lasting effect on the world. A minimum of historical awareness tells the audience of *Tamburlaine* that his empire vanishes almost as soon as he stops talking about it. His boys really do "finish all his wants." Faustus cancels himself: "Cut is the bough that might have grown full straight"—he is a possibility that did not take place. Barabas's fear that he "may vanish o'er the earth in air / And leave no memory" (1.2.270–71) comes approximately true as Malta resumes the ordinary course of its corruption under the governor it started with. The anti-social fabric closes neatly with the death of the outsider. Dido goes out in a bloodbath she has not intended, the suicides of Anna and Iarbus mocking her claims to uniqueness of suffering, while Æneas floats toward his destiny. Edward is supplanted and revenged by the son whose existence he has barely noticed. At best, he has played his role in the fisher-king story whose hero must be the new Edward who replaces him. As he feared would happen (5.1.48), he dies and his name lives on. The Guise's sole Caesarian achievement is to activate his antagonist, Navarre. Each of them, like their ancestral Vices, is unmasked and dismissed. Each is a kind of gap in the proceedings of history, a burp at the cosmic feast.

Slapstick tragedy—Marlowe's characteristically violent form of the tragicarnivalesque—is, after all, the only kind a Vice can star in. It is in the nature of privative evil that it registers primarily as folly: a pratfall into nonexistence. Eliot was, of course, right to respond to *The Jew of Malta* as savage farce and to perceive that it is farce played out in a waste land.[25] A morality play seen from the point of view of the Vice must be an exercise in foredoomed, absurd activity: a matter of throwing firecrackers at a castle, tragedy as carnival. In the case of Faustus, it is a matter of ascending on your dragon to the ninth sphere only to find that you have, at the cost of your soul, purchased a considerably expanded cage. As the walls of that cage become visible, so does the absurdity of the creature strutting, Chauntecleer-like, within it, imagining himself a potentate. A nutshell, no matter how large, will not make you a king of infinite space. To be a ruler of the elements, as Faustus imagines himself to be, is only a larger form of being a lord of much dirt. As their purposes are progressively revealed to be delusory and frustrating, as self dissolves into permutations of unreality, the protagonists' habitual exhortations to themselves to "be resolute" begin to sound like Pozzo's cry of "Onward!" Like him they stagger toward St. Sauveur, undeterred by blindness or the fact that their wealth is a bag of sand.

The Confessions of Dr. Faustus

As will be clear by now, I regard much, perhaps most, of Marlowe's work as a sustained, skeptical gloss on Augustine: *Confessions: The Preterite Version.* For both writers, the most basic fact of human nature is the restlessness bred of privation, its normative condition is blindness, its consuming sin *curiositas* in the particular form of a passion for the worthless. The core of the self, for each, is desiring emptiness, the "hungering dark" Debora Shuger (*Habits of Thought in the English Renaissance,* 69) finds in the sermons of Tindale and Hooker: a void that could only be filled by God, but that the human ego keeps trying to fill with material goods and physical experiences. In both cases, the fate of the self is to be consumed by what it consumes, disappearing into pastness along with its experiences. What is missing for Marlowe's protagonists— indeed for virtually all his characters—is simply the divine reality that for Augustine displaces our emptiness. In the end, Faustus the preterite sinner is caught in the first stage of Calvinist conversion— recognition of the enormity of one's sins and despair at the wrath of God—without being able to advance to the second stage; the acceptance of grace (see *Institutes,* 3.3.7). This is only an emotionally intensified version of his state at the beginning of the play when he reinforces his own despair by remembering the biblical threats in Romans 6:23 and 1 John 1:8 while omitting the accompanying promises (1.1.38–43).[26] Without grace, there is no progression. In the absence of God, everything else is comically inadequate substitution. Literally in the case of Faustus, figuratively in the other cases, Marlowe shows us Augustine's universe from the viewpoint of the unredeemed.

Marlowe's slapstick tragedy of the ego and its discontents will, in fact, seem eerily familiar to readers of Augustine's *Confessions,* not merely because the chiasmic defeat of worldly ambitions in the process of their realization is so central a feature of Augustine's narrative. The education for worldly success that Patricius gives his son leads the latter to the renunciation of that success. The fulfillment of Monica's hopes for her son's conversion costs her the grandchildren who are her other hope. Dr. Faustus, as Philip Brockbank pointed out many years ago, bears the name of Augustine's Manichean rival, just as he shares his original's belief in the substantial reality and independence of evil.[27] Just as important, his career reflects that anxiety over the nature of the ego and the means of its preservation that pervades the *Confessions.* The ego, as Augustine conceives it, is of course remarkably evanescent, painfully and dangerously "distended" through time and space, always liable to fly apart or dissolve into its constituent moments or, within the present moment, into its own multiplicity. Narration for Augustine, like worship, is a constant struggle against distraction, the bane and comfort of Dr. Faustus's existence. In both protagonists, the aspiration to "be resolute" struggles against the entropic tendency of consciousness to lose itself in the solicitations of the external world.

When Augustine in book 12 imagines salvation it is as a state of permanent definedness: an unchanging simplicity in which you exist as pure adoration, reflecting God and reflecting upon Him, an ecstatic shadow. Of the present self, he could say, as he does of time,[28] "I understand it until I try to talk about it" (cf. *Conf.,* XI, 14). Augustine's narrative, in turn, continually tries to fix the self by textualizing it, turning every significant moment of his life into the realization of a text or texts, as Faustus turns his life into the conscious attempt to realize the contents of his magic books and the unconscious drive to realize the biblical texts he has dismissed in his first speech. The "I" of Augustine's narrative alters with every attempt to define it. It is variously the total contents of the storehouse of *memoria* in book 10 and the disembodied consciousness that wanders through it, at once proprietor and sightseer. It is the soul, but also a mass of accidents that must be held separate from the soul. It is your will, which is not yours but God's; and it is your perverted will, which, without existing, still pulls you away from existence; and it is the worldly self—Augustine the Professor—created by that perversity. Crucially, it is that lump of something that is left when you have seen through and renounced the worldly self: the lump God shapes, informs, teaches, speaks to and through in order to make the "real" you. You discover your mortality, as we have seen, by dissolving that social identity—deconstructing it—a process that produces the proof of your damnation and the hope of your salvation.

Faustus's twenty-four year struggle to stabilize and realize his ego, to constitute it out of unreality, is the perfect, manichean shadow of Augustine's: the narrative of the damnation without the completing narrative of the salvation, a version in which the better angels are shouted down. If not to enforce the analogy, why else should Marlowe latinize Faust into Faustus?[29] All Marlovian comedy because its central subject is the construction of false consciousness, is Augustinian comedy. For that reason, it is also the carnivalesque comedy of masking and unmasking. (Anyone seeking the tradition of comedy to which Eliot assigned *The Jew of Malta* need look no further than the first half of *Confessions*.) The trick of the devils is, of course, to show Faustus his life as show, even while deluding him with the "reality" of material possession and the "power" of performance. His Augustinian damnation is to believe in the reality of his masques, which are in fact figurations of *consuetudo:* to love that which he has conjured, shadows without substance.

Faustus's character is doubly carnivalesque. He is the unmasker of earthly pretensions to dignity—the uncrowner of the Pope and Benvolio, the clownish supplanter of Paris—and the hopeless thrall of pretension who imagines he *is* Paris (and Homer to boot) and whose revenge on Benvolio is an outraged response to offenses against his dignity. Not surprisingly, like carnival itself, Faustus is taken up by rulers as a pastime. He offers them a show of power that, in its insubstantiality and pointlessness, mirrors theirs. He doesn't control it, they don't control him, though both pretend to. "His" power realizes—that is, makes unreal shows of—their desires, each as silly as his own (grapes, warts: what people ask for when you offer them their heart's desire). In prior turn, of course, the pageant of the Seven Deadly Sins has shown Faustus the farce-image of his own desires. Faustus enters every court as both satirist and consoling illusionist, potentate and slave—the dialectic that provides the real dramatic interest of the magic scenes—doing tricks for the entertainment of lesser fools, being entertained as both wonder and fraud.

Habitually, the Marlovian protagonist plays the game of power parodically, as an outsider who sees it as illusion even while being captivated by it. He plays it to destroy it, even though his identity depends on it. Carnival uncrowning has no more literal advocate than the Tamburlaine of *Part 1*. (The Tamburlaine of *Part 2* comes to see himself as the official order—the ruler of the world could hardly do otherwise—and thus comes to the attention of death-the-mocker.[30]) Edward, who wants to turn his kingship into narcissistic pageantry, also wants to be a king of substance. Barabas mocks Christian machiavellism while imitating it and succeeds in embodying it as farce: Satan as Mr. Punch. In each case, the Marlovian protagonist is the agent of carnival unmasking, with all its burden of Augustinian significance, and the persistent victim of masks, without which he is nothing, a perfect shadow on a sunshine day. The illusion of your own reality is dependent on exposing the unreality of others, the principle being that if your consciousness can be shown as false, mine will seem real. Carnival is meant, like a neutron bomb, to demolish the world and leave it standing.

Marlowe's protagonists, as we have seen, survive by willed self-ignorance, by the increasingly desperate refusal to remove the masks that displace them while seeming to substantiate them. That crucial Augustinian point at which you renounce your own unreality, kill the old Adam to save the new, is thus forestalled, literally and figuratively, beyond death. Their deaths instead recapitulate (as farce) the lives of their false selves: Barabas boiling and Edward buggered, Tamburlaine crawling over the map, Faustus orating, and Dido burning. They act out the suspicion that haunts and puzzles Augustine: that people prefer death through unreality to life through God. Their mask is their God. Revenge tragedy, we will soon see, is the drama of what happens when the masks of official identity are forcibly removed.

5

"A Crafty Madness": Carnival and the Politics of Revenge

"Here's fine revolution, and we had the trick to see't"

Hamlet (5.1.90–91)

THE STATE OF TRAGIC PLAY

IN drama as in life, revenge is dangerous, not just to the practitioner and his victim, but also to the state. "Great men were gods if beggars could not kill 'em," says Vindice, grasping the political point more firmly than almost any of his colleagues (*Revenger's Tragedy*, 2.2.93).[1] Revenge is about killing monarchs; it is about treason and what to do with it. More than almost any other form in English, it is the drama of political violence and its containment. Practically speaking, there is no such thing as private revenge; revenge is the action of the private citizen against a public order he feels has wronged him. Though it may spring from personal injury and almost necessarily takes secret forms, publication is a necessary part of its fulfillment. Hamlet must be completed by Horatio. Plays within plays habitually act, as they do in *The Spanish Tragedy, The Revenger's Tragedy,* and *The Maid's Tragedy,* as the means by which the private grievance is made public and political in the moment of avenging it. The revelation of the monarch as murderer and usurper inevitably has the effect of demystifying the monarchy itself. That's one reason why the new rulers who appear at the end of revenge—the Child in *The Duchess of Malfi,* Antonio in *The Revenger's Tragedy,* Fortinbras in *Hamlet*—are customarily figures of diminished or dubious authority, King James to some previous Tudor. In Hamlet's terms, Hyperion is not only displaced by the satyr, but also demystified into the hobbyhorse. Revenge tragedy as a species of the carnivalesque dramatizes, with particular vividness and political emphasis, the passage from "heroic" to "ironic" vision that Northrop Frye finds in Shakespearean tragedy generally.[2] I wish to argue that it also dramatizes the passage from prelapsarian community—Denmark before Gertrude fell into secret love—to present separation, the community of spies and actors that is Claudius's court.

The political orientation of Elizabethan theater has been a subject of particularly intense debate since the publication of Jonathan Dollimore's *Radical Tragedy* in 1984. For Dollimore, of course, that orientation is starkly adversarial and skeptical. Renaissance dramatists "were actively engaged in challenging ideology."[3] He argues that Elizabethan drama, using proto-Brechtian devices of alienation, pervasively demystifies and denaturalizes the social and cosmic order. It questions the existence of a coherent, essential soul, habitually showing that "men are as the times are," that social roles and power relations determine behavior more than inherent character does. By dramatizing cosmic injustice and showing religion to be a tool of Machiavellian statecraft, it demonstrates "the disintegration of providentialist belief" (83). Not surprisingly, Dollimore finds in revenge tragedy a drama of alienation: "revenge action is not a working out of divine vengeance, but a strategy of survival resorted to by the alienated and dispossessed" (29). Unfortunately, Dollimore never turns this argument into a developed theory of revenge tragedy, contenting himself with disconnected chapters on *Antonio's Revenge* and *The Revenger's Tragedy,* neither of which he considers generically. Along similar political lines, Michael Bristol has argued that "the Elizabethan theater is . . . a creation of the plebian culture of the Renaissance," which incorporates its critical attitude toward institutions of power.[4]

Other recent students of the politics of Elizabethan theater have given very different, less consoling interpretations. Richard Wilson, for example, argues that it operated as "an instrument of division," benefiting from (and contributing to) the suppression of folk carnival and of "the subversiveness of artisanal culture."[5] The true images of this theater and the cultural process it represents are to be found in *Julius Caesar:* in the suppression of the plebians' rebellious festivity by the Tribunes, in the crowning of Caesar as an exploitive "Carnival King, a Lord of Misrule" (37), and in Antony's manipulation of the mob through promises of wealth and festivity. Jonathan Haynes, using a different model, *Bartholemew Fair,* sees a similar logic of suppression: Jonson, by putting the legally harassed and increasingly commercialized fair on the stage, distances us from its anarchic violence even as he memorializes it: "the audience is legally separated from the stage, made physically (if not mentally) passive, turned into consumers of a commodity rather than participants in a ritual."[6] Haynes sees Jonson as central to a process by which the artist is constituted as "an individual . . . of austere independence" (662), distanced from his audience and the "memories of a primitive communism" (650) that are embodied in carnival. The history of Elizabethan drama, for Haynes, is marked by the increasing privatization of art and the increasing individualization of the artist. More of Osric's party than Hamlet's, it offers not a radical critique of emergent capitalist society, as Dollimore wishes it to, but a mirroring of that emergence.

No one doubts that the elements of carnival were present in Elizabethan popular culture or that they were incorporated into the drama. The question is whether they (or carnival generally, as we saw in chapter 1) can be read, in the politically wishful ways of Dollimore and Bakhtin, as institutionalized "fine revolution." Leah Marcus's book on "the politics of mirth," for example, studies how Elizabeth and the Stuarts consciously incorporated such festivity into royalist public relations, arguing that "the appeal to 'public mirth' in the Stuart period was an appeal to royal authority."[7] Leonard Tennenhouse describes how, in Shakespearean history plays, "the popular energy embodied in carnival legitimizes authority, provided that energy can be incorporated in the political body of the state."[8] Peter Stallybrass and Allon White, while endorsing the *"demystifying* potential" of carnival, also warn against "the false essentializing of carnivalesque transgression" as either *"intrinsically* radical or conservative."[9] "[C]arnival often violently abuses and demonizes *weaker,* not stronger, social groups— women, ethnic and religious minorities, those who 'don't belong'" (19). What is clear from this debate is what is fundamental to my argument: that carnival, *pace* Bakhtin, has no necessary political valence, despite its intensely political significance. LeRoy Ladurie's account of the 1580 events in Romans, where aristocratic and popular factions formed rival, and eventually warring, carnivals, demonstrates that the forms of carnival are equally available to peasant and aristocrat, for revolution or for reaction. Carnival, like revenge, is dangerous. Ladurie, as we saw in chapter 1, concludes that the violence in Romans may have represented "the essence of the institution."[10] That Shakespeare understood the violence latent in festive activity as well as the ways its apparent transgressions can be incorporated into a myth of state power will be clear to anyone familar with the *Henriad.*[11]

The significance of carnival to Elizabethan comedy has been long established, particularly by Barber's discussion of May Day festivities, comic inversion, holiday, and the Lord of Misrule in *Shakespeare's Festive Comedy*. Barber himself incorporates *Henry IV, Part I* into this pattern of festive comedy in the famous chapter that treats Hal and Falstaff in terms of the struggle between Lent and Carnival. In his final pages, however, Barber dismisses *Hamlet*, for all its "wonderful fooling," as requiring "a different movement" than the patterns of comic festivity (261). That judgment more than any other may have put revenge tragedy out of play in subsequent explorations of carnival in Elizabethan theater.[12] And that judgment is, I submit, wrong. Revenge tragedy absorbs and reapplies the patterns of carnival because it too is "linked to moments of crisis . . . of death and revival, of change and renewal."[13] When we see that connection, we will begin to see what is most peculiar about revenge as tragedy: that revengers habitually see the events around them as comedy and themselves as both comic and doomed.[14] Oedipus does not find his situation funny, though, God knows, he might: Hamlet, Vindice, Hieronimo, even Evadne do. Revengers and Lords of Misrule practice what Guildenstern accuses Hamlet of using: "a crafty madness" (3.1.4), which turns out to mean a subversive disordering of the discourses of both state and self.

My basic argument here is that revenge tragedy is about the radicalization of the revenger: his sudden perception of the social world as fundamentally disordered, unjust, and false. In a society that identifies sanity with the acceptance of degree, hierarchy, place, and providential control, such a perception will "naturally" appear as insanity.[15] At the same time, it will also appear to *us* as individuation: the discovery of self-in-separation, political, theological, and psychological. The revenger has just discovered, after all, the gap between himself and his place, his identity has been decentered, his powerlessness revealed to him; if he is not, in Vindice's terms a "great man," he might still be one of the "beggars" who can kill them. A revenge play, as Barber and Wheeler remark of *Hamlet*, "situates its hero, and its audience, at the node of despair and revolutionary protest."[16] The revenger acts verbally and physically on a vision of the world as chaotic, valueless, fluid. He operates predominantly as comic, mimic, parodist, decoding the apparent order of the world around him, as Hamlet deconstructs through ridicule Claudius's assertions of order and normality in the first court scene. Alexander may indeed pass—in carnival mockery of a royal progress—through the guts of a beggar, enacting a basic imperative of carnival, the eating of the rich, part of the meaning of Mardi Gras.[17] Significantly, Horatio—the prototypically sane man of his society—refuses to follow Hamlet as close to the nihilism of radical individualism and materialism as Hamlet is willing to go. He remains outside Hamlet's deconstructive logic, even as he remains outside the ceremonies of Claudius's court. The things Horatio has not dreamt of are demonic. The revenger, by acting on the imperatives of a crazy world, invokes the spirit of carnival, which acts out inversion, disordering, unmasking, and the chaotic fluidity of identity. The victim of misrule comes to control and embody it; he becomes, like Tamburlaine, a lord of misrule. Thus, Hamlet comes to control the chaos around him, as Claudius seems to do in the first half of the play. Hamlet, dressed in his antic costume, a king of shreds and patches, contends with that other "king of shreds and patches," Claudius, acting out the contention, through ridicule and violence, that is the basic action of carnival. But the carnival pattern also ensures the containment of the anarchic force that the revenger represents. The lord of misrule will be displaced by a new ruler: Fortinbras, Antonio, or the Duchess's child. The order that is restored, however, is one that has been demystified, desanctified. Fortinbras is king by accident, election, the threat of force, but not king by blood or nature. Revenge tragedy is thus politically very ambivalent, neither "radical tragedy" nor conservative co-optation.[18] It incorporates the folk rituals of rebellion into the formal culture. In so doing it neutralizes them (at least formally or ostensibly), but it also incorporates their subversiveness: The madmen enter the castle, as they do literally in both *The Duchess of Malfi* and *The Changeling*. Revenge tragedy is about inmates taking over asylums. Appropriately enough for the literature of a pre-revolutionary period, it entertains the most violent solutions while recoiling from them. It enacts an intense emotional ambivalence reflected in its characteristically gruesome comedy, tragic farce, instability of tone and register: the ambiguity of a form that embodies both anarchic rebellion and reactionary control: the wedding of Vanessa Redgrave and Newt Gingrich.

HAMLET AS UNLICENSED FOOL

Like most revenge tragedy usurpers (for example, the Duke in *The Revenger's Tragedy*), Claudius is a lord of misrule, the characteristic activity of whose court is drunken festivity. At the same time, his court mimics normal order and the appearance of his brother's reign with the same queen on the throne, the same prince waiting as heir, the same Lord Chamberlain, and the same allies and enemies abroad.[19] At the same time, however, this state represents (to Hamlet at least) a radical, carnivalesque inversion of natural and moral order: Hyperion displaced by the satyr; a king of substance ("he was a man, take him for all in all": 1.2.187) replaced by "a king . . . of nothing" (4.2.28–30). In Hamlet's mind and perhaps in fact, Claudius's reign is the revenge of the low on the high, body on soul, appetite on reason, figured in the displacement of the love between his father and mother by the lust between his uncle and mother and figured later in the overwhelming of Ophelia's mind by visions of seduction, betrayal, and incest. "Things rank and gross in nature / Possess it [the world, the court, human nature] merely" (1.2.136–7). Claudius himself presents his reign as an interregnum (or interlude) between the two Hamlets, insisting on his successor's compelled presence. Claudius's opening speech figures the court as a grotesque mask, "with an auspicious and a dropping eye" (1.2.11) and as a place of disordered ritual (or ritualized disorder): "with mirth in funeral, and with dirge in marriage" (1.2.12). In the same way, the play figures Claudius's kingship as masking, in which performance, his smiling villainy, hides the performer's private face. A "Carnivalesque Lord of Misrule," he is a tyrant in the name of festivity (presiding sequentially over a marriage and coronation, a drunken revel, a play at court, and a fencing match) as well as by public approval.[20] His first appearance in the court scene of act 1, scene 2 is a combination of masking and masquing, of acting the benevolent king while is court acts out a ritual of normalcy. As Bakhtin says, "the official feast asserted all that was stable, unchanging, perennial" (9). In the Mousetrap scene, of course, Hamlet as the presenter, commentator on, and covert author of the play displaces Claudius, the ostensible master of this particular revel: The victim of misrule asserts his mastery of it through (in several senses of both words) subversive play, what Bristol accurately calls "abusive counter-festivity" (*Carnival and Theater*, 186). In the process he disrupts not only Claudius's pretense of control, but also the ceremony of Claudius's court, as his mimicry and his theatrically antitheatrical mourning have done in the first court scene.

There and elsewhere before the final fencing scene, Hamlet stands ostentatiously outside the revelry of the Claudian court. The cultural process that has carried the pattern of carnival festivity into the tragic literature of the period (a process paralleled in the separation of increasingly professional and artistically self-conscious Elizabethan actors from the community that made up their audience) has separated the hero from the community he none the less feels himself to represent. Hamlet's career is marked by a series of abortive gestures toward the public whose popular favorite he is. Typically, he addresses the Players as "good friends" (2.2.422) even while asserting his authorial superiority over them and imposing his secret plans on them. Vindice "acts for" (but in isolation from) Antonio and his late wife, Gloriana, Castiza, and the public at large. Hieronimo acts for the people he has thrown out of his courtroom as well as for Horatio, Isabella, and himself.

As Stallybrass and White have demonstrated, carnival did not just disappear, it underwent "migrations, concealments, metamorphoses, fragmentations, internalizations and neurotic sublimations" (*Transgression,* 176). The revenger, one of the most literarily important of these mutations, is a radical example of psychological individualism and isolation; only in the lost past could he feel at one with his public role and the community figured in it. Typically, the world has in one degree or another approved the crime and become an accomplice in it: Claudius *was* elected, Gertrude's marriage approved. Balthazar is the heir apparent. The Duchess of Malfi's very servants share Ferdinand's lecherous misogyny. Hamlet's desire to save Denmark and his sense of himself as "the Dane" have to coexist with a radical alienation from the community around him. The world at large pursues its corrupt, illegitimate festivity while the revenger in secret prepares his own "play": "Soliman and Perseda," "The Murder of Gonzago," Vindice's masque of revengers, or the "thing I have seen in a play" (5.5.94–95) that Bosola enacts in the darkened cockpit of the Cardinal's quarters.[21] Hamlet dies before "the still unknowing world" in a court that thinks him a traitor. Acting on behalf of a remembered order, the revenger enacts not a ritual of community but of loss, separation, unwilling individuation: the movement from that nameless figure of princeliness Ophelia remembers to the disordered Hamlet she sees before her, holding her hand at arm's length, staring at her from an unimaginable distance, antic in costume, tragic in isolation.

Ophelia, of course, has another vision of Hamlet, this time of that lost, remembered Hamlet who was the ideal integration of self and role:

> The courtier's, soldier's, scholar's, eye, tongue, sword,
> Th' expectation and rose of the fair state,

The glass of fashion and the mould of form,
Th' observ'd of all observers.

(3.4.151–54).

This is, in the terms of an earlier chapter, Hamlet as pentangle, not least because it presents him as a thing observed, the billboard of his interpretive community, giving back an idealized image of itself and its authority, not unlike the idealized image Hamlet attaches to his father. Ophelia's Hamlet is not merely an abstract form, notably without a name; he is the "mould" from which an ideal might be cast: the abstraction of an abstraction. He not only gives forms to the state, but also grows organically from it: the "rose of the fair state." The figure represents apparently stable hierarchy, unvarying and natural princely perfection if you imagine it as pure emblem, but transience if you imagine a living rose. Rigidly conceptualized, this figure is presented as something entirely known, a sign that *is* its signified, though the confusion of Ophelia's grammar suggests otherwise. The parallelism of her first line seems to present Hamlet as the courtier's eye, the soldier's tongue, and the scholar's sword: two figures suggesting Osric, one suggesting Horatio, but neither suggesting Hamlet past or present (her grammar, of course, suggests Bottom). Real or not, this figure is lost: "That noble and most sovereign reason / Like sweet bells jangled out of time, and harsh" (3.1.157–58): bells that remind us of the antic and the lunatic quite as much as of the church.

The pantomime Dane who has accosted Ophelia at her sewing, however, is emphatically personalized—"Lord Hamlet, with his doublet all unbrac'd, / No hat upon his head, his stockins fouled, / Ungart'red" (2.1.75–77)—because he is now seen as individuated, a person not a form, and separated from any supporting or defining system. This new Hamlet figures mystery as well as the disorder implied by his carefully deranged costume. He is the product not of ideal and public patterns of behavior, but of private, unseen motives. He has, in Bakhtinian terms, uncrowned himself (not to mention the Ghost, whose pallor, silence, and fixed eyes give the model for his son's performance). We know, of course, that the madness is at least partly histrionic, an "antic disposition" (something felt) but also "put on" (not felt). He is performing a dumb show, as his actors will later do. As Ophelia describes it, he has provided himself with a shock entrance and an elaborately "dramatic" exit: "He seem'd to find his way without his eyes / For out a' doors he went without their helps, / And to the last bended their light on me" (2.1.95–97). Hamlet is representing, acting out, madness, in a form that allows him to punish Ophelia and observe her at the same time. His performance communicates the fact that it is not communicating.[22] Hamlet the antic acts out radical separation from his would-be interpreter as well as social displacement; in Victor Turner's terms, he is a liminal (displaced, disoriented) man performing a liminoid (playful, satiric) act.[23] Since Ophelia is also acting, however, playing the part her father has given her, we have one of the play's most important emblematic images: two actors, mutually baffled, watching each other from the ramparts of their separate performances.

Revenge is about acting as power, but it is also about the actor as isolated performer, signifying in a code his audience, like the one at The Mousetrap, frequently cannot understand. Acting is a weapon, but it is also a mirror that reflects the actor's performance back to the audience of himself. Often, that performance seems to be coded in a way meant to prevent outsiders from reading it: Hamlet rewrites "The Murder of Gonzago" in such a way that it will seem to a neutral observer, Rosencrantz, say, to mean the opposite of what it means to Hamlet, Horatio, and Claudius. (A nephew murdering his uncle only signifies a man murdering his brother to those who have been told the code.) Ophelia finds the dumb show incomprehensible; Gertrude watches the Player Queen with no apparent understanding that she's watching an image of herself. When Vindice plays "Vindice" before Lussurioso, he plays himself as a country bumpkin for the private amusement of himself and his brother. Since Lussurioso does not recognize the name, let alone the man, Vindice's performance can only be for its own ludic sake; it is acting as secret humiliation. Actors, like chefs, always have the power to spit in the soup they are about to serve. Here, as in *Hamlet,* acting is shown as an attack on its audience, a professional's scorn for amateurs, but also as an expression of the professional's isolation.

In a fundamental sense, then, revenge tragedy is the dramatization of estrangement, of alienation in its usual and its Brechtian sense, and of the theatricalization of identity that goes with that estrangement. Hamlet has that within which passes show. Though his exterior seems—nay, is—meant to express, to dramatize, that within, he still insists on the disconnection of the two, denying in the process both the connection between actor and role and that between performance and audience. Actors are conundra: an idea Hamlet returns to in the Hecuba soliloquy where the actor's grief is apparent but also inexplicable and unreachable. You believe in it as an act of faith, but you can't reach it through the performance that seems to convey it. While presiding over most of the elements of carnival—the mimicry, the abuse, the violence, the maskings and unmaskings—the revenger lives in a world of separation radically unlike the world of carnival. There are no footlights in carnival, Bakhtin says (*Rabelais,* 7), but the revenger sees every person as performing behind his private footlights. At the same time, however, the isolated revenger remembers community. Whether with his father-uncle, his mother-aunt, his "lover" Ophelia, his "friends" Rosencrantz and Guildenstern, Hamlet taunts his antagonists with the memory of relationships lost and travestied. The revenger's carnival both mocks and memorializes true carnival's sense of community. Far from being at one with that community, the revenger mocks his audience's—any audience's—presumption of a secure, knowing relationship with the performance before them or with each other. Here, as Laroque says of the role of carnival in Elizabethan tragedy, "festivity loses its power of natural symbiosis and instead becomes a vehicle of discord, exclusion and chaos" (*Shakespeare's Festive World,* 175).

Revenge is a form of desperate play. The situation of the revenger is, after all, liberating, as radicalization usually is. The revenger uncovers the protean multiplicity within himself through the process of disguise, through carnival; his identity is in play and shaped through play. At the same time, he discovers both the possibility of freedom from hierarchy and the possibility (usually illusory) of freedom from ethical, social, and natural constraints. In place of the-king-your-father is the-usurper-your-uncle: an authority you can not kill is replaced by one you must kill. The crown is desanctified for Hamlet, however much the relatively primitive Laertes may go on believing in it. The appropriate response is mockery, the response of carnival. If there is no Law, why should Hieronimo uphold the law? The revenger discovers a world in which everything is "in play." The result, naturally enough, is liminal giddiness as well as horror. The desanctification of the world, which unmans you, also empowers you by removing taboo.

For this reason, revengers tend to become children in the process of becoming tragic. While acquiring an overwhelming Duty, they are liberated from other duties and proprieties, starting of course with common politeness. Hamlet may be "no Vice," as Robert Weimann says, but he acquires, in spades, the Vice's "satiric aggression" toward the established order.[24] When you realize that the wisdom of age is represented by Polonius, you no longer have to respect your elders. As in the case of the new king, you have acquired a duty to mock. If the old king, your father, is now a ghost who may also be a demon, then mockery—"Well said, old mole!" (1.5.162)—may be as appropriate a response to him too as filial piety. If Ophelia *is* a slut, you can do (verbally at least) all the things to her that you could not do when she was Ophelia the beloved. Indeed, Ophelia's madness seems to incorporate that sense of having been desanctified: she internalizes Hamlet's devaluation of her. "Let in the maid that out a maid / Never departed more" (4.5.54–55): in the world of her madness, all fathers are dead and all love is seduction and betrayal. Her response, as we have seen, mirrors the revenger's, but she is destroyed by the entropic dissolution of the official order rather than empowered by it.

While carnival is in progress, Bakhtin reminds us, it seems to have no boundaries; its freedom is *the* law, not just its law. The progress of virtually every revenger is toward the loss of restraint in himself and the discarding of constraints outside himself. In decoding the restraints of the social world, he discovers the possibility of a world without restraint; that way, as Dr. Faustus demonstrates, lie both despair and the playfulness that is, paradoxically enough, a natural reaction to it. Hamlet discovers a desert of freedom and with it—as we see in his dances round Polonius or Rosencrantz and Guildenstern—at least a measure of *jouissance*. When he rediscovers the possibility of a providential order, he of course ceases to be a revenger and submits to being an agent. The return of subordination is the end of carnival.

THE REVENGER'S MASQUES

In the meantime, the revenger presides over the carnival that's available. Revenge does not merely take place in public; more importantly and specifically it involves the appropriation and subversion of public occasions. It is a usurpation of festivity: by Hamlet in the first court scene or at the play within the play; by Evadne in *The Maid's Tragedy;* or by the various revengers in the masque at the end of *Women Beware Women.* Hieronimo, the Knight Marshal of Spain, is also in practice its Master of the Revels, the man in charge of the "league, and love, and banqueting" of which the Ghost of Andrea complains (*Spanish Tragedy,* 1.5.4).[25] Indeed, Elizabeth Maslen describes the Hieronimo of the 1982 National Theatre production as behaving like "a licensed fool."[26] In *The Spanish Tragedy* he presents two shows: the triumphal masque in act 1, scene 4, which precedes the murder of Horatio, and "Soliman and Perseda," which accomplishes the revenge of Horatio. The first, created by Hieronimo and presented as part of the King's feast of victory and reconciliation is elaborately coded—as with the dumb show version of The Mousetrap, its critically naive audience at first needs the "mystery" (1.4.139) explained to them—but without private meaning. Its significance is directed to the celebrants in their public roles as part of the official feast: "This is another special argument," says the King, once he has caught the drift, "That Portingale may deign to bear our yoke, / When it by little England hath been yoked" (1.4.158–60). Through the masque, Hieronimo speaks as a public man, in his role as courtier, not as father or avenger. Whatever coded meaning it may have for an English audience is divorced from any private feelings or intentions Hieronimo himself might have.

In the case of "Soliman and Perseda," however, the public occasion—the celebration of the marriage of Balthazar and Bel-Imperia—is taken over by the private motives of the revenger, who inscribes it with such an elaborate set of personal meanings that it is unclear to its stage audience even after two explanations (not to mention the murder of Castile). Where the earlier pageant has included its audience, drawing the King and Ambassador into interpreting its readily accessible gestures, "Soliman and Perseda," from its Babel-like mixture of tongues on through the screening action that disguises murder as play, excludes even its own performers, not least Hieronimo, who shows no recognition of the self-condemnation implicit in casting himself as the Bashaw. What is presented as entertainment for the court is in fact an assault on it, an act of aggression that moves from mimicry of the injustice (and linguistic confusion) of the court world, through the hidden murders of the children of its most important watchers, to the presentation of Hieronimo's private grievances, and finally to direct attack on one of that audience, Castile. Hieronimo, as lord of misrule, takes over the King's revel to destroy the court in which it takes place. As Hieronimo says before the performance: "Now shall I see the fall of Babylon" (4.1.195). The anarchic violence of Hieronimo's and Bel-Imperia's play, by eliminating the heirs of both Spain and Portugal, destroys the order that contains it. By acting apart from the community he seeks to represent, the revenger almost necessarily acts against it; acting on his alienation and exclusion, he acts against all who are not excluded.

To his fellow courtiers, Hamlet's most visible actions are his repeated subversions of Claudius's attempts at festivity. He appropriates the installation scene, for example, simply by refusing to take part in it. In revenge tragedy, to a striking extent, the separation of the revenger-actor from his audience *is* the subject. Simply by his silent presence, like Banquo's ghost, he takes over the feast. By refusing to play the part allotted to him, Hamlet forces first Claudius and Gertrude, later Polonius, Ophelia, Rosencrantz and Guildenstern et al., to interpret the part he is playing. What begins as Claudius's performance, his ritual of false community, becomes Hamlet's ritual of separation, his insistent withholding of his private feelings from the interrogation of his "parents," a performance that insists on the opposition of private to public that Claudius has been at pains to deny. Repeatedly, Hamlet usurps the usurper's ceremonies. This first court scene passes from public ritual, to a quasi-private family conference (a public show of concern masking private, but unsuccessful coercion), to Hamlet's soliloquy, to his conference with Horatio, Marcellus and Bernardo: a structure that leaves Hamlet in control of the stage for the second half of the scene.[27]

Throughout the play, Claudius, that pompous man of forms, notably without any sign of humor, plays *alazon* to Hamlet's *eiron;* more specifically he plays Malvolio—who also dreams of usurping and marrying his lady—to Hamlet's Feste.[28] Feste, too, is a revenger, of course, and, like Hamlet, a master of disingenuous verbal subversion. Claudius, in turn, is a killjoy in both the sense of being humorless and of having murdered Yorick's master and with him the festivity of the old order, for which he substitutes his sinister rituals: coercive shows of concern, maimed funeral rites, poisoned duels, just as he substitutes the show of authority for its reality. From the installation scene on, Claudius is the natural target for Hamlet as both revenger and comic.

The Mousetrap scene allows Hamlet to usurp not only the King's celebration, but also Polonius's nominal control over the revels by acting as chorus, director, and coauthor of the entertainment while using this usurped authority, carnival fashion, to present a ritual mimicry that both depicts uncrowning (showing Claudius as regicide and illegitimate monarch) and enacts it (by driving Claudius from the throne room). Both mimicking and abusing his nominal lord, Hamlet appoints himself the court's Lord of Misrule: "your only jig-maker," as he describes himself to Ophelia just before The Mousetrap (3.2.125), an act immediately recognizable as a charivari or skimmington, directed, as they often were, against a remarried widow.[29] Like Hieronimo with his play, Hamlet becomes "author and actor in this tragedy" (*Spanish Tragedy*, 4.4.147), not to mention its audience. Cut off from the shared community of carnival, the revenger absorbs all its aspects into himself, then incorporates others into the show of which he is both contriver and spectator. In the process he turns the Players' tragedy into the "comedy" that "the king like[s] not" (3.2.293–94). Claudius is swallowed by the show he thought he was watching.[30] From Hamlet's point of view, of course, Claudius *is* the show: "The Murder of Gonzago" is "The Unmasking of Claudius," the culmination of the ritual abusing and stripping of Gertrude, Ophelia, Polonius, and the King that Hamlet has been conducting throughout the scene. As so often in revenge tragedy, the relation between actor and audience is reversed. Hamlet, like the characters of The Mousetrap, "poison[s] in jest" (3.2.234). His carnival, as carnival should, mimics the world around it:

> For thou dost know, O Damon dear,
>   This realm dismantled was
> Of Jove himself; and now reigns here
>   A very, very—pajock
>
> (3.2.281–84).[31]

Hamlet reacts not to order, but to the travesty of order, making a jig out of a jig. In dismantling the usurped world, of course, the revenger repeats its original dismantling. Hamlet's play both rehearses the murder of his father and predicts the eventual killing of his uncle.

At least thee points about this process are relevant to the subject of carnival. First, except for Hieronimo, who adapts the play he wrote as a student, based on "chronicles of Spain" (4.1.108), revengers almost never write their own plays-within-plays. Hamlet doesn't write "The Murder of Gonzago," he rewrites it; taking over a prior text and altering it to express his private meaning, as Hieronimo has done with his selection and casting of "Soliman and Perseda." The revenger privatizes public property. In so doing, Hamlet takes over the Players while pretending to join them (possibly one meaning of Horatio's remark that Hamlet deserves only half a share in the company, 3.2.279). The Players, after all, think they are entertaining Claudius, their official host. As usual in revenge tragedy, the revenger's masque is at someone else's—usually the victim's—behest. You do not make your own occasion, you take over someone else's; to the extent, in Hamlet's case, of giving the speech that actually causes the King to rise (at 3.2.265). Bakhtin's "official feast" is countered and subverted by the unofficial one.

Second, as has long been noted, Hamlet's "antic disposition" makes him, as Barber puts it (*Festive Comedy,* 261), Claudius's "all-licensed fool" (or "antic"); to revenge his father he usurps the role of that other dead father figure, Yorick. Clowns are, of course, licensed critics, but they are also one-man carnivals: the element of misrule contained within the court to reinforce its rule. The clown, says Bakhtin, quoting Veselovsky, "is the lawless herald of the . . . truth" (*Rabelais,* 93). Clowns mirror the kings they serve, parodying them but also (at least in Shakespeare) completing their awareness, adding the consciousness of the low and physical. By feeling the cold, the Fool makes Lear feel it and know what wretches feel. Clowns are, after all, voices of the powerless and afflicted. Rabelais's favorite clown had two names: Fevrial, associating him with cold, and Le Triboulet, associating him with trouble (Bakhtin, 8). Feste is left out in the wind and the rain, Lear's Fool is sick, and Yorick, of course, dead. In *Hamlet,* the Prince, stripped of power, takes on the role of the jester, that token representative of the dispossessed, and in so doing acquires the temporary power of the lord of misrule, enabled not just to mock Claudius but to dethrone him. Thus, Frank Kermode speaks of the language of the play, its hero's especially, as "liable always to the irruption of carnival."[32] Listening to Hamlet, we recognize the festive laughter, of course, as we recognize the vocabulary of carnival—Bakhtin's "continual shifting . . . parodies and travesties, humiliations" (*Rabelais,* 11)—we are only surprised at the source, until, that is, we remember that Hamlet is also the (god-)son, as Sterne surely understood, of Yorick. Certainly, Hamlet's memories of Yorick (5.1.184 f.) have an intimacy, an element of physical contact nowhere evident in his memories of his actual father.[33] But the clown is dead and the role has passed to the boy on his back, the estranged and solitary prince. Yorick, who "set the table on a roar" (5.1.190–91), *was* carnival; Hamlet, joking in the graveyard to his tiny community—two grave diggers, Horatio, and a skull—is its ghost. It is too simple to say, with Bristol, that "the happy festive community to which the prince belonged as a child is dead and buried" (*Carnival and Theater,* 192): One part of it has just been unburied, another representative is coming to take her place in Yorick's grave, and Hamlet is putting new jokes in its dead mouth. The death of that community is still going on and is, indeed, a major action of the play.

"Adieu, remember me," as the other Ghost says. Here and elsewhere, revenge tragedy enacts the death of carnival, memorializing its spirit while translating its forms to new and sinister meanings, authentic festivity being characteristic of its lost past. To Hamlet, at least, that specialist in what Bakhtin calls "grotesque realism" (19), Yorick's ultimate, anarchic, leveling joke is his death. That is why he is grinning. He can now tell Gertrude or perhaps the newly dead Ophelia "to what favour she must come." "Make her laugh at that" (5.1.194–95), says his alter ego, who now speaks *for* him as well as to him, composing the new jokes appropriate to Yorick's present condition. Hamlet enacts his carnival with a difference. The favorite theme of his joking, of course, is the delusions of hierarchy. His jokes explore the possibility of everything resolving to a dead level. Where Yorick's community was the banquet hall, Hamlet's is death, that community to which we all ultimately belong, equally. As Prosser points out, the term *antic* associates Hamlet with the grotesque and through it with "the grinning skull and the tradition of Death laughing all to scorn."[34]

Third, Hamlet's play is itself symbolic murder; that is why, unlike Vindice's or Hieronimo's, it need not contain the actual revenge. Mimicry, as every savage or statesman knows, is a necessary prelude to violence because it de-sanctifies the intended victim. It is the foreplay of assassination. Hamlet virtually never mocks anyone he is not eventually going to kill, directly or indirectly; neither does Vindice nor Bosola. Thus, Hamlet's last mocking encounter with Polonius (3.2.374–86) comes only a few moments before he kills him. Mimicry, after all, is theater's—and carnival's—special form of violence.[35] It has the peculiar power to annihilate its object in the process of mirroring him because it reduces the victim to a set of gestures that the mimic controls and the victim does not. One can step out of the role, the other cannot. The logic of mimicry is: I act you, therefore I become you, therefore I displace you. If I am doing "you," who are "you" doing? Or as Hamlet puts it: "The King is a thing. . . . Of nothing" (4.2.28–30).[36] Since Claudius is himself a player king—all rite and no right, we might say—to unmask him, to disrupt his act, is to kill him. One reason for Hamlet's failure to murder Claudius after The Mousetrap is that, in an important sense, he just *has* killed him. The balance of power shifts in the moments just after Claudius has been driven from the play because at that point Hamlet has done as much as a lord of misrule can do: He has won the war of actors. He spends most of the rest of the play trying to discard the role. Carnival depends for its meaning on a return to the order it mocks, that order Hamlet memorializes, longs for, and has ceased to believe in.

CONTAINING (AND KILLING) CARNIVAL

Revenge tragedy is the enactment of anarchic violence, but also of its containment: the double *ludus* of the tragi-carnivalesque. Hamlet is, after all, the play's most constant proponent of hierarchy; his mimicry aims at the destruction of disorder. He represents the sternest of official and Lenten values even as he embodies the most extreme forms of carnival playfulness, trying to move through entropy and play to order. He tries to reinvert what Claudius has inverted. He clowns to kill clowning. Ophelia's self-destructive madness, a degradation in the Bakhtian sense of the reassertion of lower and bodily, is the other most prominent manifestation of carnival in the play, a movement through entropy to death. If Yorick is carnival's past, she is its present: She will be buried, of course, in his grave. Typically, the flowers associated with her madness begin with rosemary for remembrance (4.5.175) and end with "long purples / That liberal shepherds give a grosser name / But our cull-cold maids do dead men's fingers call them" (4.7.169–71): a pointed conjunction of the phallic and the funereal. And the owl was a baker's daughter. The movement downward, enacted even in the mode of her death, threatens to absorb all consciousness and all difference. The First Gravedigger, hip-deep in the earth, employs a language of relentless literalness, especially where Ophelia is concerned: she "was a woman . . . but, rest her soul, she's dead" (5.1.135–36). Degradation "digs a bodily grave" but not, in this world at least, "for a new birth" (Bakhtin, 21). Throughout the play, carnival disorder is linked to the pervasive imagery of disease, poison, and madness. Hamlet's antic disposition is either a performance indicating a disease or a disease taking the form of a performance. In either case, it mimics the dissolution of the world, as Ophelia's madness does.[37] Hamlet's wordplay decodes the nonmeaning, the babble, of those around him: Claudius's politic evasions, Polonius's scrambled cant, Rosencrantz and Guildenstern's formulaic imitations of casual and friendly speech, Osric's empty courtly formulas. The inverted sign systems of carnival are an appropriate register of the revenger's world, where the norm of speech is liable to be the Machiavel's equivocations (Lorenzo's, Claudius's, Lussurioso's). They signify the entropy of language, however, not its renewal.

Carnival, as Bakhtin constructs it, is a celebration of the fluid, the protean, and the subjective. Its motto might be Ophelia's "we know what we are, but not what we may be" (4.5.43–44), but Ophelia's line is a lament for the loss of stability and degree without which she dies. The revenger (and Ophelia as his mirror) takes in the disorder of the world around him; he puts on its antic disposition. He does not, as the Halletts think, "reshape" his inner world, because "the objective world resists the changes the revenger would impose on it" (*Revenger's Madness*, 10). In their formulation, the revenger drifts into madness in the process of giving way to his inner passion. But just as there is no such thing as purely private revenge, so in revenge tragedy is there no insanity separable from that of the outside world. Ophelia's "mad" vision of seduction, betrayal, incest, and murder figures quite precisely the emotional contours of the world around her. It contains, after all, the very elements Hamlet rebels against and Claudius feels infected with. There is, in fact, no objective world in the play, as Maynard Mack suggested a long time ago.[38] There are no facts without interpretations. Hamlet must construct the murder once he "knows"—to the extent he ever does—the fact that it occurred; he must construct the motive of the murderer, the involvement of Gertrude, the time sequence, and so forth. When he does construct that world, always tentatively, seldom reliably, it turns out to be one of mysterious degradations, carnival transformations downward: Hyperion replaced by the satyr, the loving wife turned to whatever (adulteress? would-be adulteress? accomplice?). In all cases, of course, what he sees around him is change without process, unexplainable transformations like Gertrude's: change that, depending on how you read it, either falsifies the order of the world or reveals that the order was always false. Ophelia was his lover, she is, or seems to be, a spy. In the world around Hamlet, funeral dresses as marrage, mourning as festivity. That is not a disguise he "imposes on the world" (Halletts, 95); that is the carnival as *danse macabre* in which Hamlet finds himself. Carnival in its pure form sanctions the putting off of social identity, permits the impermissible, for the better health of the community. In revenge, however, that later and more sinister stage of carnival, the low destroys the high. "What we may become," as Ophelia will soon find out, is dead. What follows from the setting aside of daytime identity is figured in her bizarrely festive suicide: the singing figure, dressed in "fantastic garlands" and "crownet weeds" drifting to oblivion (4.7.168,172).

The revenger, of course, "loses himself," but not, as in pure carnival, to find what is normally lost, to reattach himself to bodily health and be reborn. The masking of the revenge carnival is figured most clearly and schematically in Piato, Vindice's Mr. Hyde, whose name means "plated" or "masked." "A mask is treason's license," as even Supervacuo can understand (*Revenger's Tragedy*, 5.1.174). All sins in this play seem to be aspects of carnival: Antonio's wife, of course, is murdered in a masque; Spurio suspects he was conceived in a "whispering and withdrawing hour" after a drunken feast (1.2.186). "It were fine," Vindice/Piato says to the poisoned skull, "[t]o have thee seen at revels, forgetful feasts / And unclean brothels" (3.5.89–91). Indeed, those two basic elements of carnival experience, feasting and forgetting, are important and complex parts of the language of the play. In keeping with the pattern of adaptation we have been tracing, however, both appear in perverted form, deathly rather than healthy. Every feast is an occasion for treachery and cannibalism: The Duchess and Spurio pass the dying Duke on their way to what they euphemistically describe as a "banquet" (3.5.217), talking of eating sin (203) and administering poison (210).[39] Meanwhile Vindice's poison has "eaten out" the Duke's tongue (191). Vindice, who is obsessed with the need for his victims to remember and recognize him (see 3.5.163–70 at the Duke's death; and 5.3.73–79 at Lussurioso's), has begun to "travel" from himself as early as 1.1.116, using a metaphor of self-loss whose significance is confirmed by Castiza's refusal to "travel" (2.2.41). By act 4, scene 2, even Hippolito has noticed that "we lose ourselves" (202). It is partly to this effect that Dollimore refers when he describes the play's subject as "life lived obsessively and destructively within the dislocated 'minute'" (*Radical Tragedy*, 147). The festive presentness of carnival is shown as a form of death in life.

Throughout, *The Revenger's Tragedy* dramatizes the spurious liberation of entropy, the playfulness of dissolution. Most famously, Vindice, whose life feels unnatural to him "as if I lived now when I should be dead" (1.1.120), puts on the mask of Piato, "the child o'th'court" (1.3.4) whose counterpart is Spurio—"an uncertain man / Of more uncertain woman" (1.2.134–35)—who wonders whether his father was a Duke or a groom, only to conclude that he was sired by a feast (1.2.180–203). When Vindice tries to return to himself (in order to murder his alter ego), he returns as a clown (4.2.42–195), a self-travesty. He becomes, in a pun the play forces upon us, a Spurious man. Few of the characters, aside from Antonio and Hippolito, have human names: The rest are either nameless—Duke, Duchess, Youngest Son, Fourth Lord, and so forth.—or type named, like the Duchess's children, all of whom are in fact lecherous, ambitious, and stupid despite the apparent distinction of their names. The topsy-turvy-ness of carnival language pervades the play: Lussurioso wants to "enter" Piato who, in turn, will "be as a virgin, close" with Hippolito (1.3.86,137). Sexual desire levels the most basic social distinctions: Sons are seduced by (step) mothers, brothers entice sisters, masters enter servants. The play's present action begins with a revel in which a nameless, masked Youngest Son rapes a religious but also nameless woman, a carnival "sport" for which he hopes to "die in jest" (1.2.66); it ends with another revel in which four nobles, three of whom are nameless, are murdered by four masked men (two nameless), who escape just before four other masked men enter with the intention of committing the same murders. In between, of course, the Duke is murdered by Gloriana's masked and costumed skull: poisoned bone hidden by carnival mask. In Vindice's black-carnival world, of course, we are all skulls in disguise; when Gloriana was apparelled in her flesh she tempted the Duke to destruction as she now does in her mask. What is missing, of course, is the face, the human Gloriana as opposed to the *momento mori.* Vindice in turn is possessed by that "witch" (5.3.118), Piato; he is entered by a mask. The surrendering of one's conscious, daytime, hierarchical identity does not restore one's humanity but destroys it. The pattern of degradation that turns love into sex also turns sex into death. As in *Hamlet,* the patterns of carnival are transposed into *danse macabre.* Carnival release is death; carnival anarchy is its own containment.[40]

Certainly and explicitly, the play enacts rebellion. Few revengers see, even momentarily, the political significance of their action as clearly as Vindice: "Great men were gods if beggars could not kill 'em" (2.2.93); "dukes' groans are thunder's watchwords" (5.3.43). As the generality of both statements suggests, one reason for Vindice's inability to stop at just one duke is that he comes to act against the office as much as against the man. Both statements lend weight, certainly, to Antonio's assumption that "you, that would murder him, would murder me" (5.3.104). Yet, Vindice *has* changed the order of his world, a fact registered, paradoxically, by the new order's condemnation of the man who has enabled it. Antonio's "virtuous" government cannot tolerate or recognize the murderousness on which it is founded. (His reign, like Lussurioso's, begins with the rash execution of the one witness who could explain the murder of the previous Duke.) Vindice will survive as the regime's dirty secret, a secret constituted by the play itself. Antonio, presented throughout as a man of peace who foregoes revenge, begins his reign with three summary executions, at least one of an innocent man who has done nothing worse than defend his lord. The process of power once demystified is not easily remystified.

Can we, then, talk about *The Revenger's Tragedy* as "radical tragedy"? Not, I am afraid, in the committed, Brechtian sense that Dollimore wishes to impose on it and so much else of Elizabethan and Jacobean drama. To interrogate an order is not the same as to reject that order, though it is a necessary step toward doing so. Similarly, to invoke the grotesqueness of "providential" action is not the same as denying providence. Vindice's stage-prompted thunder may, as Dollimore (149) argues, parody "the hypocrisy and deception of the pious," but it may equally parody conventions that themselves travesty the idea of an operative divine justice as something that can be represented by noises off. At the same time, the thunder, prompt on Vindice's mocking demand, may be a monitory indication that Vindice's carnival of revenge is nearing its end. Lords of misrule tend to think of themselves eventually as real lords, "gods" whom beggars cannot kill. Vindice's demands for thunder and heavenly applause conflate God with the theater audience, making Him a willing, subordinate collaborator in Vindice's shows. In similar fashion, the Lord of Misrule incorporates the actual lord into his performances. As the action of carnival insists on their resemblance, however, so the end of carnival insists on their difference. Carnival is, after all, only the people's "second life"; its parodic license is predicated on the return of the first. As we all know, Vindice convicts himself and accepts Antonio's sentence: "We have enough / I'faith, we're well . . . / We die after a nest of dukes—adieu" (5.3.123–25). While retaining a kind of class hostility toward "a nest of dukes," Vindice emphatically declares his own containment. To my ear, at least, the Looney Tunes style of that final line—Th-th-th-that's all, folks!—leaves it ambiguous whether we are being asked to laugh at the revenger or at the order that replaces him.

Of course, the role of Lord of Misrule contains its own delusion of control, as Hamlet should know from watching that other fool obsessed with control, Polonius. Nobody controls chaos; if anyone did, it would cease to be chaos. Hamlet is controlled by his madness as much as he controls it, as his failure to get the crucial, whodunnit facts from Gertrude in the closet scene reminds us. His (more or less) controlled performance, The Mousetrap, sets off its chain of uncontrolled consequences: Claudius's "praying"—the proof of the limitations of Hamlet's ability to read him correctly—Polonius's spying, Hamlet's blind stabbing through the curtain. Vindice, as Mercer shows (*Hamlet and the Acting of Revenge*,

90–117 passim), habitually congratulates himself on his control of what has come to him accidentally, such as the circumstance of Spurio's affair with the Duchess. The revenger learns to mimic and to use disorder, but that in turn leads him to the fatal illusion that he has mastered it: the revenger's *hubris* as it is the Machiavel's. The Mousetrap, in fact, reveals Hamlet's *hubris* as much as it does Claudius's guilt. The Lord of Misrule is himself a clown, after all. And, at least in English versions of the Summer Lord Game (see Barber, *Festive Comedy*, 44–45), he usually dies at the end of the ritual. That "fine revolution" Hamlet finds in 5.1.90–1 is death. The activity of carnival is comic, but its pattern, ending in judgment and death, is more closely akin to tragedy.

Ultimately, of course, the revenger's carnival must be politically ambiguous because carnival itself is: both the expression of rebellious violence and the means of its control. Hamlet enacts disorder in the name of order. In the carnivalesque double *ludus*, the revenger usurps the role of Lord of Misrule to overthrow the "real" Lord of Misrule: Lorenzo, Claudius, Lussurioso. Rather than reversing the disordering process, he completes it, usually confounding himself with his victims. Hamlet's final usurpation is to use the King's wine against him: a killing that invokes the travestied carnival of Claudius's drunken reign.

And yet Vindice *has* murdered his nest of dukes. He has proved the great men not gods because the beggar has killed them. And that is, both psychologically and politically, different from leaving them to kill one another. Though many critics of *The Revenger's Tragedy* fail to grasp the point, there is a great difference between waiting for a tyrant to die and killing him *pour encourager les autres*. This way the state is purged but also demystified. That is one reason why revenge, though ostensibly "private" must always be made public. You can't make Mercer's (95) distinction between private and selfish revengers and public-spirited satirists. The revenge is not complete without the revelation. Horatio is a necessary part of Hamlet's plan because Horatio is the bearer of the tale, the text Hamlet has composed for the future education of Denmark, a role the amanuensis has already begun to assume in his final speeches to Fortinbras (5.2.372–95). That text has already become a bit garbled with the death of its author, but no one has the privilege of becoming their own book. Through Horatio, Hamlet, who cannot restore his father, can at least remove the illusion of divinity from his uncle, that other beggar who has made his point by killing a "great man."

In the last analysis, perhaps the impetus to change is "a crafty

madness." To deconstruct the "sanity" of an old order is to construct the sanity of a new. To deconstruct the academic babble of
Polonius—that direct descendant of the *commedia*'s Dottore—or
the diplomatic formalities of Claudius is to recreate the possibility
of thought. As even Polonius dimly suspects, there is meaning in
Hamlet's madness. In the obscure, unstable world of the play, a
world of shifting masks over unfathomable motives, Hamlet's instability, his willingness to acknowledge misrule and uncertainty, is
the highest form of sanity. Carnival, as Bakhtin tells us, celebrates
fluidity and change; it mocks the forms that embody the illusion
of stable hierarchy, as Hamlet mocks the categories ("tragical-
comical-historical-pastoral"!) and proverbs that serve Polonius in
place of wisdom. While Polonius "defines" madness ("what is't but
to be nothing else but mad?": 2.2.94), Hamlet experiences it as
process, as exploration, and perhaps as controllable performance.
If the end of that exploration is silence and death, that is also
part of the process of carnival, which demonstrates the limits of
conscious language as well as of the social order it embodies. If the
title of Horatio's tale "of accidental judgements, casual slaughters"
(5.2.382) turns out to be "A Mad World, My Masters," he will not
entirely have missed the point. Hamlet's solitary exploration of
that madness, however, has none of the communal and physical
comforts of true carnival.

In Bakhtin's tragic history of festivity, of course, the celebratory
consciousness of carnival, "the joy of change" (*Rabelais*, 48), gives
way to a culture of alienation. "Such is the peculiar drama of the
material bodily principle in Renaissance literature—the drama that
leads to the breaking away of the body from the single, procreating
earth, the breaking away from the collective, growing . . . body of
the people" (23). This particular change may be difficult to locate
in empirical history, though analysts of the period, from Knights
to Greenblatt and beyond, have located innumerable related crises
in the institutions of the period.[41] One could point out that the loss
of a warm collective past, Northrop Frye's passage from "heroic"
to "ironic," is a perennial myth. Chaucer inscribed it two hundred
years before Shakespeare in the *General Prologue* to *The Canterbury Tales*. I hope I have demonstrated, at least by implication,
that Bakhtin's polarity of carnivalesque and individualistic, light
and dark, is far too simple. The two are synchronous, as they are
in Hamlet and his play. It is nonetheless certain that revenge tragedy enacts what the Elizabethans perceived as a crisis in the relation of the individual to the institutions that governed him (or her).
This crisis figures in one major text after another: in the fall into

chaos of Spain in Kyd's play, in the passage from Antony's Rome to Octavius's, or in the self-destruction of Lear's family. It is also figured in Hamlet's casual remark to Rosencrantz and Guildenstern that prefaces "what a piece of work is man": "I have of late—but wherefore I know not—lost all my mirth" (2.2.295–96). And "the hobby horse is forgot," a phrase Laroque (*Shakespeare's Festive World*, 130) reminds us was proverbial for the decline of festivity. The death of carnival is a central expression of this myth of loss as it is a central figure of revenge tragedy, a form that uses the motifs of carnival, that sees the world in terms appropriated from it, but that combines nostalgia for carnival with an anticarnivalesque spirit: individualistic, skeptical, hostile to body and instinct, preoccupied with the need for control and exclusion, even at the cost of installing a Fortinbras. It expresses festive rebelliousness, as it does regicide, while insisting on the need to put it aside. Carnival requires Lent, after all; it is only meaningful as part of that dialogic, dialectic relationship. Once Hyperion—the validating figure of hierarchic stability and intrinsic value—has been demystified and leveled with the hobbyhorse, he must somehow be remembered and remystified. Otherwise, we are left with a world of hobbyhorses, a world without difference. Faced with the dead level of the graveyard, Hamlet must, like Gawain turning the lace back into heraldic emblem, restore logocentric order. Carnival inversion and subversion depends on re-version.

At the same time, to see that revenge tragedy takes its most basic forms—the release of restraint, the casting off of customary identity, the ritual mockery of authority, masking and unmasking, crowning and uncrowning—from carnival is to see something that is not apparent in the critical literature: why revenge should be, in a quite literal sense, hysterically funny. It explains why revengers should so customarily see their "tragedy" in terms of comedy and why they should find in the role of clown a natural correlative to the role of revenger. Carnival and revenge both enact the possibility of radical, even apocalyptic, change: a possibility at once exhilarating and terrifying. "The people's second world," as Bakhtin repeatedly calls carnival, can be enjoyed in security so long as it remains only a holiday. When it becomes a genuine possibility, then carnival begins to destroy itself. Every man's disorientation is private. To experience the loss of social identity that Hamlet experiences is to lose the secure sense of any relationship of blood, of love, or of community; it is to pass from the banqueting hall to the graveyard, from the reign of King Hamlet to the reign of Claudius. In that isolation the revenger—lord of misrule as prince of the wasteland—retains the forms of carnival as both memory and weapon. Using it against the community that has excluded him, demystifying before murdering, the revenger enacts what we can best call *tragedia dell'arte:* elegy performed as farce, Ophelia buried in Yorick's grave. Revenge plays dramatize a process of loss, diminishment, and separation for the individual and the society that is inevitably a tragedy to the one who watches but (also) a comedy to the one who suffers.

As should be apparent from the preceding chapters, the most remarkable thing about the paradigm of the Augustinian carnivalesque is its persistence over a great stretch of literary and cultural history. Whether in fourteenth- or in seventeenth-century literature, the prevalence of carnival registers a sense of the instability and fictionality of social identity and the political structures that define it, as well as a continuing interrogation of the relation between exterior and interior: between inky cloaks and that within them, between birthmarks or confessions and the character they purport to register, between pentangle and knight, or between Tamburlaine's empire and the inward compulsions that create it. These uncertainties are, of course, constants of an Augustinian world-view, as present in the *Confessions* as in *Dr. Faustus.* They are also reminders that in at least this fundamental sense the English Renaissance is continuous with, not separate from, the later Middle Ages. Hamlet's skeptical subjectivity is not a new creation of the Renaissance but an inheritance from a tradition reaching back to the Augustine who proved his existence by his capacity to error: "si fallor sum" (*City of God,* 11.26). *Antony and Cleopatra* is a Renaissance text not in presenting some new theory of the self, but in projecting the ontological concerns of orthodox Augustinianism back upon pre-Christian Rome, Augustine's *civitas terrena,* and laterally upon Elizabeth and James, both notoriously incorporated into the figures of Egypt and Antony.[42]

6

Enthroned in the Marketplace: The Carnivalesque *Antony and Cleopatra*

> Every act of history was accompanied by a laughing chorus
> —Bakhtin, *Rabelais,* 474

CARNIVAL is, of course, the festivity of the marketplace and transaction is central to its view of the world. Carnival parody depends on the assumption that rank, hierarchy, and identity are transposable, therefore negotiable. A bishop who can be replaced by a boy bishop can, by extension, be replaced by another bishop or no bishop. On top, as the Wife of Bath has discovered, is a position that can be purchased, even if that purchase turns out to be subject to the fluctuations of the market, as purchases are. The fluidity Bakhtin celebrates in carnival is necessarily that of commerce, in which the value of a thing is a matter of shifting agreements between buyers and sellers, not an intrinsic quality, just as the return to Lenten stability may reflect, not oppression, but recoil from a world of unlimited negotiability, whose immediately recognizable literary analogue is the potentially endless process of deconstruction.

Not surprisingly, given these facts, the language of commerce pervades the texts I have been discussing: from the Wife's *chaffare* and her interwoven careers as weaver and wife; to *Gawain and the Green Knight*'s games of exchange and debates on the *prys* of heroes and *costes* of love; to Tamburlaine's buying, selling, renting, and stealing of kingship and love, or to Faustus's devilish contracts; and to Hamlet's revulsion at hire and purchase and the commercial ethics of a Polonius. Since transaction is the element of carnival most censored by Bakhtin and most central to its leveling, demystifying processes, I want to conclude this study by showing how that element functions in a play once known, among other things, for its characters' aristocratic superiority to considerations of trade: *Antony and Cleopatra*. That play, I contend, is a pervasively carnivalesque text not only in the senses we have been considering, but also in opening up, for tragicomic inspection, a world of barter.

WHOREDOM, AGAPE AND CARNIVAL

In act 4, scene 15 of *Antony and Cleopatra*, as most readers intuit and few critics admit, the Whore of Babylon tries her hand at the imitation of Christ. And a very good hand it turns out to be. The occasion for Cleopatra's short hint of what she can do in the sublime is a grotesque mock-apotheosis in which Antony, dying to this world, is hauled aloft on ropes by three grunting women, one of whom is comforting him with a volley of salacious humor that ends with a startling, if unsuccessful, attempt at *agape:* "Die where thou hast liv'd, / Quicken with kissing" (4.15.37–38)[1] Coleridge's *feliciter audax* is one term for this; *blasphemy* is another. With invocations of Revelations and Isaiah at every turn, but without putting off the body of carnality, she puts on the mantles of the Faithful and confronts the Antichrist: the Gospels' Cæsar, Augustine's Cæsar, everybody's Cæsar.[2]

This is not the first time a Christian audience of the play has been subjected to this kind of outrage. Antony has begun his career by asking for "new heaven, new earth," like Isaiah (1.1.17; compare Is. 65:17 and 2 Peter 3:13), and envisioning the dissolution of the earthly city, like John in Revelations (1.1.33–35; cf. Rev. 21:1–4). Charmian has asked for a child "to whom Herod of Jewry may do homage" (1.2.28–29; compare Matt 2:7–8). John Middleton Murry noted many years ago that Antony stages a last supper and that Enobarbus serves as his Judas.[3] No one will need reminding that Antony and especially Cleopatra come to see themselves as renouncing the world for love and losing life to gain it: out of "desolation . . . to make a better life" (5.1.1–2). After Antony's death, at least, Cleopatra "hourly learn[s] / A doctrine of obedience" (5.2.30–31). She spends the last act determinedly rendering unto Cæsar the things that are Cæsar's, including land, children, and the treasure she pretends to withhold. "I send him," she tells Proculeius, "the greatness he has got" (5.2.28–29). Dying with the serpent—whose "biting is immortal"—at her bosom, she evokes both the first Eve and the second. It is impossible, I argue, to understand this extraordinary conjunction of the sacred and the obscene—Cleopatra's ability to combine Venus, Isis, the maid that

milks, the progenitive slime of the Nile, and the Virgin Mary—
without recourse to the carnivalesque. "Royal Egypt" is also a
gypsy as the "Emperor Antony" is also a strumpet's fool.

To characterize Cleopatra, as much of the criticism does, in
terms of her identification with Isis and Venus is to privilege the
elevation at the expense of the degradation, the "Eastern star" at
the expense of the "lass unparalleled." Cleopatra is of the earth:
identified with birth and decay, the cycles of the Nile, "she represents," as Andrew Fichter puts it, "the unbroken circle of appetitive nature."[4] She is also what Philo sees as "a tawny front" (1.1.6),
and what she herself describes: a woman "with Phoebus' amorous
pinches black / And wrinkled deep in time" (1.5.28)—in Elizabethan eyes at least, a grotesque. "A brow of Egypt" is Theseus's
antithesis to "Helen's beauty" (A Midsummer Night's Dream,
5.1.11). A figure of such extreme and pervasive sexual voracity
that Romans from Philo on habitually regard her as debilitating,
she figures, like the Wife of Bath, sexual appetite abnormally pro-
longed as well as heightened. She is also, at various times, a shrew,
a virago, an ostentatious and self-glorifying liar, a beater of servants and brow-beater of lovers: a crowned version of the husband-
beating wife of the skimmingtons. As Leonard Tennenhouse is virtually alone in noting,

> Shakespeare has represented her in much the same terms Bakhtin uses
> to identify the grotesque—or popular—body in Renaissance culture.
> Shakespeare clearly endows her with all the features of carnival.[5]

While she may be "stigmatized" by this identification, as Tennenhouse goes on to argue, she is also glorified by it. "In this tradition," Bakhtin says, "woman is essentially related to the material
bodily lower stratum; she . . . degrades and regenerates simultaneously."[6] Cleopatra, I need hardly add, gives birth to a new, sexualized Antony in the process of subverting the old one. "Egypt,"
moreover, rules and is metonymically associated with a country
defined by carnival festivity and carnivalesque inversion, a national
expression of what Marilyn French calls the "outlaw feminine principle."[7] Egypt everywhere acts out that basic trope of carnivalesque subversion: women on top. Cleopatra "angles," Antony
is the fish (2.5.10–15); she drinks him to bed and wears his "sword
Philippan" (lines 21–23). In the most fundamental dynamic of the
play, carnivalesque femininity confronts masculine officialdom.

If Cleopatra is carnival, crabbed, parsimonious Cæsar, who typically regards feasting his victorious army as "waste" (4.1.16), is

Lent, a contrast Shakespeare has heightened by omitting Plutarch's testimony to the historical Octavius's affability and fondness for plays and women.[8] She is, of course, everywhere identified with feasting, a trope Clare Kinney calls "Cleopatra the Comestible."[9] It is her "lascivious wassails" that Cæsar pretends to call Antony back from (1.4.55–56). She is at various times "a morsel for a monarch" (1.5.31), an "Egyptian dish" (2.6.126), "a morsel cold upon / Dead Cæsar's trencher" (3.13.116–17), even—in her youth—a green salad. Breakfast in her house is "eight wild boars roasted whole" for twelve people (2.2.179). She herself, of course, "makes hungry / Where most she satisfies" (2.2.240–41). As the language of the play repeatedly insists, she is not only the purveyor of feasts, but also Feast itself, the literary descendent of Gargamelle as much as Venus.[10] When Octavius wants to praise the former Antony, he seizes on the most antifestive kind of feasting: "thou didst drink / The stale of horses . . . eat strange flesh, / Which some did die to look on" (1.4.61–68). The tyrant, not surprisingly, regards the proper relation of will to body as tyrannical. For Cæsar, privation is virtue; bodies, like kingdoms, exist to be conquered. Lenten in his youth, so far as we can trust Roman memories, Antony has become carnivalesque in middle age.[11]

In keeping with its pervasive category subversion, *Antony and Cleopatra* presents us with one of those polarities that look easy to read but are not. If, for example, you associate Rome with public life and Egypt with private, you run immediately into the problem that Egyptian private life is played out in public and has public consequences.[12] Sleeping with Roman generals is, after all, Cleopatra's defense policy. Taunting Antony into a public profession of love is a political gesture, whatever its private function may be. Comparably, Roman public affairs are private wars disguised. Fulvia goes to war, so Antony claims, to get her husband's attention. Pompey makes speeches about "beauteous freedom" (2.6.17), but negotiates about the family house. Octavius claims to be conquering the world as a way of avenging a slight to his sister.

If, on the other hand, you follow Northrop Frye and try to define the polarity of the two cultures in terms of Apollonian and Dionysian, you create a rigid opposition between two forces that mingle with and mimic one another throughout the play: an Alexandrian feast in Rome, a Roman suicide in Egypt. You have to create a "Dionysian" Antony out of the unresolvable, shifting figure before you.[13] The inability of Romans to be what they think they are is, of course, fundamental to the play, which is why Janet Adelman's attempt to contrast a world of fact with a world of dream also creates more problems than it solves.[14] Virtually every fact about Rome—its history, its honor, its public spirit, its male bonding, its respect for women—turns out to be a fiction. Even Octavius's power is belied by his physique, his arguable dependency on fortune, his potential vulnerability to any stray assassin like Menas. Tennenhouse's myth of an aristocratic Roman body traduced by Egyptian fleshliness forces him to read the play as rejecting and punishing Cleopatra, despite her fifth-act victory over Cæsar, and as endorsing Octavian patriarchy, despite the play's numerous anticipations of the next "Eastern star" to mock Roman authority.

A carnivalesque paradigm, on the other hand, inscribes a shifting, dialectical relationship between the two poles. The carnivalesque order mirrors the official one, is incorporated within it (as carnival is within the church year), and both subverts and reinforces it, as Egypt does with Rome. To see that relationship is to see why travesty—right down to Cæsar's imitation of Hymen in marrying the dead lovers—should play such a large part in the play. It is also to see how great tragedy can be based on an oscillation between the literal, theatrical, and carnal senses of "to die," an oscillation that helps account for the play's notorious generic instability. More important, perhaps, it will explain the remarkable prevalence of the carnivalesque blasphemy I noted earlier. Cleopatra, Agrippa famously says, "made great Cæsar lay his sword to bed; / He ploughed her, and she cropp'd" (2.2.227–28). As Clare Kinney, at least, has noted, Cleopatra beats swords into ploughshares.[15] The Augustinian carnivalesque offers at least one explanation of why Christ and Carnality should find themselves in such intimate alliance against Cæsar, especially a Cæsar so identified with chaste bodily denial. In so doing it will help to explain in more than the familiar Freudian terms the threat posed to Rome by Egypt. Throughout the play Rome is identified with a masculine, body-denying tyranny of the human (as opposed to divine) will; Egypt, the body, and the feminine are identified with carnival and thus with escape from that control. Egypt enslaves ego—Cleopatra is at various times, of course, fetters, serpents, enchantress ("the Great Fairy," for example, at 4.8.12)—because it releases emotion, dream, libido. Egypt will free you from the confinement of playing "Antony" but will not allow you to assert that ego-based Antony. In Rome, conscious will tries to enslave instinct; in Egypt, instinct threatens to enslave conscious will. "Rome" is a structure of internal and external control, threatening tyranny; Egypt" is the carnivalesque principle of resistance, threatening entropy. Egypt will thus appear to Rome as both life and death, liberation and madness, expansion and dissolution.

That Egyptian principle emerges directly from the marketplace, the traditional site of carnival, where Antony sits "enthroned" (2.2.214) waiting for his first meeting with Cleopatra and where Antony and Cleopatra proclaim their (nominally, her) empire:

> I' th' marketplace, on a tribunal silvered,
> Cleopatra and himself in chairs of gold
> Were publicly enthroned.
>
> (3.6.3–5)

From their first pageantlike entrance on, Antony and Cleopatra's affair is played out as public spectacle, available for promiscuous observation and participation, presenting itself as both royal and common. Enobarbus "saw her once / Hop forty paces through the public street" (2.2.229). In act 1, scene 1 Antony completes the process of offending Cæsar's ambassadors by leaving them in order to "wander through the streets, and note the qualities of people" (1.1.53–54), characteristically, at Cleopatra's request. As Julian Markels writes: "Cleopatra and 'the public street' are ornaments to each other, and they measure each other's value."[16] The leveling effect of doing it in the street is one of the first charges Octavius brings against Antony:

> to sit
> And keep the turn of tippling with a slave,
> To reel the streets at noon, and stand the buffet
> With knaves that smells of sweat.
>
> (1.4.18–21)

Antony, engaged in carnival games at carnival hours, is indistinguishable from the other players, from slaves and knaves, or from the Antony who "tumble[s]," clownishly prostrate, "on the bed of Ptolemy" (line 17). Carnival dissolves hierarchy and suspends official rank. Cleopatra, hopping those forty paces in the public street, may be Egypt's queen, but she is also Egypt's carnival, no more than the most interesting of street shows: They, like Enobarbus, can "note the qualities" of her. Significantly, at Cydnus, Antony, who is still the agent of Roman authority and trying to stage a Roman official visit, is left alone in the market by a crowd that flocks to see the real show, a barge that is somewhere between a Lord Mayor's Day pageant and a parody of one: a carnival float. He is drawn into carnival, she *is* carnival. She leads him through the streets, drinks him to bed, puts her mantles on him. Carnival fluidity is the medium of her character.

EGYPTIAN BUSINESS

Commerce, as most readers will know by now, is the dirty secret of Bakhtin's carnival—the element he most consistently tries to suppress—and Cleopatra's fluidity is also that of the market. After "gypsy," "strumpet" is the first and most frequent term of Roman abuse thrown at her (1.1.13), women who sell themselves being a threat to the men who wish to sell them. She, of course, "trade[s] in love" (2.5.2), not merely by getting armies in return for her favors. At their first meeting, as Enobarbus describes it, Antony "for his ordinary, pays his heart / For what his eyes eat only" (2.2.225–26). Their moment-to-moment relationship is a constant extortion of tribute, whether in the form of pearls, protestations, or empires. "If it be love, tell me how much" (1.1.14): from her first words Cleopatra makes it clear that love is a measurable commodity and subject to fluctuation. The commodity is obtained by what we might call the negotiability of Cleopatra's character. Her moods are determined by the market: "If you find him sad, / Say I am dancing" (1.3.2–3). The principle may be that the customer is always wrong, but the transaction nonetheless makes Cleopatra vulnerable as the purveyor of a product always subject to rejection. The "morsel for a monarch" can easily become the "morsel cold" on the dead monarch's trencher and despised by the next purchaser.

At the same time, however, Cleopatra is the restauranteur as well as the meal. Octavia is only a commodity (however mystified), traded by males; Cleopatra is an entrepreneur. This conjures the possibility of a world, outside Rome, where women are independent agents. It also makes Cleopatra and carnival the embodiments of a free market of private traders, as opposed to Octavius, whom Thidias celebrates as "the universal landlord" (3.13.72). As his rivals find, Octavius aims for monopoly. In his new world order values will be fixed because there will be only one purchaser. His empire is a vast enclosure movement, driven, like enclosure, to maximize profit and control by eliminating subdivision. By the end of the play, he can assert that "Cæsar is no merchant, to make prize with [Cleopatra] / Of things that merchants sold" (5.2.183–84): an assertion of aristocratic superiority to the market that actually declares the market closed. The "sole sir of the world" (line 120), though still one of the "factors of the gods," no longer needs to bargain. The plutocrat retires to his mansion and, like Ben Jonson's usurer, curses trade. Throughout the play, Cæsar plays to end "play," in both the carnival and market senses. Cleopatra bids; Octavius forecloses.

Cleopatra assumes that all relationships are functions of desire; Octavius assumes that they are functions of control. Cleopatra's appetitive world is comic because it asserts that all desires (hence, all relationships) are renewable. One of the play's most startling moves is to equate that comic renegotiability and deferral of closure with the market: "play" of body and feeling with "play" of commercial value. What else does it mean to "trade in love"? What is not sold today can be sold tomorrow. Even a "morsel cold" can be reheated. Any emotional deal can be restructured. He who is sunk today can be refloated tomorrow. By contrast, Cæsar insists on finality not because he has a "tragic sense of life," but because his drive for control can only be fulfilled in universal stasis, to which both Cleopatra and the market represent vitality and resistance. Cleopatra maintains a comic world in which consequences are perpetually suspended. She no more expects her flight from the battle to cause his than she expects her feigned death to cause his real one. Cleopatra's vision of a perpetually festive afterlife with Antony and the suicide it facilitates are the ultimate extensions of this comedic principle of escape, eternity being, of course, the ultimate deferral. She gives leave "to play till doomsday" (5.2.232), play that takes the final form (319–20) of Charmian's mocking farewell to Octavius's soldiers. The play's generic instability is a direct function of Cleopatra's insistence—beyond death— on the commercial, comic, and carnivalesque.

As Janet Adelman and others have well and truly established, Octavius epitomizes a Roman mentality that sees the world in terms of hierarchy and the rigid boundary definitions that usually go with it.[17] Official Rome acts pervasively to restrict the play of values (what is "manly"?), of meanings (what is "a man"?), and of identities (what is "Antony"?). Rome aspires to a dictatorial control over terms as well as lands, a universal stabilization of categories. To Philo and to the Roman lobe of Antony's brain, Antony's "real" identity is fixed and unproblemmatical (albeit gone missing), something that can be represented by plated armor or heroic statuary. Romans (and Egyptians imitating them) imagine themselves as marble-constant; Egypt and Cleopatra are liquid, flowing, and unstable. Rome's mental world is vertical, like a command structure; Egypt's is horizontal, like a floodplain or a marketplace, both places of promiscuous mingling. The Nile's floods, as Antony reminds Lepidus in act 2, scene 7, produce crops and crocodiles with equal fluency. Egyptians overflow, like Antony in his dotage (1.1.2); Romans (think they) are contained. "According to Cæsar's distinctly Roman economy of the self," Adelman writes in her most recent book, "plenty constitutes self-waste, compromising the stringent self-withholding that is his ideal."[18] Octavius's praise for Antony's self-mortification after Modena has nothing to do with any transcendent, otherworldly value. He praises discipline for discipline's sake and for its immediate military utility, though his praise may imply the ontology—I am my containment—on which the Empire is built. To Philo and Demetrius, Enobarbus, Octavius, the Roman Antony, anything that dissolves barriers threatens not only the self, but also the construction of the world on which that self depends. You must, for ontological as well as personal reasons, keep "your square" (2.3.6), as Antony says a moment before deciding to desert his wife. If you drink with slaves, you may become a slave. If Antony consorts with women, then he "is not more manlike / Than Cleopatra; nor the queen . . . / More womanly than he" (1.4.5–7). When captains can become women, how shall the world be ordered?[19]

Of course, Egypt's relation to Rome is dialectical, as carnival's relation to officialdom always is. To the extent that Egyptian festivity depends on the protection of the elder Pompey, Julius Cæsar, Antony, and their armies, it can be said to be sponsored by Rome. That is another aspect of Cleopatra's negotiability. Certainly, no one apotheosizes the warrior Antony more fervently than she— Eros does not arm him so well—and no one envies Octavia's official status as wife more intensely. Still, Cleopatra—She Who is Permitted to Laugh—comprises the psychological loyal opposition, seeing the fictionality of Rome and enjoying its heroics as sexual fantasy and sexual comedy, as game. Politically, that is, Egypt embodies the love of the ruled for the ruler as well as rebelliousness. Cleopatra's most rampant sexual images ("oh, happy horse to bear the weight of Antony") picture a rapturous acceptance of phallic domination.

At the same time, Cleopatra, figuring the self not as fixed but as infinitely various, represents the most fundamentally carnivalesque threat to that control. She lives, as we all know, in a cloud of double entendres—from "ram thou thy fruitful tidings in my ears" (2.5.23) to "the soldier's pole is fallen" (4.15.65) and even to the elision of "asp" (for death, lover, Antony) and "ass" (for death, enemy, Cæsar) in her dying words. Cleopatra's puns—and Enobarbus's puns about her—destabilize language by degrading. In the words of Michael Bristol, "the basic principle of grotesque or Carnival realism is to represent everything socially and spiritually exalted on the material bodily level."[20] "Here's sport indeed! How heavy lies my lord!" (4.15.32), says Cleopatra. As we have seen, the play is an elaboration of the triple entendre of Cleopatra's "celerity in dying" (1.2.144), which culminates in a suicide that is simultaneously an allusive, carefully staged, theatrical dying; an orgiastic sexual dying, "as sweet as air, as soft as balm" (5.2.311); and a literal dying. It is both the confirmation and the refutation of Enobarbus's first-act abuse.

Her puns, like her constant and ostentatious self-theatricalization, figure a self that is both multiple and indeterminate. Her death is, of course, both Roman suicide and Egyptian mockery of Roman solemnities. Even her royal title "Egypt" unfolds into "gypsy": the high and the low conflated. The Queen herself enacts an Egyptian—and carnivalesque—sense of self as process, something reinvented from moment to moment in performance. In her dying moments, despite her claims to Roman constancy, she flickers through the roles of lover, wife, mother, lass, even while freezing into the (staged) image of Isis and Egypt. Kinney (177) notes that more than forty different titles are applied to Cleopatra during the play. She embodies that "antitaxonomic energy" Terry Castle sees in masquerade, subverting "the vision of a classifiable cosmos."[21] That subversion is the very fear Octavius expresses when, leaving the revelry on Pompey's yacht, he complains that "this wild disguise hath almost / Antick'd us all" (2.7.124–25), a phrase that links festivity to theatrical playing and to madness, and both to loss of self. Cleopatra's carnivalesque being-in-process figures an Egyptian world in which boundaries dissolve, like those of Antony's "cloud that's dragonish" (4.14.2). Thomas McAlindon writes that in the Egyptian world,

> so close to "the primal state" (1.4.41), there is an inevitable blurring of the distinction between the human and the animal. When lost in folly or passion, the protagonists are likened to . . . horse, mare, nag, ox, lion and mallard. Shameful and grotesque though it may be, the implied transformation never seems horrifyingly unnatural. . . . [It is] as if the whole natural order were a single ontological category in which motion, mingling, and change are the norm.[22]

What McAlindon describes as a natural process, however, is primarily a linguistic and theatrical one. Nothing *literally* dissolves in the play. "Dissolution" is a way of imagining the world as fluid performance.

ROMAN ORDERS

Naming is, of course, the most fundamental stage of ruling; to define is to control. To conceive of the world and the self as fluid is a way of evading domination, as Cleopatra habitually evades Antony's control—as Bertilak's Lady does with Gawain—by switching roles (for example, from theatrical dying to scolding to tongue-tied oblivion to noble resignation during their parting in act 1, scene 3). Rome, on the other hand, is built on dominion expressed characteristically through fealty and contractual alliance. It has seldom been noticed how closely the play's Rome is modeled on that described in *The City of God,* St. Augustine's great memorialization of the death of the world order founded by Augustus. At the very beginning of the book Augustine defines Rome as "a city which aims at dominion, which holds nations in enslavement, but is itself dominated by that very lust of domination."[23] Rome's historical pursuit of dominion is the subject of Augustine's book 3. In Augustine as in Shakespeare, Rome is a culture whose greatest achievement is the law; whose greatest passion is conquest; and whose greatest institution is the self. The *civitas terrena,* of which Rome is the prototype, "was created by self-love reaching the point of contempt for God, the Heavenly City by the love of God carried as far as contempt for self . . . . [The earthly city] loves its own strength shown in its powerful leaders" (14.28; p. 593). That city, he adds, in what amounts to a remarkably concise summary of Octavian policy:

> desires an earthly peace for the sake of the lowest goods; and that is the peace it longs to attain by making war. For if it wins the war and no one survives to resist, then there will be peace, which the warring sections did not enjoy when they contended . . . for the things which they could not both possess at the same time.
>
> (15.4)

Octavius, who famously desires to "possess" (2.7.101) the time rather than enjoy it, embodies precisely that cold ruling in apartness characteristic of Augustine's Rome and Bakhtin's official feast. (Time, like everything else to Octavius, is an object, a species of property, the "much dirt" he is lord of.) Significantly, Octavius never identifies himself with the physical Rome as Cleopatra does with Egyptian soil. It is the thing he rules, not himself: a chaos upon which he imposes order, "this common body" (1.4.44) on which he inflicts a repressive will, like his version of Antony in the wilderness. Octavius's new Rome—the political expression of its master's cold knowing in apartness—will also be a purely secular order. Antony's god leaves him, but Cæsar has no god except his own personified destiny. Like Bakhtin's official feast, Rome creates "no second life" (*Rabelais,* 9) because it acknowledges no order of values beyond its own. As J. L. Simmons has written, "Shakespeare . . . represents Rome as a pagan world in which the characters must perforce operate with no reference beyond the Earthly City."[24] That better than average citizen of the earthly city, Dolabella, is not asked whether Antony was like Cleopatra's dream, but whether he thinks that "there . . . might be such a man" (5.1.93) as the one she dreamed. He can't.[25] Thinking isn't dreaming. The Empire manages to be both spiritually and carnally impoverished—like Octavius's personal life or Antony's Roman marriage—while being materially powerful.[26] Cleopatra's Egyptian carnival is opposed and absorbed by a "monolithically serious" (Leggatt, 176) order we might call, combining Augustinian and Bakhtinian terms, the *civitas officialis.* Antony's role in the play is to be the locus of that conflict.[27]

With Antony, as with Cleopatra and Octavius, the carnivalesque paradigm enables us to see familiar ground in an unfamiliar way. Like Sir Gawain, and for the same logocentric reasons, Antony needs to believe in a version of himself that is at once subjective and substantial, an unchangeable essence that is also visible to others, like a pentangle. Both men externalize that identity as glowing armor, the enclosed body signifiying an enclosed, and thus stabilized, essence. In both cases, the armor, while seeming to signify and be identical with the man wearing it, represents the collective and unstable judgment of his community. It signifies their willingness to mythologize the wearer as a representative of themselves. Rome, as Augustine says, loves the image of its own strength reflected in its leaders: an image physically assembled before us in act 4, scene 4 by Eros and Cleopatra. Both heroes discover that the armor is removable—"happed on" the man, not organically related to him—and that its taking off signals the dissolution of the self it seemed to contain. What seemed an emblem is (also) a disguise. Antony's Egyptian experience deconstructs that "visible shape."

Even more ruthlessly than Gawain, Antony is shown that what

he has regarded as his personal identity is a locus of fictions, his own as well as other people's.[28] He is the object of a common need to believe in and exalt honor, courage, heroism, and the Roman virtues: another version of the hero as billboard. Antony is Rome's as well as Cæsar's "spacious mirror" (5.1.34): not loved for what he is so much as invented so he can be loved. As with Kurtz and his admirers in *Heart of Darkness,* the need for a hero is universal, but the definition of one varies from one worshipper to the next: Philo remembers battlefield prowess, Cæsar a surreal exaggeration of Lenten self-denial, Cleopatra a more affable version of heroic self-assertion. Even his bounty, the quality of Antony that everyone except Octavius agrees on, is undercut by his theft of Pompey's house (though Antony, Cæsar's "mirror," shows an Octavian gift for handsome apology where handsome behavior has been lacking). Few readers will need reminding that the generous and spontaneous Antony is also an actor who (in act 4, scene 2) manipulates his captains into weeping, then denies he meant it. Pompey's Menas and Antony's Enobarbus greet each other as fellow pirates (2.6.84–96).[29] For that matter, Enobarbus remembers Antony weeping over those he has destroyed as Cæsar now does. Antony's subsequent behavior mocks Octavia's willingness to identify him with his honor and Scarus's willingness to identify him with courage. To Octavius, in any case, physical courage only makes one an "old ruffian" (4.1.4). The point is precisely that none of these versions of Antony is more or less real than the others. Cæsar's hero of abstention may even be truer, looking at the whole of Antony's life, than Cleopatra's happy horseman, or the jealous bureaucrat Ventidius serves and mocks. The past Antony, of course, exists only in stories. That one, as the saying goes, is history; and history, the play shows us, is a collocation of lies or, to put it more politely,of self-interested subjective versions, such as Cæsar's manipulative contrast of Antony past and present or Pompey's memorialization of Cassius and Brutus as courtiers of freedom, like himself. If history is a field of unreality, identity is and must be both collective and dispersed, not a coherent unit but a sum of imaginings. Antony's experience teaches him a basic carnivalesque lesson he cannot accept without losing his fiction of self-containment and ceasing to exist as a Roman: our selves we do not own.

The heroically coherent Antony exists, and can only exist, in the mind of Cleopatra. The world of fact denies it; Cleopatra herself, as Charmian reminds her in act I, scene 5, has exalted other generals before. In a movement entirely characteristic of the Augustinian carnivalesque, the play dissolves Antony's ego-based social identity to relocate his being in the egoless, instinctual bodily sphere and in a transcendent sublimation of that: Cleopatra's dream-fiction of an Emperor Antony, her master builder. That dream, like Hilde Wangel's final version of Solness, is not in the man himself and is not communicated to him. The absence of the literal object is its necessary precondition. Notoriously, of course, Antony is Cleopatra's fool when he is there, her god when he is away. Only in his absence are they a genuinely "mutual pair": He—or rather his after-image—provides the stimulus, she provides the informing myth, which, because history is a system of myths, may be the most real of the Antonys he leaves to posterity and is, in any case, the one Octavius decides to bury. The past can and will be turned into romance and epic because both the winners and losers want it that way: the "romance" of Antony and Cleopatra's defeat is a necessary part of the "epic" of Octavius's victory. In his curtain speech, Cæsar is already stabilizing the genres: "Their story is / No less in pity than his glory [i.e., mine] which / Brought them to be lamented" (5.2.361–63). The instability of his grammar, however, suggests a different romance in which "his glory" is as much an object of pity as "their story."

In Antony's present and presence, however, things are liable to take a different generic turn. Their myth was Roman gossip before it was mythologized and bedroom farce before it was gossip. (Enobarbus's barge speech is remarkable not least because it holds all three phases in suspension.) Cleopatra as the embodiment of carnival seems bent on deconstructing the Roman Antony even as she honors it. Psychologically, we might assume, she needs to destroy his previous, publicly determined self-image—precisely because it is not his but Rome's—to replace it with one dependent on her (his identity will still not be *his*). The idol of his troops will be reconstructed as the idol of Cleopatra: a process strikingly encoded in his invitation to her to "leap . . . / Through proof of harness to my heart, and there / Ride on the pants triumphing" (4.8.14–16). The hero imaginatively abandons himself to a ravishment in which his Roman armor is not only cast asunder, but also dissolved. She can "leap through" it "to his heart" because the image figures feeling as real and its containment as not. In this figure, which we might call disproof of harness, it is habitually his armored self she bursts through and his sword she appropriates, just as it is his official self she most consistently mocks and, as it were, privatizes, publicly turning the Empire's Viceroy in Egypt into a doting lover in the first scene and a henpecked husband in the third. Her original way of attracting his attention, of course, was to stage a show that left him, a mock-king, "enthroned" in the deserted marketplace, "whistling to the air" (2.2.219).[30] In her games, he is alternately the fool who catches the salt-fish (2.5.15–18) and a caught fish himself (2.5.10–15). The woman who "rides on the pants triumphing" is, literally and figuratively, woman on top.

There, like Gawain, "he watz despoyled with spechez of myerthe." To appropriate Antony's victorious sword, however, is to acknowledge its power even as one seems to neutralize it. A king would not be worth mocking if he were simply unreal. Cleopatra's mockery, instead, externalizes that power and thus creates a gap between it and the mutual imaginative construct they (sporadically) agree to call "Antony." His authority is not him but something he wears: not the heart but the harness (O, unhappy horse). As in the case of Gawain, a rigid, masculine construction of the self is replaced by a liquid, feminine one. In the process, the ground of his being is transferred from dead metal to living soil (or living mind, depending on whether you see him living in her flesh or her imagination). Antony, in either case, relocates his manhood in Cleopatra, who is throughout identified with fluidity: the sea, the Nile, and its mud. If "his delights were dolphin-like" because they "show'd his back above the element they liv'd in" (5.2.88–90), that element is her. Cleopatra degrades to exalt, bringing Antony down to the bodily level where we all necessarily live to lift him above it, as the dolphin is supported by the element it partly rises above. The speech in which this image occurs is devoted to reconstructing a colossal Roman Antony who, nevertheless, exists at that point only within her dreaming. My master-building!

TRAGICARNIVALESQUE

We are seeing, of course, the familiar double *ludus* of the tragicarnivalesque. Egyptian festivity mocks and subverts official Rome to construct a new Romanness, reconnected to the physical and the sexual, the popular and the feminine, an order inaugurated in the marketplace, though destroyed, literally at least, in the monument. Cleopatra's imaginatively (re)constructed Antony is Roman in stature but Egyptian in multiplicity and indefiniteness: posed statuary but also swimming dolphin, an unstable mixture of dream and (asserted) reality, attributable equally to nature and art. His bounty is an unending autumn, "no winter in it" (5.2.87–88): an image both of fertility and of endless deferral. Cleopatra's towering, bounty-dripping Antony is as unmistakably phallic as the asp that will take her to him. What goes down, as Cleopatra knows better than anyone, must come up. Degradation inverts hierarchy; it doesn't destroy it.

If Egypt, with its transvestite queen wearing Antony's sword or costuming herself as an admiral, parodies Rome, Rome's official feast travesties Egyptian festivity, enacting the usual relationship of carnival and official feasts. As the former debases to exalt, the latter exalts to debase, honoring Octavia's holy, cold femininity in order to prostitute it. As Carol Neely has pointed out, Antony and Octavius enact a parody of the marriage ceremony—giving hands, pledging fidelity, and embracing—every bit as sexually transversive as (and considerably more perverse than) anything Cleopatra performs. The marriage, Neely adds, "exaggerates the sociopolitical function of marriage to secure male alliances and eliminates its sexual and emotional purposes."[31] That marriage and the treaty arising from it are celebrated by the "Alexandrian feast" (2.7.96) staged on Pompey's barge: a travesty of reconciliation in a society at (temporarily cold) war; a travesty of bonding in a society where increasingly the only functioning bond is political self-interest; and a travesty of festive release in a society where loss of self is death. Here Pompey "laugh[s] away his fortune" (2.6.104–5). This bacchanal, of course, excludes women and thus leaves room only for bonding among male competitors. Carnival release here is figured not as fertile Egyptian "ooze," but as the sterile "quicksands" of drunkenness where, Antony warns Lepidus, he will sink (2.7.22,59–60). Here carnival play is not release from self but nervous, self-protective game playing: Antony's teasing of Lepidus, Octavius's grudging, self-reserved participation. Like all Roman occasions, this one is a test of one's power of containment. In the midst of this "play," of course, Menas offers to cut the throats of "these three world-sharers" (2.7.75), carnival uncrowning with a vengeance, and an offer that demonstrates how fictional the solidity of Octavius's official order (not to mention, the inevitability of his personal destiny) is. To let go of yoursef even momentarily, as Lepidus and Pompey do, is to lose your place in that fiction, as they do.

As the play figures it, the absorption of carnival is the focal process of Cæsar's leveraged buyout of the world because the carnivalesque embodies both the carnal and spiritual orders that refuse to acknowledge Cæsar's power. For the people of the play, epitomized by Enobarbus, Egypt is the "second world." In its fictions Octavius figures as an ass unpolicied (5.2.307–8), a lord of much dung (lines 7–8), or the paltry knave of Fortune (lines 2–3). Octavius, however, maintains his own coherence (and the power it conveys) by the ruthless, exclusionary proprietorship of his own legend ("Go with me to my tent, where you shall see / How hardly I was drawn . . . / How calm and gently I proceeded": (5.1.73–75). There must be only one fiction of Octavius. The carnival feast must be turned into a parade, the "solemn show" of Antony and Cleopatra's funeral (5.2.364), in and after which they will serve, as Cleopatra has said, as his "scutcheons and . . . signs of conquest" (5.2.135): emblems not only of his power, but also of a world reduced to objects.

The solemn funeral is only plan B, however. Plan A was the staged triumph, co-opted carnival in which Cleopatra will be not a scutcheon, but a "puppet" (5.2.208). It is a measure of how important carnival is in the play that Antony and Cleopatra, but equally Eros, Iras, and Charmian, regard it as the ultimate weapon, more threatening than Cæsar's army. Cæsar's shows will, of course, be hostile, exclusionary, and in the service of the official order; derisive rather than celebratory: a display of his power from which, like the feast for his troops, he will be absent. He doesn't play, but he owns and uses those who do. Nonparticipation both signifies and facilitates absolute control. To be included in their shows as an exhibition is to be excluded as a participant, doubly or triply excluded in Cleopatra's case because her gender is excluded as well as herself. She will be "boy[ed]" as a "whore" (5.2.220–21): at once excluded and pinned down. The speech is one of the rare moments where a recognition of how alienating the Elizabethan theater must have been for female spectators appears in the texts. To "boy" Cleopatra is to complete, in a particularly humiliating way, the subordination and silencing of female Egypt by male Rome. At the same time, the image registers the persecutory power of popular mirth—its usefulness, as in the skimmington, as a mode of repression, especially of transgressive sexuality—and the ambivalence of Antony and Cleopatra toward it. Within the Egyptian carnival they are central, defining participants; in the Roman one they will be defined objects. The former condition gives them general love, registered most conclusively by the deaths of their attendants; the latter deprives them of it. To be registered in vulgar fame is both the greatest desire because it offers you the prospect of an unofficial countermyth, history written by the losers, and the greatest fear because it is the means by which history will be manipulated against you by an absent power shaping vulgar fame through intermediaries. If Octavius can not make them a show, he will build them a monument, in both cases to his own glory.

To a Roman, Elizabethan, or modern audience, of course, the historical Cleopatra is an absence, who- or whatever is representing her. Within the play, the carnivalesque Cleopatra figures plenitude, whereas the Augustinian one figures privation. That doubling, seen also in Alisoun and Falstaff, is perhaps the most characteristic sign of the Augustinian carnivalesque. Cleopatra *was* a woman, as the grave digger says, but, poor thing, she's dead. Long before her death, however, she has embodied the privation of fleshly life at the same time as its satisfactions. She "makes hungry / Where most she satisfies" (2.2.236–37): She is the generator of emptiness, endlessly converting fulfillment into need. Cleopatra's failed attempt at *agape,* trying to "quicken" the dying Antony with kissing (4.15.39) must inevitably remind us of Faustus wanting Helen to make him "immortal with a kiss" (*Dr. Faustus,* 5.1.99).[32] In the language of this play, Cleopatra is habitually associated with the Egyptian earth figured as an element both dead and alive, material but also generative. Even in Octavius's final speech, the earth "clips" the lovers as it entombs them. Spontaneous generation—the capacity of dead matter to produce life—is as central to the imagery of the text as spontaneous combustion is to *Bleak House.*

That death can perform "some loving act" (1.2.143–44) would have come as no surprise to Augustine. Cleopatra is the embodiment of the mind assimilated to what it loves, enslaved to *consuetudo,* but also of the mind that hungers for a reality beyond its objects. She figures that great Augustinian concept of the earthly self as both void and locus of desire. As her imagination sexualizes everything—turning ears into wombs and messages into sperm—it also vivifies everything. Antony *is,* in a sense, reborn from her kissing: recreated in dream and converted into a speech that is clearly shown to have further redemptive functions. It causes a grief that "smites" Dolabella's "very heart at root" (5.2.104–05) to release his (significantly sexualized) compassion. Both in absorbing Antony and in imposing her dream of him on Dolabella, Cleopatra breaks down separation. In the prison house of self she dreams her escapes. In the terms of Augustinian orthodoxy, *eros* and *agape* are at once opposed—love wrongly versus love rightly directed—and linked by degree. Both, of course, are expressions of incompleteness, responses to privation. The lesser still reflects the greater and, as we have seen in the ending of both the Wife of Bath's *Prologue* and *Tale,* aspires to become the greater. As Andrew Fichter observes, "Antony and Cleopatra . . . assert for themselves a love transcending death and a triumph emerging from defeat that we are meant to recognize [as] an impulse that is completed in Christian miracle."[33] We should not, however, historicize that in a way that, as in Fichter's reading, merely ironizes and discounts their experience. The soul's entombment in the flesh is not a process that ended with the Nativity.

Similarly, Rome is both the deceased Empire and the perennial institution—Augustine's earthly city and Bakhtin's official feast—against which flesh and spirit make common cause, essentially that of vital energy against dead form. Each seeks escape from and overthrow of a world governed by the private human will. Cleopatra's imagination, however much it officially values Roman hierarchy, order, and stability, characteristically reaches beyond them, as it tries to reach beyond self to some larger ground of vitality that is simultaneously God and the physical nature celebrated in carnival, spiritual love as sexual. Rome, literal and figurative, is the very embodiment of the dead forms of the material world and the habits of mind Augustine calls *consuetudo*. The play's Octavius is, of course, busily assembling the Empire whose fall would occasion *The City of God,* the great hidden text of *Antony and Cleopatra,* the one that defines the play's Rome and completes the historical process begun in the play's action. That double image—Rome's fall figured in the moment of its consolidation, material victory as spiritual defeat—is the essential, chiasmic pattern we have seen in both the medieval and Renaissance versions of the carnivalesque. The conjunction of the earthly city's completion and the birth that enables both its fulfillment and its end is the great, paradigmatic double *ludus* of Augustinian historiography.

The beginning of that end is, also of course, the Nativity, the appearance of another star in the east. The startling rhetorical figures that make Cleopatra a type of Christ, a pattern of the faithful, and an image of the Virgin triumphing over the serpent (and vice versa, of course), are neither accidental nor incidental. Israel, we might say, is in Egypt. "Blasphemy" mirrors piety (even if the mirror's image is reversed). *Antony and Cleopatra* is a demonstration of the need to integrate the two paradigms and to see how the politics of Augustinian theology and popular carnival reinforce as well as criticize one another. Historically, as we know, the Augustinian church authorized carnival and carnival took its forms—boy bishops, mock communions, feasts of the innocent, paschal laughter—from the church, because, I would argue, both operate to subvert the forms of the earthly city and the private self, the forms that carnivalesque literature embodies in Claudius, Bajazeth, and Octavius.

That subversion coexists with an acknowledgment of the inevitability of Octavian victories and the succession of Fortinbras and Callapine. *Antony and Cleopatra* enacts with particular clarity a distinction I have stressed throughout this book between carnival and the carnivalesque. Antony and Cleopatra's Egyptian carnival, considered as an extratextual phenomenon that is only recreated in the text, accomplished nothing except its own defeat. Octavius's Empire, unsubverted, swallows their story, indeed converts it by a familiar gastric process into the stuff of Cæsar's greatness. Carnival is conservative, as Marcus, Tennenhouse, Stallybrass and White, have argued: It is incorporated into and reinforces the official order.[34] In the carnivalesque, however, in the textual struggle for control and definition of terms, Egypt is victorious and Rome subverted. So, for that matter, is Plutarch because Shakespeare has shown us the public relations process by which Roman "destiny" is and was constructed. Rome's measure is taken by both Augustinian and carnivalesque standards. Roman order is revealed as a fiction of, let us say, very qualified necessity. The Empire's historical epic is bracketed between this play and the Gospels at its beginning and *The City of God* at its ending. It is not Antony and Cleopatra who are maginalized, ironized, demythologized, so much as Cæsar. Cleopatra's trick with the treasure depends, remember, on Cæsar confusing desire for wealth with desire for life. Egypt's ontology—like Carnival's and Christianity's—is more complex than that. It asserts that there is or might be a life elsewhere. Thus, carnivalesque *is* subversive. "This wild disguise" *does* "antic us," in text if not in fact, unpolicying the ass Cæsar while leaving him Emperor. We need, of course, to remember that textual and empirical history are not (exactly) the same: what is subverted in one survives in the other. This text enacts simultaneously the defeat of carnival and the victory of the carnivalesque. Whose glory, as Octavius's grammar asks, is to be pitied?

NOTES

PREFACE: "BARNSLEY MAIN SEAM"

1. Geoffrey Chaucer, *General Prologue* to *The Canterbury Tales,* in *The Works of Geoffrey Chaucer,* general ed. Larry D. Benson (New York: Houghton-Mifflin, 1987), lin. 1.746, p. 35.

CHAPTER 1. THE VARIETIES OF *LUDUS*

1. Mikhail Bakhtin, *Rabelais and His World,* translated from the Russian by Helene Iswolsky (Cambridge: MIT Press, 1968; reprint, Bloomington: Indiana University Press, 1984). The work was completed in 1940, but not published in the Soviet Union until 1965.

2. On Bakhtin's *Rabelais and His World* as a response to Stalinism, see Terry Eagleton, *Walter Benjamin or Towards a Revolutionary Criticism* (London: Verso, 1981), 144–46; and particularly Katerina Clark and Michael Holquist, *Mikhail Bakhtin* (Cambridge: Harvard University Press, 1984), 305–20, for whom *Rabelais* "represents Bakhtin's most comprehensive critique to date of Stalinist culture" (305).

3. See Aron Gurevich, *Medieval Popular Culture: Problems of Belief and Perception,* trans. Janos M. Bak and Paul A. Hillingsworth (Cambridge: Cambridge University Press, 1988), especially chapter 6, 176–210, where this critique is developed.

4. *Rabelais,* 10. Further references appear within parentheses in the text.

5. Terry Castle, "The Carnivalization of Eighteenth-Century English Narrative," *PMLA* 99 (1984): 912. Somewhat less enthusiastically, Michael Gardiner, in *The Dialogics of Critique: M. M. Bakhtin and the Theory of Ideology* (London: Routledge, 1992), describes Bakhtin's praise of carnival humor as "at times . . . embarrassingly fulsome and naive" (180).

6. Ken Hirschkop, "Introduction," in *Bakhtin and Cultural Theory,* ed. Hirschkop and David Shepherd (Manchester: Manchester University Press, 1989), 35; cf. Bakhtin's comment that the "very brevity of [carnival] freedom increased its fantastic nature and utopian radicalism" (*Rabelais,* 89).

7. Caryl Emerson, "The Tolstoy Connection in Bakhtin," in *Rethinking Bakhtin: Extensions and Challenges,* ed. Gary Saul Morson and Caryl Emerson (Evanston, Ill.: Northwestern University Press, 1989), 154. In English-language criticism at least, the view of Bakhtin as a fundamentally religious thinker (and of *Rabelais* as an allegorical attack on Stalinism) is primarily associated with Clark and Holquist, *Mikhail Bakhtin,* especially chapter 5, "Religious Activities and the Arrest." They describe Bakhtin as "a religious intellectual from the Orthodox tradition" in spite of the "palpable anticlericalism of his Rabelais book" (120), which they take to be both populist and covertly anti-Stalinist. In "The Politics of Representation," *Allegory and Representation: Selected Papers from the English Institute, 1979–80,* ed. Stephen Greenblatt

(Baltimore: Johns Hopkins University Press, 1981), 162–83, Holquist develops the idea that Bakhtin habitually expressed Christian views in Marxist language. Holquist's and Clark's views, which entail an elaborate debate about what Bakhtin wrote and what he intended when he did so, are disputed by Morson and Emerson, *Rethinking Bakhtin*, 31–49. Ann Shukman discusses Bakhtin's interest in the "human need for God" (143) in "Bakhtin's Tolstoy Prefaces," in Morson and Emerson, 137–48. My own view, it will be clear, is based less on assertions of specific influence or of covert Christian allegory than on my general sense that Bakhtin habitually attributes transcendental and restorative qualities to carnival. I am not arguing that Augustinian theology influenced Bakhtin theory causally, but that the two modes of thought converge.

8. Emerson, "Tolstoy," 157.

9. For a more conventionally Christian account of the customary medieval distinctions between holy fooling and satanic mimicry and subversion, see Rachel Billington, *A Social History of the Fool* (Brighton, UK: Harvester, 1984), especially chapter 2, "Theological and Philosophical Attitudes to the Fool," 16–31.

10. Thus Terry Eagleton remarks that "Bakhtinian carnival . . . at once cavalierly suppresses hierarchies and distinctions, recalling us to a common creatureliness . . . and at the same time does so as part of a politically specific, sharply differentiated, combatively one-sided practice—that of the lower classes." See "Bakhtin, Schopenhauer, Kundera," in Hirschkop and Shepherd, 188.

11. Gurevich, *Medieval Popular Culture*, 179.

12. On this pattern of containment see Anthony Gash, "Carnival against Lent: The Ambivalence of Medieval Drama," in *Medieval Literature: Criticism, Ideology and History*, ed. David Aers (Brighton: Harvester, 1986), 74–98. Concerning the institution of carnival in Elizabethan England, Howard Felperin, *The Uses of the Canon: Elizabethan Literature and Contemporary Theory* (Oxford: Oxford University Press, 1990), 117, concludes that "Bakhtinian 'carnival' occupies a position more dialogic than revolutionary in relation to the conservative authority of church and state that permits it." Michael Gardiner, *Dialogics of Critique*, 187, remarks that Bakhtin "generally fails to see the degree to which popular culture is permeated or at least circumscribed by elements of the dominant culture and ideology."

13. Paul Strohm, *Hochon's Arrow: The Social Imagination of Fourteenth-Century Texts* (Princeton: Princeton University Press, 1992), 45. Strohm's chapter 2, "'A Revelle': Chronicle Evidence and the Rebel Voice," 33–56, demonstrates how the terminology of carnival was used by the chroniclers to "discredit the social standing, judgement, and objectives" (34) of the participants in the so-called Peasants' Revolt of 1381. At the same time, Strohm argues, the carnival "schemes wielded by the chroniclers to stigmatize rebel actions were elements of 'mutual knowledge,' available to—and in fact employed by—the rebels for the production of oppositional acts" (52).

14. Leah Marcus, *The Politics of Mirth: Jonson, Herrick, Milton, Marvell and the Defense of Old Holiday Pastimes* (Chicago: University of Chicago Press, 1986), 8.

15. Leonard Tennenhouse, *Power on Display: The Politics of Shakespeare's Genres* (New York: Methuen, 1986), 79. This safety-valve theory of carnival is summed up with typical pungency by Terry Eagleton: "Carnival, after all, is a *licensed* affair in every sense, a permissible rupture of hegemony, a contained popular blow-off as disturbing and relatively ineffectual as a revolutionary work of art. As Shakespeare's Olivia remarks, there is no slander in an allowed fool" (*Walter Benjamin*, 148).

16. Peter Stallybrass and Allon White, *The Politics and Poetics of Transgression* (London: Methuen, 1986), 18, 14. The italics are theirs.

17. Emmanuel LeRoy Ladurie, *Carnival in Romans* (New York: George Braziller, 1979), 229.

18. I allude, of course, to the title of Dover Wilson's famous book (Cambridge: Cambridge University Press, 1935), though my account of "what happens" (see my chapter 4) differs from his.

19. Mikhail Bakhtin, *The Problems of Dostoevsky's Poetics,* trans. by Caryl Emerson (Minneapolis: University of Minnesota Press, 1984); see especially chapter 4, "Characteristics of Genre and Plot Composition in Dostoevsky's Works," 101–80, which places Dostoevsky in relation to menippean satire and "carnivalesque folklore" (107).

20. 3.2.135 in *The Riverside Shakespeare,* ed. G. Blakemore Evans and others (Boston: Houghton-Mifflin, 1974). Further references, in parentheses, are to this text.

21. For a brilliant analysis of the myth of change from a heroic past to a complex and ironic present in Shakespeare's tragedies, see Northrop Frye, *Fools of Time: Studies in Shakespearean Tragedy* (Toronto: University of Toronto Press, 1967). For my version of the relevance of that myth to the carnivalesque in *Antony and Cleopatra,* see chapter 6 below.

22. Terry Castle, *Masquerade and Civilization: The Carnivalesque in Eighteenth-Century English Culture and Fiction* (London: Methuen, 1986), 102. Bakhtin, with less jargon than Castle, asserts that carnival participants become part of "the oneness of the grotesque world" (*Rabelais,* 33).

23. Thus Eagleton, "Bakhtin, Schopenhauer, Kundera," 184, describes the carnivalesque as "that aggressive onslaught on the fetishism of difference that ruthlessly, liberatingly reduces back all such metaphysical singularities to the solidarity of the flesh."

24. The best-known version of this reading is William Beatty Warner, *Reading "Clarissa": The Struggles of Interpretation* (New Haven, Yale University Press, 1979); see especially chapters 1 to 4, 3–120.

25. The echo of "vulgar Marxism" in the phrase "vulgar Augustinianism" is intended and relevant. In the period on which I will be focusing—roughly 1350–1650—one did not so much learn Augustine as inherit him or, more accurately perhaps, inhale him. We do not have to have read Marx to refer to the proletariat or know the term commodity fetishism to take it as a fact of life. The same is or was true of Augustinian theology. It is probably significant that only the latest writer I discuss, Milton, knows Augustine with a scholar's thoroughness (and a rival genius's penetration). For the rest, with the partial exception of Marlowe, I neither assert nor deny any detailed knowledge of the *opera.* It would not be necessary. Even in the case of Marlowe, I would not guarantee more than a brilliant, if understandably preoccupied, undergraduate's knowledge of the most famous passages of *Confessions* and a clear-headed sense of the Manichean and Pelagian alternatives to Augustinianism. I am interested, in other words, in Augustine as part—not the whole—of the inherited framework of a culture. For that reason, I do not try to trace in detail the evolution of Augustine's thought or the variations between, say, an early text like *De libero arbitrio* and a late one like the *Enchiridion,* though, as most Augustinian scholars do, I distinguish sharply between the early Augustine and the more authoritarian and pessimistic later one. I have also decided, with the appropriate apologies to genuine theologians and Latinists, to cite Augustine in the most readily available English translations.

26. St. Thomas Aquinas, *Summa Theologiæ: A Concise Translation,* ed. and trans. by Timothy McDermott (London: Methuen, 1989), 8.48.1: "Badness . . . cannot be a particular sort of existence or form or nature; it cannot be anything but the absence

of good" (91). See also Charles Journet, *The Meaning of Evil,* translated from the French by Michael Berry (London: Geoffrey Chapman, 1963).

27. All references to *City of God* are to John O'Meara's edition of Henry Bettenson's translation (Harmondsworth: Penguin, 1984), using their sectioning and the abbreviation *CG.*

28. See the useful summary in Etienne Gilson, *The Christian Philosophy of St. Augustine,* trans. L. E. M. Lynch (London: Gollancz, 1961), 144–45. "Evil," he concludes, "is the privation of a good which the subject should possess, a failure to be what it should be and hence, a pure nothingness" (144). See also Henry Chadwick, *Augustine* (Oxford: Oxford University Press, 1986), 19–20.

29. Gillian Evans, *Augustine on Evil* (Cambridge: Cambridge University Press, 1982), 75.

30. References to *Paradise Lost* are to the edition of Alistair Fowler (London: Longmans, 1968).

31. On *Paradise Lost*'s enactment and criticism of the Augustinian definition of desire as a response to the sense of lack or impairment, see Bruce Thomas Boehrer, "*Paradise Lost* and the General Epistle of James: Milton, Augustine, Lacan," *Exemplaria* 4:2 (fall 1992): 295–316. Milton's debt to Augustine has long been recognized. See, for example, Peter Fiore, *Milton and Augustine: Patterns of Augustinian Thought in "Paradise Lost"* (University Park: Pennsylvania State University Press, 1981).

32. For *aversio,* see Evans, 116.

33. The same lesson is taught to Peer in *Peer Gynt:* The serpent tells Eve roughly what the Old Man of the Mountains tells Peer: "*Trol, vaer dig selv—nok*" ["Troll, be thyself, only"] (Oslo: Gyldendal Norsk Forlag, 1991), 45. I cite the parallel as a sign of the continuity, in this case via Lutheran Protestantism, of the doctrine of privative evil and its associated assumptions. The larger pattern of the play—the pursuit of Peer's phantasmal earthly self at the expense of his soul—is, of course, an eminently Augustinian one; it is the pattern, in fact, of the pre-conversion half of *Confessions.*

34. Gilson, *The Christian Philosophy of St. Augustine,* 145.

35. St. Augustine, *Confessions,* trans. by Henry Chadwick (Oxford: University Press, 1992), 29. All further references are to this edition (abbreviated *Conf.*), and use its sectioning. The first number represents book the second represents the chapter, and the third represents the variant sectioning.

36. Henrik Ibsen, *Rosmersholm,* trans. by James McFarlane (Oxford: Oxford University Press, 1969), 304; cf., Augustine on the tendency of beings created out of nothing to return to nothing: *CG,* 14.13.

37. "God is the author of natures, though he is not responsible for their defects" (*CG,* 13.15).

38. Donald Cress, "Augustine's Privation Account of Evil: A Defense," *Augustinian Studies* 20, no. 1 (1989): 109.

39. Gerard O'Daley, *Augustine's Philosophy of Mind* (Berkeley and Los Angeles: University of California Press, 1987), 150, claims that "we almost tangibly sense the absence of . . . the recognition of the unconscious" in Augustine.

40. Thus Emilie Zum Brunn, *St. Augustine: Being and Nothingness* (New York: Paragon, 1988), 51, writes that for Augustine "the soul can only turn toward 'nonbeing' by means of a mistake, thinking it will find there substantial nourishment."

41. Robert Meagher, *An Introduction to St. Augustine* (New York: New York University Press, 1978), 105 [his emphasis].

42. Kenneth Surin, *Theology and the Problem of Evil* (Oxford: Blackwell, 1986), 10.

43. On the role of "perversity" in Augustine's concept of sin, see Jonathan Dolli-

more, *Sexual Dissidence: Augustine to Wilde, Freud to Foucault* (Oxford: Clarendon, 1991), 128–47.

44. In *Augustine: Later Works,* trans. John Burnaby, The Library of Christian Classics, vol. 8 (London: S. C. M. Press, 1955), 81.

45. In *Christopher Marlowe: Complete Plays,* ed. J. B. Steane (Harmondsworth: Penguin, 1969), 330–31. Further references to Marlowe are to this edition.

46. St. Augustine, *On Christian Doctrine,* trans. D. W. Robertson (New York: Bobbs-Merrill, 1958), 88. All further references are to this edition.

47. Stanley R. Hopper, "The Anti-Manichean Writings," in *A Companion to the Study of St. Augustine,* ed. Roy Battenhouse (New York: Oxford University Press, 1955), 168.

48. See, for example, Wallace Matson's dismissal of privative evil as "a play on words, an unfunny joke," in *The Existence of God* (Ithaca: Cornell University Press, 1965), 143. For a more serious consideration of the charge that Augustine's account of evil is simply "insufficient" to events like the Holocaust, see John Hick, *Evil and the God of Love* (London: Macmillan, 1966; reprint. 1977), 53–58. An Augustinian might, of course, ask what account of evil *is* "sufficient" to the Holocaust.

49. Evans, *Augustine on Evil,* xi.

50. Christopher Kirwan, *Augustine* (London & New York: Routledge, 1989), 71, 70.

51. Leo C. Ferrari, *The Conversions of St. Augustine* (Philadelphia: Villanova University Press, 1984), 75.

52. Gilson, *The Christian Philosophy of St. Augustine,* 152.

53. John D. Cox, *Shakespeare and the Dramaturgy of Power* (Princeton: Princeton University Press, 1989), 13, cites Stephen Greenblatt's use of the ruin image in *Renaissance Self-Fashioning* (Chicago: University of Chicago Press, 1980), 2, to dismiss the idea that Augustine (or the Augustinian tradition) was interested in the "fashioning" of identity. Cox rightly objects that "Augustine's sense of self is extraordinarily complex and subtle." That is largely because, however, the construction of self out of carnal desire and habituation (*consuetudo*) is the chief activity of the fallen state. Augustine's concern with the self—what is constructed and explored for much of the first half of *Confessions*—is a function of the threat that self, the dead shell of existence, poses to the soul trapped within it. The self (Augustine the rhetorician) constructed in the early books is what is exploded by Augustine's conversion. Thus, while Cox is right to stress the continuity of interest in "self-fashioning" through the Augustinian tradition, Greenblatt is also correct in asserting Augustine's skepticism about the utility of the exercise. Cox's book, which is primarily concerned with the *Henriad* and the problem comedies, remains, however, one of the few to give serious attention to the Augustinian influence on Elizabethan drama. Where he is concerned to establish the continuity of an Augustinian tradition of social criticism, I am interested in relating that tradition to the carnivalesque.

54. Charles Taylor, *Sources of the Self: The Making of the Modern Identity* (Cambridge: Cambridge University Press, 1989), 136.

55. Robert McMahon, *Augustine's Prayerful Ascent: An Essay on the Literary Form of the "Confessions"* (Athens: University of Georgia Press, 1989), 144. The reference to chiasmic structure of *Confessions* is on the same page.

56. Kenneth Burke, *The Rhetoric of Religion: Studies in Logology* (Berkeley and Los Angeles: University of California Press, 1970), 94.

57. To the best of my knowledge, for example, it has not been noted that Dr. Faustus's renunciation scene (act I, scene 1) parodies Augustine's account of his conversion in the garden in Milan. Both scenes enact the injunction *tolle, lege,* "pick up and read" (*Conf.,* 8, 12, 29). Faustus, however, picks up Jerome's bible only to put it down. He

reads—two isolated passages, as Augustine does—not to meditate on them, but to forget them in fantasy. In book 8 of the *Confessions* Augustine is delivered from concupiscence, the "old loves" symbolized by the fig tree under which the conversion takes place. The upshot of that conversion is the realization that he "did not now seek a wife" (12, 30). Faustus, of course, renounces religion for concupiscence. The first use he will try to make of magic is to ask for a wife, "for I am wanton and lascivious" (I.5.145), the last use will be Helen. Evil, as Augustine insists it always does, acts as a grotesque inversion of good. The parallel identifies Dr. Faustus not only with his Manichean namesake [as Philip Brockbank notes, *Marlowe: Dr. Faustus* (London: Edward Arnold, 1962), 15]; it also makes him a preterite version of the preconversion Augustine. Marlowe's Faustus is, of course, pre-eminently a rhetorician, who has made the "schools ring with *sic probo*" (I.2.2) and who prides himself, as the young Augustine did, on conquering Christians in debate, "gavell[ing] the pastors of the German Church" (I.1.112). The parallel, of course, implicitly questions the justice that bestows grace on one doctor and not the other.

58. Peter Brown, *Augustine of Hippo: A Biography* (London: Faber, 1967), 240; the description is echoed by R. A. Markus, *Sæculum: History and Society in the Theology of St. Augustine* (Cambridge: Cambridge University Press, 1970), 134. Markus's chapter 6, 133–53, gives a thorough doctrinal account the later Augustine's acceptance of coercion.

59. Cox, *Dramaturgy of Power*, 13.

60. Brown, *Augustine of Hippo*, 383–84.

61. See Elaine Pagels' summary judgment in *Adam, Eve, and the Serpent* (New York: Random House, 1988): "Augustine's dark vision of a human nature ravaged by original sin and overrun by lust for power rules out uncritical adulation and qualifies his endorsement of imperial rule" (118).

62. See *CG*, 19.1.

63. Herbert A. Deane, *The Political Ideas of St. Augustine* (New York: Columbia University Press, 1963), 134. Deane's view of Augustine's theory of the state is contained in chapter 4, 116–53.

64. See Harold Baynes, *The Political Ideas of St. Augustine's "De Civitate Dei"* (London: G. Bell & Sons, 1936), 5–6.

65. Martin Luther, *De Servo Arbitrio* (WA 782–783), in *Luther and Erasmus,* trans. and ed. E. Gordon Rupp and Philip S. Watson, Library of Christian Classics, vol. 17 (London: S.C.M. Press, 1969), 327.

66. Alasdair MacIntyre, *Three Rival Versions of Moral Enquiry* (London: Duckworth, 1990), 89; for Abelard, see 89–91.

67. Romand Coles, *Self/Power/Other: Political Theory and Dialogical Ethics* (Ithaca: Cornell University Press, 1992), 51–52.

68. John Calvin, *Institutes of the Christian Religion,* ed. John T. McNeill and trans. Ford Lewis Battles, 2 vols., Library of Christian Classics, vols. 20, 21 (London: S.C.M. Press, 1960), 2:1519. The classic study of the simultaneously authoritarian and revolutionary impact of Calvin is Michael Walzer, *The Revolution of the Saints: A Study in the Origins of Radical Politics* (Cambridge: Harvard University Press, 1965). See also Roland Mushat Frye, *The Renaissance "Hamlet": Issues and Responses in 1600* (Princeton: Princeton University Press, 1984), 61–70, for a concise summary of Calvinist doctrine on resistance to tyranny.

69. D. W. Robertson, *A Preface to Chaucer* (Princeton: Princeton University Press, 1962), viii. For an extreme example of what sort of criticism this legislative approach produces, see "A Medievalist Looks at Hamlet," in *Essays in Medieval Culture* (Princeton: Princeton University Press, 1980), 312–31.

70. Brown, *Augustine,* 270, paraphrasing *De Baptismo,* 2.4.

71. See C. L. Barber, *Shakespeare's Festive Comedy: A Study of Dramatic Form and Its Relation to Social Custom* (Princeton; Princeton University Press, 1959; reprint. Cleveland: World, 1968); see especially 6–10.

72. A small but significant indicator of the debt I refer to is the fact that the references to Augustine in the index to McNeill and Battles's edition of the *Institutes* take up fourteen columns.

73. Lee Patterson, *Chaucer and the Subject of History* (London: Routledge, 1991), especially the introduction, 3–46; David Aers, "Medievalists and Deconstruction: An Exemplum," in *From Medieval to Medievalism,* ed. John Simons (Basingstoke: Macmillan, 1992), 24–40; see especially his comments on the "traditions of negative theology" (35) Chaucer inherited from Augustine.

74. The evidence of the skimmington and the charivari suggest, once again, that Bakhtin is significantly wrong about the historical practice of carnival, if not about the literary carnivalesque. The charivari was, of course, a form of sexual policing, more often meant to punish than to liberate feminine self-assertion. In addition to Stallybrass and White, *Transgression,* see Natalie Zemon Davis, *Society and Culture in Early Modern France* (Stanford: Stanford University Press, 1965; reprint. Cambridge: Polity Press, 1987), especially chapter 5, 'Woman on Top," 124–51; and Michael Bristol, "Charivari and the Comedy of Abjection in *Othello,*" *Renaissance Drama* 21 (1990): 3–22.

75. Compare John Ganim's comment in *Chaucerian Theatricality* (Princeton: Princeton University Press, 1990), 53, that "the Wife seeks constantly (though not always consciously) to accomplish the reversal of the carnival world," especially in transposing bodies and their authority with books and theirs.

CHAPTER 2: "VANYSSHED WAS THIS DAUNCE, HE NYSTE WHERE": ALISOUN'S ABSENCE IN THE *WIFE OF BATH'S PROLOGUE AND TALE*

1. See Carl Lindahl, *Earnest Games: Folkloric Patterns in the "Canterbury Tales"* (Bloomington: Indiana University Press, 1987), especially part 1, 19–70, "The Shape of Play and Society." For a reading of the *Tales* as a subversive text, opposing to a hierarchic society "a set of values based upon an individual and collective freedom of speech," see Jon Cook, "Carnival and *The Canterbury Tales:* 'Only Equals May Laugh' (Herzen)," in *Medieval Literature: Criticism, Ideology, and History,* ed. David Aers (Brighton: Harvester, 1986), 169–91.

2. Line references are to *The Riverside Chaucer,* general ed. Larry Benson (Oxford: Oxford University Press, 1987). I have also consulted the notes in *The Works of Geoffrey Chaucer,* ed. F. N. Robinson (Cambridge, Mass.: Riverside, 1957).

3. C. David Benson, *Chaucer's Drama of Style: Poetic Variety and Contrast in the "Canterbury Tales"* (Chapel Hill: University of North Carolina Press, 1986). My disagreements with Benson are outlined in my review of the book in *AUMLA* 73 (1990): 235–40.

4. A particularly ambitious attempt to do justice to the complexities of subjection in the *Canterbury Tales* is Lee Patterson, *Chaucer and the Subject of History* (London: Routledge, 1991).

5. Robertson's famous discussion of the Wife as heretical "exegete" and figure of carnality is in the his *Preface to Chaucer,* 317–31. Burlin's section on Alisoun

is in *Chaucerian Fiction* (Princeton: Princeton University Press, 1977), 217–27. The description of her as "battered" is on 218. Kenneth Oberembt's sympathetic reading of Alisoun is in "Chaucer's Anti-Misogynist Wife of Bath," *Chaucer Review* 10, no. 4 (1976): 287–302. Delany's chapter, "Strategies of Silence in the Wife of Bath's Recital," in *Medieval Literary Politics: Shapes of Ideology* (Manchester: Manchester University Press, 1990),112–29, concludes with the insistence that the *raptus* of Cecily Chaumpaigne should be understood as literal rape (128–29). Louise Fradenburg, "The Wife of Bath's Passing Fancy," *Studies in the Age of Chaucer* 8 (1986): 31–58, discusses the Wife as "an image of the absent, the regressive, the heart's desire" (32) with primary reference to Lacan's "God and the *Jouissance* of the Woman" in *Feminine Sexuality: Jacques Lacan and the Ecole Freudienne,* ed. Juliet Mitchell and Jacqueline Rose (New York and London: Norton, 1982). Walter Long, "The Wife of Bath as Moral Revolutionary," *Chaucer Review* 20, no. 4 (1986): 273–84, compares the Wife's objections to labeling of women with Mill (278–79) and quotes Mill on "the 'sultan-like . . . sense of superiority' men have traditionally felt over women" (280). Barrie Ruth Strauss, "The Subversive Discourse of the Wife of Bath: Phallocentric Discourse and the Imprisonment of Criticism," *ELH* 55, no. 3 (fall 1988): 527–54, draws heavily on Irigaray's *This Sex Which Is Not One* and on Julia Kristeva. See Strauss, 551, n. 11.

6. John Alford, "The Wife of Bath versus the Clerk of Oxford: What Their Rivalry Means," *Chaucer Review* 21, no. 2 (1986): 110 (my emphasis).

7. Marjorie Malvern "'Who Peynted the Leon, Tel Me Who?': Rhetorical and Didactic Roles Played by an Aesopic Fable in the *Wife of Bath's Prologue,*" *Studies in Philology* 80, no. 3 (summer 1983): 238–52; Bernard Huppe, *A Reading of the "Canterbury Tales"* (Albany: State University of New York Press, 1964),107–35.

8. Mary Carruthers, "The Wife of Bath and the Painting of Lions," *PMLA* 94, no. 2 (March 1979): 209–22; Dorothy Colmer, "Character and Class in the *Wife of Bath's Tale,*" *JEGP* 72 (1973): 329–39; David Aers, *Chaucer, Langland and the Creative Imagination* (London: Routledge and Kegan Paul, 1980), 83–89, 146–52.

9. Peggy Knapp, "Alisoun Weaves a Text," *Philological Quarterly* 65:3 (Summer 1986): 387–401; reprinted as "Alisoun Looms" in Knapp's *Chaucer and the Social Contest* (London: Routledge, 1990), 114–28; Delany, *Medieval Literary Politics.*

10. Robertson, *A Preface to Chaucer,* 330.

11. As Hope Phyllis Weissman says, "with a characteristically late medieval richness of determination, Chaucer summons the materials of both experience and authority to supply the concrete details of the portrait": "Antifeminism and Chaucer's Characterization of Women," *Geoffrey Chaucer: A Collection of Original Articles,* ed. George Economou (New York: McGraw-Hill, 1975), 105.

12. Lee Patterson, "'For the Wyves Love of Bath': Feminine Rhetoric and Poetic Resolution in the *Roman de la Rose* and the *Canterbury Tales,*" *Speculum* 58, no. 3 (July 1983): 656–95; Knapp, "Alisoun Weaves a Text"; and Strauss, "Subversive Discourse.

13. Beryl Rowland, "On the Timely Death of the Wife of Bath's Fourth Husband," *Archiv* 209 (1972–73): 273–82; D. J. Wurtele, "Chaucer's Wife of Bath and the Problem of the Fifth Husband," *Chaucer Review* 23, no. 2 (1988): 117–28. On the marital customs of the landholders, see Carruthers, "The Painting of Lions."

14. Susan Crane, "Alison's Incapacity and Poetic Instability in the Wife of Bath's Tale," *PMLA* 102, no. 1 (January 1987): 26.

15. H. Marshall Leicester, "Of a Fire in the Dark: Public and Private Feminism in the *Wife of Bath's Tale*," *Women's Studies* 11 (1984): 157–78. The quotation is from 175.

16. Hereafter, line references to the Wife's text refer to Ellesmere Fragment 3. Other references are by fragment and line number. On Midas and the barber, see Patterson 1983, 657.

17. Carolyn Dinshaw, "Eunuch Hermeneutics," *ELH* 55, no. 1 (Spring 1988): 27–52; quotation is p. 27. Dinshaw elaborates her version of the Wife as text in *Chaucer's Sexual Poetics* (Madison: University of Wisconsin Press, 1989), 113–31.

18. Crane, "Alison's Incapacity," 20.

19. Jill Mann, *Chaucer and Medieval Estates Satire* (Cambridge: Cambridge University Press, 1973).

20. P. M. Kean, *Chaucer and the Making of English Poetry* (London: Routledge and Kegan Paul, 1972), 217–18 [Pardoner], 267–75 [Wife].

21. Burlin, *Chaucerian Fiction*, 226.

22. Susan Schibanoff, "The New Reader and Female Textuality in Two Early Commentaries on Chaucer," *Studies in the Age of Chaucer* 10 (1988): 71–108, extends this body of observation by considering Chaucer as the possible originator of the glosses on the *Wife of Bath's Prologue and Tale* in the Ellesmere manuscript and Alisoun herself as a figure for the new, private reader. Delany discusses the problem of trying to construct the Wife as a "resisting reader" of clerical antifeminism (*Medieval Literary Politics*, 112–29).

23. Patterson, "For the Wyves Love of Bath," 687.

24. Thomas Hahn, "Teaching the Resistant Woman: The Wife of Bath and the Academy," *Exemplaria* 4, no. 2 (fall 1992), 433. Hahn's essay, which appeared shortly after my article in *ELH*, proposes a version of the Wife, as a "discursive site" (434) representing Woman as the resistant other who energizes masculine discourse while being excluded from it, which is closely complementary to mine. The orientation of his argument is toward Irigaray, however, rather than toward Bakhtin or Augustine.

25. Peggy Knapp, "Alisoun and the Reappropriation of Tradition," *Chaucer Review* 24, no. 1 (1989): 45–52.

26. The major sources mentioned here (Jerome *Adversus Jovinianum*, Walter Map, the relevant passages of the *Roman de la Rose*, Gower's "Tale of Florent," "The Marriage of Sir Gawaine," "The Weddynge of Sir Gawain and Dame Ragnell") are given in *Sources and Analogues of Chaucer's "Canterbury Tales"*, ed. W. F. Bryan and Germaine Dempster (Chicago: University of Chicago Press, 1941). The section concerning the *Wife of Bath's Prologue and Tale*, 207–68, is edited by B. J. Whiting.

27. Robinson, 697–704. The notes to this text in the *Riverside Chaucer*, 864–74, record much the same body of information. Schibanoff's discussion of the glosses in the Egerton and Ellesmere MSS. indicates that Chaucer's earliest editors recognized that the *Prologue* and *Tale* are a tissue of intertextual references ("The New Reader and Female Textuality," see especially 71–92).

28. The argument for Matheolus as the source of the passages usually ascribed to Deschamps is made by Zacharias P. Thundy, "Matheolus, Chaucer, and the Wife of Bath," in *Chaucerian Problems and Perspectives: Essays Presented to Paul E. Beichner*, ed. Edward Vasta and Zacharias Thundy (Notre Dame: University of Notre Dame Press, 1979), 24–58.

29. Jill Mann, *Geoffrey Chaucer* (Hemel Hempstead: Harvester, 1991), 51–54. The quotation is 51.

30. Abelard's account of the *dissuasio* is reprinted by Robert P. Miller, *Chaucer: Sources and Backgrounds* (New York: Oxford, 1977), 447–51. The covering section, "The Antifeminist Tradition" (397–473) includes Heloise's primary source, Jerome *Adversus Jovinianum,* and the relevant passage from the *Roman.*

31. Chaucer's only other female source, Marie de France, whose fable of the lion is referred to at 3.692, is not, in the original, concerned with women or marriage.

32. Knapp, "Reapportionment" [see note 25], 45–52 *passim.*

33. See the Riverside edition's note on this line, p. 870.

34. In the case of this text at least, I disagree strongly with Elaine Tuttle Hansen's assertion that "the Chaucerian poet . . . finally invokes the myth of female difference, through his representation of women and Woman" ("Fearing for Chaucer's Good Name," *Exemplaria* 2, no. 1 [1990]: 33; an extended version appears as chapter 2 of *Chaucer and the Fictions of Gender* [Berkeley: University of California Press, 1992], 26–57). The Wife, as (mis)interpreter of her own text, mystifies the difference. The text minimizes practical differences, even while insisting on the ultimate unknowability of female experience to a male author. You can, of course, insist, as Hansen does, that this is a case of Chaucer suppressing "the very real threats to the male poet" (33) posed by a recognition of his similiarities to women. Here, however, it is more obviously a case of the author revealing and the character concealing.

35. Alisoun's substitution of her commodified body for her self is noted by Strauss, 535–36, and by Aers, *Chaucer, Langland,* 149–50. I would add that commerce, including sexual commerce, is a carnival activity, a point I take up at greater length in chapter 6.

36. See Wurtele, "The Problem of the Fifth Husband," *passim.*

37. Oberembt, "Chaucer's Anti-Misogynist Wife of Bath," 295.

38. I think Dinshaw confuses the issue when she argues that "the appropriative nature of glossing has a particularly masculine valence." As Dinshaw concedes in the next paragraph, the Wife is "a glossator herself" (*Chaucer's Sexual Poetics,* 123). Appropriation, whether of Alisoun by Jankyn or of the knight by the hag, is what Alisoun's text is all about.

39. Jankyn's name ("Johnny") is the diminuitive of John, as in "Sir John", the cant name for a priest, applied to both the Monk (7.1929) and the Nun's Priest (7.2810) by Harry. See the Riverside gloss on "John," 1319. Alisoun refers to Jankyn's reading from the book of wicked wives as "prech[yng]" (3.641).

40. I have borrowed the description of Alisoun as a frustrated code user from Philip West, "The Perils of Pauline Theology: The Wife of Bath's Prologue and Tale," *Essays in Arts and Sciences* 8 (1979): 8.

41. Britton J. Harwood notices a somewhat simpler version of this pattern: "having been dishonored, the maiden becomes a hag. When honor is vested in her once more, she becomes a maiden again," in "The Wife of Bath and the Dream of Innocence," *Modern Language Quarterly* 33, no. 3 (September 1972), 272.

42. See, for example, Delany, *Medieval Literary Politics,* 125: "It is what logicians term a non-question, a pseudo-problem."

43. See Crane, "Alison's Incapacity," 23; also Robert Kaske, "Chaucer's Marriage Group," in *Chaucer the Love Poet,* ed. Jerome Mitchell and William Provost (Athens: University of Georgia Press, 1973), 52.

44. The most famous explication of the contradiction between the hag's answer

and her later behavior is by Charles A. Owen, "The Crucial Passages in Five of the *Canterbury Tales:* A Study in Irony and Symbol," in *Chaucer: Modern Essays in Criticism,* ed. Edward Wagenknecht (Oxford: Galaxy, 1959), 259–64.

45. Robert Sturgis, "The *Canterbury Tales'* Women Narrators: Three Traditions of Female Authority," *Modern Language Studies* 13, no. 2 (spring 1983): 41–51, thinks benignly that Alisoun draws other women into "an ever-expanding community of women bound by female solidarity against male domination" (45). There are, however, no women present who could be drawn into an alliance of wives. In that sense, Alisoun addresses a phantom audience. Their function, like that of Jankyn's authorities, is to allow the speaker to declare herself a majority. Given the make-up of the pilgrim audience, exclusion is surely more the point than inclusion. Alisoun's claims of universality are a projection of solipsistic isolation: the mirror-image of "clerkes . . . in hire oratories."

46. Crane, "Alison's Incapacity," 23; cf., Peggy Knapp, *Chaucer and the Social Contest,* 127: "embedded deep in this story is the untraditional idea that men must learn from women."

47. In Marlowe, *The Complete Plays,* ed. Steane, 354.

48. For Satan's declaration of himself as "self-begot, self-raised," see *Paradise Lost,* ed. Fowler, 5.860

49. The hag's transformation reflects a remarkable mixing of the codes of romance and carnivalesque. She is returned to the lower bodily level: from talking, reasoning hag to silent, sexually desirable young woman; at the same time, however, she passes from grotesque to romantic object.

50. Barrie Strauss, "Subversive Discourse" (545–47), discusses the hag's transformation as a "complex doubling of [the knight's] desire" (545); he does not see her reality, "he sees his desire" (546).

51. Warren Ginsburg, "The Lineaments of Desire: Wish-Fulfillment in Chaucer's Marriage Group," *Criticism* 25, no. 3 (Summer 1983): 203, citing Augustine's belief that "language has its origin in desire," argues that "ultimately the Wife's desires make her a metaphor for language itself." Lady Bertilak, as we will see in the next chapter, is subject to the same identification.

52. Robertson, *A Preface to Chaucer,* 381.

53. See the Riverside editor's note to 3.880, p. 873.

54. The ambiguity of carnivalesque performance operates even here, however, to destabilize categories. If Alisoun the wife represents how authority defines woman, then Alisoun the entrepreneur, pervasively greedy and intransigent, can be read as representing how the same clerical and literary authority defines her class.

55. Wayne Shumaker, "Alisoun in Wanderland: A Study in Chaucer's Mind and Literary Method," *ELH* 18 (1951): 88.

CHAPTER 3: "THER HE WATZ DISPOYLED, WITH SPECHEZ OF MYERTHE": CARNIVAL AND THE UNDOING OF SIR GAWAIN

1. All references to the text are to *Sir Gawain and the Green Knight,* ed. J. R. R. Tolkien and E. V. Gordon; 2nd ed., ed. Norman Davis (Oxford: Oxford University Press, 1967).

2. John Halverson, "Template Criticism: *Sir Gawain and the Green Knight,*" *Modern Philology* 67 (1969):138.

3. Larry D. Benson, *Art and Tradition in "Sir Gawain and the Green Knight"* (New Brunswick, N.J.: Rutgers University Press, 1965); see, for example, 218.

4. John Burrow, *A Reading of Sir Gawain and the Green Knight* (London: Routledge and Kegan Paul, 1965).

5. Geraldine Heng, "Feminine Knots and the Other *Sir Gawain and the Green Knight*," *PMLA* 106 (1991): 500–14; R. A. Shoaf, *The Poem as Green Girdle: Commercium in "Sir Gawain and the Green Knight"* (Gainesville: University Presses of Florida, 1984).

6. Ivo Kamps, "Magic, Women, and Incest: The Real Challenges in *Sir Gawain and the Green Knight*," *Exemplaria* 1, no. 2 (1989): 313–36; the quotation is at 314.

7. Derek Brewer, *Symbolic Stories: Traditional Narratives of the Family Drama in English Literature* (Cambridge: Brewer, 1980), 72.

8. A. V. C. Schmidt, "'Latent Content' and The Testimony in the Text'" in *Sir Gawain and the Green Knight*," *Review of English Studies*, n. s. 38, no. 150 (1987): 145–58.

9. Stephen Manning, "A Psychological Interpretation of *Sir Gawain and the Green Knight*," in *Critical Studies of Sir Gawain and the Green Knight*, ed. Donald Howard and Christian Zacher (Notre Dame: Notre Dame University Press, 1968), 279–94; Virginia Carmichael, "Green is for Growth: Sir Gawain's Disjunctive Neurosis," *Assays* 4 (1987): 25–39.

10. David Farley Hills, "Gawain's Fault in *Sir Gawain and the Green Knight*," *Review of English Studies*, n. s. 14 (1963): 124–31; P. J. C. Field, "A Rereading of *Sir Gawain and the Green Knight*," *Studies in Philology* 68 (1971): 255–69.

11. Heng, "Feminine Knots"; Shoaf, *The Poem as Green Girdle* [for both, see note 5 above]; A. Kent Hieatt, "*Sir Gawain*: Pentangle, *Luf-Lace*, Numerical Structure," *Papers on Language and Literature* 4 (1968), 339–59; Robert W. Hanning, "Sir Gawain and the Red Herring: The Perils of Interpretation," in *Acts of Interpretation: The Text in Its Context 700–1600*, ed. Mary J. Carruthers and Elizabeth D. Kirk (Norman, Okla.: Pilgrim, 1982), 5–23. For an extremely sophisticated Lacanian reading which concentrates on gaps and fissures in the text, see Elizabeth Scala, "The Wanting Words of *Sir Gawain and the Green Knight*: Narrative Past, Present and Absent," *Exemplaria* 6 (1994): 305–38. I am particularly indebted to my former student, Geraldine Heng, whose work on *Gawain* stimulated me to begin writing up my own. Heng's reading of the poem in terms of feminine versus masculine texts is also followed in Gayle Margherita's *The Romance of Origins: Language and Sexual Difference in Middle English Literature* (Philadelphia: University of Pennsylvania Press, 1994), chapter 6, "Father Aeneas or Morgan the Goddess," 129–51.

12. James Joyce, *Ulysses* (New York: Random House, 1966), 24, "Nestor."

13. I am arguing particularly, if implicitly, against the kind of thing Ross G. Arthur does when he insists that "signs such as the pentangle . . . are capable of being 'read' in a variety of ways, but instead of leaving us in a relativistic quandary the poet has succeeded in building a properly orthodox hierarchy of such readings," *Medieval Sign Theory and "Sir Gawain and the Green Knight"* (Toronto: University of Toronto Press, 1987), 3. As the repeated presence of unresolved dualities—Is the Green Knight monstrous or beautiful? Is Hautdesert massive or insubstantial?—should indicate, the poem offers no such illusory comforts. The unclassifiable has a marked tendency to remain unclassified, as the appearance of the castle may be the product either of Gawain's prayer or Morgan's curse. Professor Arthur's assumption that the poem's sign system is ultimately readable

is a common one, however. See, for example, John Plummer, "Signifying the Self: Language and Identity in *Sir Gawain and the Green Knight*," in *Text and Matter: New Critical Perspectives of the "Pearl"-Poet*, ed. Robert J. Blanch, Miriam Youngerman Miller, and Julian N. Wasserman (Troy, N.Y.: Whitston Publishing, 1991), 195–212, who argues that the Green Knight and the Lady complicate Gawain's heraldic view of the world without really undermining it.

14. One of the most concise and persuasive readings of the doubleness of the opening remains Alfred David, "Gawain and Aeneas," *English Studies* 49 (1968): 402–09. See also Thomas L. Reed, "'Boþe Blysse and Blunder': *Sir Gawain and the Green Knight* and the Debate Tradition," *Chaucer Review* 23 (1988): 140–61.

15. See Bakhtin, *Rabelais and His World*, especially chapter 1.

16. Robert Levine, "Aspects of Grotesque Realism in *Sir Gawain and the Green Knight*," *Chaucer Review* 17 (1982): 65–75.

17. Sandra Billington, *Mock Kings in Medieval Society and Renaissance Drama* (Oxford: Clarendon Press, 1991), especially 30–38.

18. Schmidt, "Latent Content,'" 157 (see note 8).

19. C. L. Barber, *Shakespeare's Festive Comedy* (Princeton: Princeton University Press, 1959), 6–11.

20. The classic study of the significance of the form of the pentangle remains Hieatt, "*Sir Gawain:* Pentangle, *Luf-Lace,* Numerical Structure" [see note 11 above].

21. Stephanie J. Hollis, "The Pentangle Knight: *Sir Gawain and the Green Knight*," *Chaucer Review* 15 (1981): 273.

22. Thus Kathleen M. Ashley, "'Trawthe' and Temporality: The Violation of Contracts and Conventions in *Sir Gawain and the Green Knight*," *Assays* 4 (1987): 16, remarks that "the pentangle is so blatantly allegorized, calling attention to its meaning so insistently, that the reader should be put on guard."

23. For those associations, see John F. Kitely, "'The Endless Knot': Magical Aspects of the Pentangle in *Sir Gawain and the Green Knight*," *Studies in the Literary Imagination* 4, no. 2 (1971): 41–50.

24. Gawain's various "interpretive communities" are discussed by Sarah Stanbury, *Seeing the Gawain-Poet: Description and the Act of Perception* (Philadelphia: University of Pennsylvania Press, 1991), 96–115.

25. On the figures of the chess game and the specific chess problem called "jeu parti" in the Hautdesert section of the poem, see Thomas Rendall, "Gawain and the Game of Chess," *Chaucer Review* 27, no. 2 (1992), 186–199.

26. For Robert Hanning, "Sir Gawain and the Red Herring" [see note 11], "the fish in its embellished state [is] the *Gawain*-Poet's supreme emblem of the civilization that nurtures, elects, deceives, tempts, and (to some extent) defeats the best knight of the Arthurian world" (22). For a closely related line of argument, see John Leyerle "The Game and Play of Hero," in *Concepts of the Hero in the Middle Ages and Renaissance*, ed. Norman T. Burns and Christopher Reagan (London: Hodder and Stoughton, 1976), 49–82. Leyerle describes the poem as "an interconnected series of one Christmas game after another" (53). Along similar lines, Rendall, 186–99, elucidates the pattern of references to chess and chess problems (*jeux partis*) in the episodes in Hautdesert.

27. See Castle, *Masquerade and Civilization;* especiallly chapter 2, "Travesty and the Fate of the Carnivalesque," 52–109. As I have earlier mentioned, Castle argues for the "antitaxonomic energy" of masquerade: its subversion of the "vision of a classifiable cosmos" based on the "desire for firm conceptual boundaries" (102).

28. For a discussion of the process by which the Lady redefines "Gawain" as "a discursive construct" (118), see Geraldine Heng, "A Woman Wants: The Lady, *Gawain,* and the Forms of Seduction," *Yale Journal of Criticism* 5, no. 3 (1992): 101–34.

29. As a fictional character, of course, Gawain's past is not an objective history so much as it is his role in previous fictions. Thus, Larry Benson, 95–97, discusses the poem's "untraditional" Gawain confronting his "traditional" reputation at Hautdesert. This poem's Gawain is presented to us, strangely perhaps, as a history detached from any specific events, possibly because unvarying perfection does not stoop to instances.

30. Hollis, "The Pentangle Knight" (note 21), Hieatt, "Pentangle, *Luf-Lace,* Numerical Structure" (note 11) and Heng, "Feminine Knots" (note 5) all argue for the emblematic flexibility of the girdle, signifying, for Heng, "mobility and transformation" (506); for Hieatt, "untroth" (344); for Hollis, imperfection (see 277).

31. Heng, "Feminine Knots," 509, argues for the girdle itself as "a signifier for language, for the operation and play of linguistic difference." The knot, however, is given and declared significant by the Lady; it may be a speech act, but she is speech itself.

32. It also perhaps subverts her husband's. John Leyerle, 53, suggests that *Bertilak* is "an onomastic pun on *berȝt layk,* 'bright game'."

33. See "The 'Syngne of Surfet' and the Surfeit of Signs in *Sir Gawain and the Green Knight,*" in *The Passing of Arthur: New Essays in Arthurian Tradition,* ed. Christopher Baswell and William Sharpe (New York: Garland, 1988), 153: "Gawain's judgement is corrupted not only by 'surfeit' but also by . . . the plethora of signs that confront him and that by their very multiplicity vex and question any exclusivity in interpretation."

34. Lawrence Besserman, "The Idea of the Green Knight," *ELH* 53 (1968): 219–39, without citing the Porter's remark, does note the parallel between the cock-crowing at lines 1412 and 2008 and "the crowing of the cock at Peter's betrayal of Christ" (223). Besserman sees the Green Knight generally as having "a parodic connection to Christ by way of the doctrine of hypostatic union" (230). My argument throughout this chapter has been that such "identifications" occur only as parts of a paratactic complex of contradictory suggestions; (i.e., they are mock-identifications). Part of what is "mock" about this one is that Gawain, who kisses and betrays, also resembles Judas. Gawain, like Peter, weeps and repents, however, and the "sifting" of Peter (see Luke 22:31) may be recalled in Bertilak's characterization of Gawain as a "perl bi þe quite pese" (2364). The poem, of course, encourages us to see Bertilak as *both* the devil who sifts and the lord who is betrayed. The doubleness of Gawain's role, here and elsewhere, looks back to Aeneas/Antenor, the "tulk . . . tried for his tricherie, þe trewest on erthe" (3–4).

35. On this point I disagree with Heng, "A Woman Wants," who assumes that the Lady can be known, at least positionally, through the game. The poem persistently reminds us that players also exist behind and separable from their tokens on the board. The Lady whom Gawain can see is playing, all right, but she is also being played. "Hit is *my* wede þat þou werez," says the Green Knight (2358).

36. For Heng, see note 5 and note 31. Sheila Fisher discusses the relationships of masculine and feminine powers in "Taken Men and Token Women in *Sir Gawain and the Green Knight,*" in *Seeking the Woman in Late Medieval and Renaissance*

Writings: Essays in Feminist Contextual Criticism, ed. Fisher and Janet E. Halley (Knoxville: University of Tennessee Press, 1989), 71–105; also in "Leaving Morgan Aside: Women, History, and Revisionism in *Sir Gawain and the Green Knight,*" in Baswell and Sharpe (see note 33), 129–51. Both essays, while right about the poem's undermining of male authority, rely on an essentializing of gender difference that I think the poem subverts.

37. See, of course, Stephen Greenblatt, *Shakespearean Negotiations: The Circulation of Social Energy in Renaissance England* (Oxford: Clarendon Press, 1988). Greenblatt, also of course, takes the idea of "dynamic circulation" from Michel Foucault, *L'Usage des plaisirs,* vol. 2 of *Histoire de la sexualite* (Paris: Gallimard, 1984), 52–53. See Greenblatt, 166n.

38. Shoaf (see note 5), 6, 8. In the later essay, "The 'Syngne of Surfet,'" Shoaf argues that Gawain comes to "a new, easy tolerance of alternative, even radically different interpretations" (165). I do not find that a persuasive account of the "antifeminist outburst" or of Gawain's exposition of the green "bende," though I am much indebted to Shoaf's analysis of the destabilization of signs elsewhere in the text.

39. Hollis, "The Pentangle Knight" (see note 21): 268.

40. I reject with some reluctance the theory put forward by Kathleen M. Ashley, "Bonding and Signification in *Sir Gawain and the Green Knight,*" in Blanch, Miller, and Wasserman, 1991 [see note 13], 213–19: "the reconstruction of the boar after dismembering may stand as a central image for the poem's theory of signs. Although meaning may appear at first as intrinsic and natural, though the signified/signifier bond may appear inevitable, the poem systematically deconstructs all such bonds and connections. It then reconstructs them, emphasizing the role played by human choice and human art. . . . Man, the maker of civilization through his art and his artifacts, is a maker of meanings. It is as free makers of meaning that I think we can understand the conclusion of the poem, which invites its readers to become resignifiers" (217). I would say that it compels us to resignify while critically distancing us from the process and from Gawain as its paradigm. To follow Ashley's metaphor, the reconstructed boar may be delicious and necessary, but it is no longer the living pig. Gawain, not the poem, reconstructs a version of the heraldic world: *his* stuffed boar, not ours or (necessarily) the poem's.

41. Schmidt, "Latent Content," 149, is one of the few to note that Gawain converts it to a heraldic "bende." John Plummer [see note 13 above] points out that the "bende," as Gawain wears it, "forms a heraldic qualification of the pentangle, 'difference,' in heraldic parlance" (205). One might add that it forms a *difference* in critical parlance.

CHAPTER 4: THE UNBEING OF THE OVERREACHER: PRIVATIVE EVIL, PROTEAN CARNIVAL, AND THE MARLOVIAN HERO

This chapter originated as a paper given at the Shakespeare Institute, University of Birmingham. My thanks to T. P. Matheson for the invitation to speak. I should acknowledge general debts to Harry Levin's *The Overreacher* (Cambridge: Harvard University Press, 1952) and Judith Weil, *Christopher Marlowe: Merlin's Prophet* (Cambridge: Cambridge University Press, 1977), whose influence on my reading of the plays is so pervasive that I have not tried to acknowledge it in specific footnotes.

1. L. C. Knights, *Drama and Society in the Age of Jonson* (London: Chatto & Windus, 1937; reprint. New York: Barnes and Noble, 1968); Jonathan Dollimore, *Radical Tragedy: Religion, Ideology and Power in the Drama of Shakespeare and His Contemporaries* (Brighton: Harvester, 1984); Francis Barker, *The Tremulous Private Body: Essays on Subjection* (London: Methuen, 1984).

2. See Philip Watson's introduction in *Luther and Erasmus,* 12–28. Alan Sinfield, *Faultlines: Cultural Materialism and the Politics of Dissident Reading* (Oxford: Oxford University Press, 1992), 152, notes that "the Reformation doctrine of grace and predestination was not new—the reformers drew continually upon the church fathers, especially Augustine." For one example among many of Calvin contending against the appropriation of Augustine by anti-Calvinists, see *Institutes,* 4.17.28 (on transubstantiation).

3. For general surveys of Marlowe's religious and intellectual background, see Paul Kocher, *Christopher Marlowe: A Study of His Thought, Learning and Character* (Chapel Hill: University of North Carolina Press, 1946); and Levin, *Overreacher.* More specifically on the religious debate in Marlowe's intellectual milieu is Harry C. Porter, *Reformation and Reaction in Tudor Cambridge* (Cambridge: Cambridge University Press, 1958). See also: Pauline Honderich, "John Calvin and Dr. Faustus," *Modern Language Review* 68 (1973): 1–13; Arieh Sachs, "The Religious Despair of Dr. Faustus," *JEGP* 63 (1964): 625–47; Joseph Westland, "The Orthodox Christian Framework of Marlowe's *Faustus,*" *Studies in English Literature* 3 (1963): 190–205. Weil, *Merlin's Prophet,* makes exceptionally thorough and intelligent use of the extensive biblical allusion in Marlowe's work.

4. Walzer, *Revolution of the Saints,* 24.

5. John Cox, *Shakespeare and the Dramaturgy of Power,* chapters 2 and 3, 22–60, gives a detailed account of the continuity of Augustinian social criticism from medieval to Tudor drama, arguing that instead of "a sacred culture suddenly giving way to secular . . . what we find is a gradual transformation of ideology" (31) within the framework of what he generally calls "Augustinian political realism." Here and elsewhere, Cox's primary concern is with explicit and implicit social commentary rather than with the doctrine of privation and its relation to the ontology of the self.

6. Line references, as before, are to J. B. Steane's edition of *The Complete Plays* (Harmondsworth: Penguin, 1969). I have used the Penguin edition because it is the one most widely available and frequently used. Since my argument does not depend on Steane's ordering of the plays or his attempts to meld the A and B texts of *Dr. Faustus,* I have preferred not to send readers to the library in search of Brooke, Greg, and others. That the phrase "the tragedy of a Jew" might have been regarded as a "contradiction in terms" by an Elizabethan audience is suggested by Malcolm Kelsall, *Christopher Marlowe* (Leiden: E. J. Brill, 1981), 135.

7. Joel B. Altman, *The Tudor Play of Mind* (Berkeley: University of California Press, 1978), 327, thinks that the "she" Tamburlaine really loves is his sword, a suggestion I might be tempted to use were I directing the play. Altman's general discussion of invention versus reality in Marlowe (321–88) is one of the best available.

8. This constant intrusion of the absurd on the would-be sublime is what causes Wilbur Sanders to complain about "Marlowe's fitful muse" in *The Dramatist and the Received Idea: Studies in the Plays of Marlowe and Shakespeare*

(Cambridge: Cambridge University Press, 1968), 205. Not even Sanders, however, suggests that Marlowe's muse deserted him *between* "my girl" and "my gold," so there must be an explanation other than fitfulness.

9. Constance Kuriyama, *Hammer or Anvil: Psychological Patterns in Christopher Marlowe's Plays* (New Brunswick, N. J.: Rutgers University Press, 1980).

10. See Una Ellis-Fermor, *Christopher Marlowe* (London: Methuen 1927; reprint Hamden, Conn.: Archon, 1967), 61–87.

11. I refer, of course, to Greg's late dating of *Dr. Faustus* in his parallel-text edition of 1950, *Marlowe's "Dr. Faustus" 1604–1616* (Oxford: Oxford University Press) and to J. B. Steane's conjectural reordering of the plays (with *Faustus* midway in the canon) in his *Marlowe: A Critical Study* (Cambridge: Cambridge University Press, 1964).

12. In chapter 2 of *Habits of Thought in the English Renaissance: Religion, Politics, and the Dominant Culture* (Berkeley: University of California Press, 1990), 69–90, Debora Kuller Shuger discusses a theme she finds in the sermons of Tyndale and Hooker: the desolated soul that seeks substantiation through "incorporation in the mystical body of Christ" (69). In these preachers "inwardness [is] constituted by the experience of absence and longing. . . . The self (soul) is not so much the creation of power but of desire" (89). Significantly, she does not trace this pattern back to the Augustinian sources I have described in chapter 1 above. Marlowe, of course, gives us the fallen soul's material parody of this process: His protagonists attempt to fill their desolation with possessions rather than spirit. Here and elsewhere, Reformation theology is more continuous than discontinuous with Augustinian tradition.

13. See my essay, "Lovelace and the Self-Dramatizing Heroes of the Restoration," in *The English Hero, 1660–1800,* ed. Robert Folkenflik (Newark: University of Delaware Press, 1982), 193–204.

14. See Dollimore, *Radical Tragedy,* especially chapter 6, 109–19; and Simon Shepherd, *Marlowe and the Politics of Elizabethan Theatre* (Brighton: Harvester, 1986), especially chapter 3, 72–109.

15. Elizabeth Forbes's translation, in *The Renaissance Philosophy of Man,* ed. Ernest Cassirer and others (Chicago: University of Chicago Press, 1948), 225.

16. Greenblatt quotes Philibert de Vienne's *The Philosopher of the Court* (1547) in praise of Protean man's ability to "change and transform himself" (*Renaissance Self-Fashioning from More to Shakespeare,* 164).

17. Karen Cunningham, "Renaissance Execution and Marlovian Elocution: The Drama of Death," *PMLA* 105, no. 2 (March 1990): 209–222, discusses Marlowe's ironizing of displays of power to create a "drama of subversion" (210). She relates this practice to the subversion of the official lessons of Elizabethan public executions by the "carnival" that accompanied them (213).

18. Greenblatt, *Renaissance Self-Fashioning,* 217: "The objects of desire, at first so clearly defined, so avidly pursued, gradually lose their sharp outlines and become more and more like mirages . . . the will exists, but the object of the will is little more than an illusion."

19. Barabas and his fellow embodiment of the sterility of evil, the Wife of Bath, stand in strikingly similar relationship to Christian authority. Both are shaped by a discourse which identifies them as Other, dangerous, evil, a source of infection; both are demonized; both are confined by a stereotype, an imposed identity that you confirm by the very fact that you resist conforming to it. Both are, in short, resisting readers of the discourse that entraps them. At the same time, both are nihilating figures because they make resistance, defection, negation, and revenge,

the principle of their being. In both cases, the political reading ("victim") and the theological one ("self-victimizer") are at odds: the one emphasizing what has been done to them, the other what they do to themselves. That ambivalence, which is seen also in Augustine's attribution of the theft of the pears both to bad company and to his own love of damnation, is fundamental to the Augustinian carnivalesque.

20. Douglas Cole, *Suffering and Evil in the Plays of Christopher Marlowe* (Princeton: Princeton University Press, 1962), 261.

21. Leo Kirschbaum discusses the "dislocation between verbal potency and accomplishment" in *Tamburlaine:* See *The Plays of Christopher Marlowe* (New York: World, 1962), 48; see also Altman, *Tudor Play of Mind,* 321–88.

22. When Orcanes attributes his victory to "justice of . . . Christ" (*Tamburlaine, part 2,* 2.3.28), Gazellus replies that "Tis but the fortune of the wars . . . / Whose power is often prov'd a miracle" (31–32). Orcanes decides to honor Christ *and* Mahomet anyway! Like the semiotician-detective in Eco's *The Name of the Rose,* he finds the pattern his mind wants to find. The misreading of signs is, of course, a major subject of Marlowe's plays, as of Augustinian literature generally.

23. Thus, Howard Felperin in *The Uses of the Canon,* 115, comments that through "conspiracy, atheism, and sodomy . . . . Marlowe's heroes, and possibly Marlowe himself, enact their ringing reiterations of a difference that sets them above the 'base slaves' . . . who are defined by obedient subjection." Felperin's brief discussion (114–18) of ludic transgression and its containment in Marlowe occupies some of the same ground as my own. He is not, however, concerned with the Augustinian nature of the pattern. We also disagree on whether carnivalesque subversion can, in any simple sense, be contained.

24. *Hammer or Anvil,* 134. Readers of Augustine will recognize that the theme is hardly peculiar to Marlowe.

25. T. S. Eliot, "The Blank Verse of Marlowe," in *The Sacred Wood* (London: Methuen, 1920; reprint 1960), 92.

26. For a shrewd analysis in Kirkegaardian terms of Faustus's despair, see King-Kok Cheung, "The Dialectics of Despair in *Dr. Faustus,*" in *"A Poet and a Filthy Play-maker": New Essays on Christopher Marlowe,* ed. Kenneth Friedenreich, Roma Gill, and Constance Kuriyama (New York: A. M. S., 1988), 193–202. A similarly fatal and carnivalesque misuse of Biblical text is Faustus's quotation of Christ's "consummatum est" when he signs the contract (2.1.73). Jan Kott, *The Bottom Translation: Marlowe and Shakespeare and the Carnival Tradition,* trans. Daniela Miedzyrzecka and Lillian Vallee (Evanston: Northwestern University Press, 1987), 10, cites this passage as an example of *parodia sacra* and refers the reader to *Rabelais,* 86.

27. See Philip Brockbank, *Marlowe: Dr. Faustus,* Studies in English Literature, no. 6 (London: Edward Arnold, 1962), 14–16. Augustine's account of Faustus, "a great trap of the devil," comes primarily in *Confessions* (trans. Chadwick) 5, 3, 3 to 7, 13, pp. 73–80.

28. Augustine famously remarks, "What then is time? Provided that no one asks me, I know." (Conf. 11, 14).

29. Anne Hunsaker Hawkins, *Archetypes of Conversion: The Autobiographies of Augustine, Bunyan, and Merton* (Lewisburg: Bucknell University Press; London & Toronto: Associated University Presses, 1985), 70, notes that in *Confessions* "Faustus and Carthage represent the false and earthly vision, whereas Ambrose and Milan represent the true and spiritual vision." With the exception

of the ignored Old Man, of course, Marlowe's play contains no figure corresponding to Ambrose. This *is* the preterite version.

30. Anthony Sher's Tamburlaine at Stratford in 1992, evolving from monkey-walking trickster to strutting, and increasingly immobile, tyrant, caught both the carnivalesque and the official roles of the character.

CHAPTER 5. "A CRAFTY MADNESS": CARNIVAL AND THE POLITICS OF REVENGE

1. In *The Plays of Cyril Tourneur,* ed. George Parfitt (Cambridge: Cambridge University Press, 1978), 39. All further references are to this edition.

2. Frye, *Fools of Time,* 6.

3. Dollimore, *Radical Tragedy,* 18. For a stringent critique of Dollimore's methodology and his interpretations, see Tom McAlindon, "Cultural Materialism and the Ethics of Reading; or the Radicalizing of Jacobean Tragedy," *MLR* 90, no. 4 (October 1995): 830–46.

4. Michael D. Bristol, "Carnival and the Institutions of Theater in Elizabethan England," *ELH* 50 (1983): 637. The argument is amplified throughout the first section of Bristol's *Carnival and Theater: Plebian Culture and the Structure of Authority in Renaissance England* (London: Methuen, 1985), 8–53.

5. Richard Wilson, "'Is This a Holiday?': Shakespeare's Roman Carnival," *ELH* 54 (1987): 43, 33.

6. Jonathan Haynes, "Festivity and the Dramatic Economy of Jonson's *Bartholemew Fair,*" *ELH* 51 (1984): 645–68. The quotation is from 659.

7. Leah Marcus, *The Politics of Mirth,* 8.

8. Leonard Tennenhouse, *Power on Display,* 79.

9. Peter Stallybrass and Allon White, *The Politics and Poetics of Transgression,* 18, 14.

10. LeRoy Ladurie, *Carnival in Romans,* 229.

11. See Tennenhouse, *Power on Display,* 83–84; C. L. Barber, *Shakespeare's Festive Comedy,* 192–221. To me, Hal's systematic co-optation and countersubversion of that apparent carnival king, Falstaff, could be a political textbook for the period. By the time Hal is King, he has not only drawn the fangs of whatever anarchic rebellion the tavern world represents, but also incorporated that into the myth of his own heroism, his authority, and his role as embodiment of the nation. He does, with comprehensive effectiveness, what King James spent twenty years trying to do: use festivity to cement authority. As Tennenhouse (83–84) puts it, in the *Henriad* "[t]he figures of carnival ultimately authorize the state as the state appears to take on the vigor of festival.

12. The only article I know to discuss *Hamlet* in these terms is Phyllis Gorfain, "Toward a Theory of Play and the Carnivalesque in *Hamlet,*" *Hamlet Studies* 13, nos. 1–2 (1991): 25–49. Gorfain is primarily concerned with the relation between the linear patterns of tragedy and the circular ones of carnival and relatively unconcerned with the matters that interest me: masking and identity, revenge tragedy as a genre, and its relation to Augustinian theology. See, however, note 37 below.

13. Bakhtin, *Rabelais,* 9. Two important essays on *Hamlet* deal with revenge as a strategy for evading death: Alexander Welsh, "The Task of Hamlet," *Yale Review* 69, no. 4 (1980): 481–502, treats revenge as an "act of mourning" (481); Robert N. Watson, "Giving up the Ghost in a World of Decay: *Hamlet,* Revenge,

and Denial," *Renaissance Drama* n. s. 21 (1990): 199–223, describes it as an expression of "the denial of death" (199). My argument is that Hamlet's rejection of his father's death naturally takes carnivalesque and politically subversive form and that this reaction is the common process of revenge tragedy. Aside from isolated chapters, such as Howard Felperin's on *Hamlet* in *Shakespearean Respresentation: Mimesis and Modernity in Elizabethan Tragedy* (Princeton: Princeton University Press, 1977), 44–67, the critical literature on revenge is more copious than inspiring. Fredson Bowers's *Elizabethan Revenge Tragedy* (Princeton: Princeton University Press, 1940; reprint Gloucester: Peter Smith, 1959) remains a standard source on the historical context of revenge. Eleanor Prosser, *Hamlet and Revenge* (Stanford, Calif.: Stanford University Press, 1967) concentrates on the relevance of "orthodox Christian concepts" (xi), especially ethical ones, to *Hamlet*. Charles and Elaine Hallett, *The Revenger's Madness: A Study of Revenge Tragedy Motifs* (Lincoln: University of Nebraska Press, 1980) are diligent, plodding, and theoretically naive. Roland Mushat Frye, *The Renaissance Hamlet,* discusses "Elizabethan attitudes toward retribution, resistance to tyranny, and tyrannicide" (29), but does not refer to carnival or the grotesque. Wendy Griswold, *Renaissance Revivals: City Comedy and Revenge Tragedy in the London Theatre 1576–1980* (Chicago: University of Chicago Press, 1986) is primarily concerned with the history of stage production and revival, and makes little attempt to develop a theory of the genre, contenting herself with a listing of "characteristics," such as court setting, trickery, and so forth (58–65). Peter Mercer's *Hamlet and the Acting of Revenge* (Basingstoke: Macmillan, 1987) is thinly researched on anything except *Hamlet* and the Senecan tradition. The Halletts are among the few who try to construct a coherent theory of the genre, as opposed to seeing it as an historical curiosity (Bowers) or an accumulation of devices (Griswold). However, their formula—basically that revenge is a passion which leads to excess and partial madness, thereby condemning the revenger regardless of the virtue of his original motives—commits the genre almost exclusively to studies in psychology. "The whole structure of revenge can be understood in terms of the revenger's efforts to free himself from . . . restraints" (9). They generally show little sense of the connections between their genre and related ones. They give no sign, for example, of seeing any connection between their formula, through release to excess and falsification of reality, and Barber's formula for comedy, "through release to clarification" (*Festive Comedy,* 4). This chapter attempts, among other things, to show that the two patterns are intimately related.

14. See Mercer's somewhat puzzled comment that "while *The Revenger's Tragedy* is not a comic experience for the audience (it is too full of horror and evil), it is something very close to that for Vindice" (106).

15. See Catherine Belsey, *The Subject of Tragedy: Identity and Difference in Renaissance Drama* (London and New York: Methuen, 1985), 5.

16. C. L. Barber and Richard Wheeler, *The Whole Journey: Shakespeare's Power of Development* (Berkeley and Los Angeles: University of California Press, 1986), 269.

17. Hamlet's reference to a royal "progress" is noted by Francois Laroque, *Shakespeare's Festive World: Elizabethan Seasonal Entertainments and the Professional Stage,* trans. Janet Lloyd (Cambridge: Cambridge University Press, 1991), 276.

18. Compare Haynes's useful statement of the political roles of Elizabethan and other carnival: "the festive moment is essentially conservative in a strong and stable society, potentially revolutionary in an unstable and sclerotic one"

(656). Haynes's formulation closely parallels the dialectical relation between carnival and the official order developed in Gurevich's *Medieval Popular Culture* (See chapter 1, note 3 above).

19. Sandra Billington, *Mock Kings in Medieval Society and Renaissance Drama,* 53, notes that during of the fifteenth and sixteenth centuries the Christmas "mock-court developed into a close copy of real government."

20. Bristol, *Carnival and Theater,* 207. Laroque, 240, calls Claudius "a tragic buffoon, a Carnival Mock King or Lord of Misrule." R. M. Frye, *The Renaissance "Hamlet,"* 295, sees Claudius's drinking as allusive to "one of the major themes of the Twelfth-Night revels in which an elected parodic monarch 'reigned' and drank."

21. The line reference is to *The Duchess of Malfi,* ed. Elizabeth Brennan (London: Benn, 1964).

22. Talking of Hamlet's puns, James Calderwood remarks that the "comedic sense of community must yield here to tragic divisions. Thus the process of cross-erasure splits the pun's meaning's down the middle, leaving Hamlet isolated with his ironies and his listeners penned in confusion": *To Be and Not To Be: Negation and Metadrama in "Hamlet"* (New York: Columbia University Press, 1983), 83. Kirby Farrell, in *Shakespeare's Creation: The Language of Magic and Play* (Amherst: University of Massachusetts Press, 1975), 168, remarks that Hamlet "calls attention to himself even as he withholds himself."

23. Victor Turner, *From Ritual to Theatre: The Human Seriousness of Play* (New York: Performing Arts Journal Publications, 1982), 41. Janet Adelman, *Suffocating Mothers: Fantasies of Maternal Origin in Shakespeare's Plays, "Hamlet" to "The Tempest"* (New York and London: Routledge, 1992), 28–29, discusses the prevalence of "boundary contamination" throughout the play.

24. Robert Weimann, *Shakespeare and the Popular Tradition in the Theatre,* ed. Robert Schwartz (Baltimore: Johns Hopkins University Press, 1978), 150, 154.

25. Line references to *The Spanish Tragedy* are to the New Mermaid edition, ed. J. R. Mulryne (London: Benn, 1970).

26. Elizabeth Maslen, "The Dynamics of Kyd's *Spanish Tragedy,*" *English* 32, no. 132 (summer 1983): 112.

27. For an interesting discussion of Hamlet's use of theatricality as a means of control and provocation, both toward other characters and the audience, see Brent Cohen, "'What Is It You Would See?': *Hamlet* and the Conscience of the Theater," *ELH* 44 (1977): 222–47.

28. One of the few critics, other than Bristol, to suggest that Claudius is less than deeply cunning and that "for just once—the hero has the edge in awareness" over the villain, is Bertrand Evans, *Shakespeare's Tragic Practice* (Oxford: Clarendon, 1979), 81. For the description of Hamlet as an *eiron,* see Susan Snyder, *The Comic Matrix of Shakespeare's Tragedies: "Romeo and Juliet," "Hamlet," "Othello," and "King Lear"* (Princeton: Princeton University Press, 1979), 94.

29. For charivari and jig as "counter-festivities," see Bristol, *Carnival and Theater,* 164–65. An Elizabethan jig was, of course, an afterpiece. Hamlet is identifying his play as the comedy that follows the tragedy of his father, who by ironic inversion becomes the forgotten "hobby-horse" (2. 134–35) of Hamlet's next speech.

30. Lawrence Olivier in his film version stages this scene with the two groups on facing platforms: Player King visually equated with "player" King.

31. "Dismantled": literally, "disrobed"; compare with Gawain's "despoyling"

by Berkilak's attendants. Claudius uncrowns Denmark, Hamlet uncrowns Claudius.

32. Frank Kermode, *Forms of Attention* (Chicago: University of Chicago Press, 1987), 46.

33. The point is made, among others, by Harry Levin, *The Question of Hamlet* (Oxford and New York: Oxford University Press, 1959), 124.

34. Eleanor Prosser, *Hamlet and Revenge,* 151.

35. Rosencrantz and Guildenstern are, of course, murdered by a letter that is a parody of official, Claudian discourse, filled with "as's of great charge" (see 5.2.33–47). To murder in jest is also to murder in deed.

36. Hamlet generally, though not consistently, takes a strictly essentialist view of male character. His father's royalty, like his paternity, is an inviolable, nontransferable quality. No amount of mere performance will identify Claudius with either role. Because Hamlet sees Claudius as a figure of privative evil, beneath the King's performance there is necessarily "nothing." Gertrude, on the other hand, is told to "assume a virtue, if you have it not" (3.4.160) on the grounds that she will acquire the quality of the part she plays. Men, it would appear, have essences; women do not. Gertrude, in her son's mind, feeds off her husbands (e.g., battening "on the moor" Claudius, 3.4.67), taking her quality from them, as they do not take theirs from her. The antiessentialist view, which sees identity as protean masking, is, of course, carnivalesque; the essentialist view, seeing it as rigidly stable, is Lenten.

37. Compare Phyllis Gorfain's reading [see note 12]: "While Hamlet can play mad, Ophelia must go mad. She lacks Hamlet's mastery over reflexive role-playing because she is inhibited, in part, by gender restrictions about appropriate female role-playing. To gain Hamlet's freedom to speak, which he gains through the symbolic role of fool in the license of his 'antic disposition,' Ophelia must speak in the licensed voice of the symbolic madman. . . . Ophelia acts out the Other into which Hamlet's misogyny places her, but she serves, in her authentic madness, as the paradigm of the Otherness into which theater, fools, carnival, and other forms of license also fit. She is a paradigm of the Female Grotesque, a double-bodied figure of exuberant excess and mortality which dominates carnivalesque texts" (34). She is more, I am suggesting, the elegiac shadow of such excess, her grotesque language separated from any empirically observable transgression but also from physical fertility.

38. Mack's great essay, "The World of Hamlet," *Yale Review* 41 (1952): 502–23 [reprinted in *Shakespeare: Modern Essays in Criticism,* ed. Leonard Dean (New York: Oxford, 1967, 242–62], focuses, of course, on "the mysteriousness of Hamlet's world" (Dean, 246), and on "the problematic nature of the relation of reality to appearance" in the play (247).

39. Compare Laroque on the imagery of cannibal feasting in *Hamlet: Shakespeare's Festive World,* 275–76.

40. For the opposing argument that revenge drama enacts denial of death because revengers necessarily seek to undo its affects, see Watson. "Giving Up the Ghost" [note 13]. I argue that it is the revenger who attempts to deny what the play around him makes omnipresent, from the first, premising murder to the final bloodbath. The revenger is, typically, in the situation of Hamlet, inventing voices for skulls, attempting to assert the fact of death his own actions attempt to deny.

41. The most casual list would include L. C. Knights, *Drama and Society in the Age of Jonson* (London: Chatto & Windus, 1937; reprint New York: Barnes & Noble, 1973), 1–173; Stephen Greenblatt, "Invisible Bullets," in *Shakespearean*

Negotiations (Berkeley and Los Angeles: University of California Press, 1988), 21–65; Stallybrass and White, *Transgression,* chapter 1 ("The Fair, the Pig, Authorship"), 27–79, on authorship and the separation of high from low cultures; Michael O'Connell, "The Idolatrous Eye: Iconoclasm, Antitheatricalism and the Image of the Elizabethan Theater," *ELH* 52 (1985): 279–310, on economic individualism, the internalized protestant sensibility, and their effects on Elizabethan drama. The books previously cited by Marcus and Tennenhouse deal with figurations of power in response to the crisis of transition from Tudor to Stuart dynasties. Annabel Patterson, *Shakespeare and the Popular Voice* (Oxford and Cambridge, Mass.: Blackwell's, 1989), especially chapters 1 and 2, 13–51, provides a useful introduction to Shakespeare and the politics of his time; R. M. Frye, *The Renaissance "Hamlet,"* provides a comprehensive overview. A truly comprehensive listing of crises and sources would, however, require a note of many pages. The argument of my own book, the reader will have already grasped, is that this particular crisis in the discourse—the sense of festivity lost and of imminent social and mental separation—is a constant of late medieval and Renaissance English literature. The heyday of carnival for writers of this period is always past, as indeed it was for Bakhtin.

42. For that identification see H. Neville Davies, "Jacobean *Antony and Cleopatra,*" *Shakespeare Studies* 17 (1985): 123–58; and *Antony and Cleopatra,* ed. Emrys Jones (Harmondsworth: Penguin, 1977), 46–47.

CHAPTER 6. ENTHRONED IN THE MARKETPLACE: THE CARNIVALESQUE *ANTONY AND CLEOPATRA*

1. All references are to *The Riverside Shakespeare,* ed. Evans and others, which, along with most editions, reads "when" for "where." Because Cleopatra is offering her lips at the time, "where" seems to me to make clearer sense. Antony's mock-apotheosis is noted by Howard Felperin, *Shakespearean Representation,* 107.

2. For the identification of Cleopatra with the Faithful of Revelations, see Andrew Fichter, "*Antony and Cleopatra:* 'The Time of Universal Peace,'" *Shakespeare Survey* 33 (1980): 99–111. Roy Battenhouse, "Augustinian Roots in Shakespeare's Sense of Tragedy," *The Upstart Crow* 6 (1986): 1–7, discusses Antony and Cleopatra's situation as "an ironic parallel to Christian paradigm" (2), especially the paradigms of Christ and Mary. The play's allusions to the Apocalypse were first identified by Ethel Seaton, "*Antony and Cleopatra* and *The Book of Revelation,*" *Review of English Studies* 22, no. 87 (1946): 219–24. The Biblical allusions throughout the play are listed by Naseeb Shaheen, *Biblical References in Shakespeare's Tragedies* (Newark: University of Delaware Press; London: Associated University Presses, 1987), 175–86. For the relation of the allusions in this play to contemporary iconography of Elizabeth and James I, see Paul Yachnin, "'Courtiers of Beauteous Freedom': *Antony and Cleopatra* in its Time," *Renaissance & Reformation* 15 (1991): 1–20.

3. J. M. Murry, *Shakespeare* (New York, 1936), 303; cited by Fichter, 105.

4. Fichter, "Universal Peace," 103.

5. Leonard Tennenhouse, *Power on Display,* 143.

6. Bakhtin, *Rabelais,* 274. The exploitation of this pattern for tragicomic purposes is hardly limited to *Antony and Cleopatra.* The aggressively sexual and copiously fertile Duchess of Malfi, otherwise so unlike Cleopatra in manner,

dignity, and domesticity, exemplifies the same trope, not least in bringing the philosophically barren Antonio to physical life and fatherhood. She is also, of course, subjected to skimmington abuse by Bosola, Ferdinand, and her servants.

7. See Marilyn French, *Shakespeare's Division of Experience* (London: Cape, 1982), especially chapter 1, 21–31.

8. The changes made to Caesar's character are summarized by Vivian Thomas, *Shakespeare's Roman Worlds* (London: Routledge, 1989), 102–3.

9. Clare Kinney, "The Queen's Two Bodies and the Divided Emperor," in *The Renaissance Englishwoman in Print: Counterbalancing the Canon,* ed. Anne M. Haselkorn and Betty S. Travitsky (Amherst: University of Massachusetts Press, 1990), 177.

10. On Gargamelle, see Bakhtin, *Rabelais,* 459–60.

11. Cleopatra, "cold in blood" (I.5.74) in her salad days, shows a similar reversal of conventional youth and age.

12. For the equation of Rome with public and Egypt with private life, see, among others, Ania Loomba, *Gender, Race, Renaissance Drama* (Manchester: Manchester University Press, 1986), 124–30.

13. Northrop Frye, *Fools of Time,* 48.

14. See Adelman's *The Common Liar: An Essay on "Antony and Cleopatra"* (New Haven: Yale University Press, 1973), passim.

15. Kinney [see note 9], 178.

16. Julian Markels, *The Pillar of the World: "Antony and Cleopatra" in Shakespeare's Development* (Columbus: Ohio State University Press, 1968), 45.

17. Adelman, *Common Liar,* elaborates the pattern I summarize in this paragraph; on measure and overflow, see 122–31. Susan Snyder, "Patterns of Motion in *Antony and Cleopatra,*" *Shakespeare Survey* 33 (1980): 113–22, contrasts images of Roman fixity, a quality she unfortunately regards as genuine, with those of Egyptian flux. Fixity in this play is a fiction.

18. Adelman, *Suffocating Mothers,* 178.

19. Tamburlaine, terrified that his sons may have been infected by the femininity of their mother (in *Tamburlaine, Part 2,* 1.4), represents the high hysterical form of this mentality. [See chapter 4 above.]

20. Bristol, *Carnival and Theater,* 22.

21. Castle, *Masquerade and Civilization,* 102.

22. T. McAlindon, *Shakespeare's Tragic Cosmos* (Cambridge: Cambridge University Press, 1991), 228.

23. Augustine, *The City of God,* book 1, preface, p. 5.

24. Joseph L. Simmons, *Shakespeare's Pagan World: The Roman Tragedies* (Brighton: Harvester, 1974), 8.

25. The subtle but important distinction in Cleopatra's speech is noted by Graham Bradshaw, *Shakespeare's Skepticism* (Brighton: Harvester, 1987), 34.

26. Alexander Leggatt, in *Shakespeare's Political Drama: The History Plays and the Roman Plays* (London: Routledge, 1988), 175–76, notes that the play gives Egypt "a more palpable texture than Rome": "In Egypt . . . the routines of life go on: music, billiards, drinking, fishing, and making love . . . . Rome . . . is here as neutral and unatmospheric as a committee room. Its entire political structure seems to consist of Caesar and his entourage."

27. Thus Ania Loomba [see note 12] observes that "Antony perceives he is only nominally the site of the conflict which is actually between Cleopatra and Caesar" (127).

28. I stress the parallels between the two figures because the disappearance

from general knowledge of the *Gawain* MS makes direct influence impossible. The similarities in the pattern of the two works thus argue a common paradigm.

29. A possible source for this is the famous passage in *City of God* (4.4), which I have discussed in chapter 1, where Augustine illustrates the principle that kingdoms without justice are only "gangs of criminals on a large scale," with the story of the captured pirate who defined the difference between his predation and Alexander's by saying that "because I do it with a tiny craft, I'm called a pirate: because you have a mighty navy, you're called an emperor" (139).

30. Enobarbus's rapturous account is as self-mockingly over the top as the performance that occasions it. Cleopatra couldn't get away with any of this stuff if she didn't make it funny.

31. Carol Thomas Neely, *Broken Nuptials in Shakespeare's Plays* (New Haven and London: Yale University Press, 1985), 143.

32. In Marlowe, *Complete Plays,* ed. Steane, 330.

33. Fichter, "Universal Peace," 100.

34. For discussions, cited in previous chapters, of the co-optation and conservative functions of carnival in Elizabethan and Jacobean England, see Leah Marcus, *The Politics of Mirth;* Tennenhouse, *Power on Display;* Stallybrass and White, *The Politics and Poetics of Transgression.*

Bibliography

Adelman, Janet. *The Common Liar: An Essay on "Antony and Cleopatra."* New Haven: Yale University Press, 1973.

―――. *Suffocating Mothers: Fantasies of Maternal Origin in Shakespeare's Plays, "Hamlet" to "The Tempest."* New York and London: Routledge, 1992.

Aers, David. *Chaucer.* Brighton: Harvester, 1986.

―――. *Chaucer, Langland and the Creative Imagination.* London: Routledge and Kegan Paul, 1980.

Alford, John. "The Wife of Bath versus the Clerk of Oxford: What Their Rivalry Means." *Chaucer Review* 21, no. 2 (1986), 108–32.

Altman, Joel B. *The Tudor Play of Mind.* Berkeley and Los Angeles: University of California Press, 1978.

Aquinas, St. Thomas. *Summa Theologiæ: A Concise Translation.* Edited and translated from the Latin by Timothy McDermott. London: Methuen, 1989.

Arthur, Ross G. *Medieval Sign Theory and "Sir Gawain and the Green Knight."* Toronto: University of Toronto Press, 1987.

Ashley, Kathleen M. "'Trawthe' and Temporality: The Violation of Contracts and Conventions in *Sir Gawain and the Green Knight.*" *Assays* 4 (1987): 3–24.

―――. "Bonding and Signification in *Sir Gawain and the Green Knight.*" In Blanch, Miller, and Wasserman, 213–19.

Augustine, Saint. *The City of God.* Translated from the Latin by Henry Bettenson. Edited by John O'Meara. Harmondsworth, U.K.: Penguin, 1984.

―――. *Confessions.* Translated from the Latin by Henry Chadwick. Oxford: Oxford University Press, 1992.

―――. *Later Works.* Translated by John Burnaby. The Library of Christian Classics, vol. 8. London: S.C.M. Press, 1955.

―――. *On Christian Doctrine.* Translated by D. W. Robertson. New York: Bobbs-Merrill, 1958.

Bakhtin, Mikhail. *Rabelais and His World.* Translated from the Russian by Helene Iswolsky. 1968. Reprint. Bloomington: Indiana University Press, 1984.

―――. *The Problems of Dostoevsky's Poetics.* Translated by Caryl Emerson. Minneapolis: University of Minnesota Press, 1984.

Barber, C. L. *Shakespeare's Festive Comedy: A Study of Dramatic Form and Its Relation to Social Custom.* 1959. Reprint. Cleveland: World, 1968.

Barber, C. L., and Richard P. Wheeler. *The Whole Journey: Shakespeare's Power of Development.* Berkeley and Los Angeles: University of California Press, 1986.

Barker, Francis. *The Tremulous Private Body: Essays on Subjection.* London: Methuen, 1984.

Baswell, Christopher, and William Sharpe, ed. *The Passing of Arthur: New Essays in Arthurian Tradition.* New York and London: Garland, 1988.

Battenhouse, Roy B. *A Companion to the Study of Saint Augustine.* New York: Oxford University Press, 1955.

———. "Augustinian Roots in Shakespeare's Sense of Tragedy." *The Upstart Crow* 6 (1986): 1–7.

Baynes, Norman H. *The Political Ideas of St. Augustine's "De Civitate Dei."* London: G. Bell and Sons, 1936.

Belsey, Catherine. *The Subject of Tragedy: Identity and Difference in Renaissance Drama.* London and New York: Methuen, 1985.

Benson, C. David. *Chaucer's Drama of Style: Poetic Variety and Contrast in the "Canterbury Tales."* Chapel Hill: University of North Carolina Press, 1986.

Benson, Larry D. *Art and Tradition in "Sir Gawain and the Green Knight."* New Brunswick, N.J.: Rutgers University Press, 1965.

Besserman, Lawrence. "The Idea of the Green Knight." *ELH* 53, no. 2 (summer 1986): 219–39

Billington, Sandra. *Mock Kings in Medieval Society and Reniassance Drama.* Oxford: Clarendon Press, 1991.

———. *A Social History of the Fool.* Brighton: Harvester, 1984.

Blanch, Robert J., Miriam Youngerman Miller, and Julian Wasserman. *Text and Matter: New Critical Perspectives of the "Pearl"-Poet.* Troy, N.Y.: Whitston Publishing, 1991.

Boehrer, Bruce Thomas. "*Paradise Lost* and the General Epistle of James: Milton, Augustine, Lacan." *Exemplaria* 4, no. 2 (1992): 295–316.

Bowers, Fredson Thayer. *Elizabethan Revenge Tragedy 1587–1642.* 1940. Reprint. Gloucester: Peter Smith, 1959.

Bradshaw, Graham. *Shakespeare's Skepticism.* Brighton: Harvester, 1987.

Brewer, Derek. *Symbolic Stories: Traditional Narratives of the Family Drama in English Literature.* Cambridge: Brewer, 1980.

Bristol, Michael D. "Carnival and the Institutions of Theater in Elizabethan England." *ELH* 50, no. 4 (winter 1983): 637–54.

———. *Carnival and Theater: Plebian Culture and the Structure of Authority in Renaissance England.* New York and London: Methuen, 1985.

———. "Charivari and the Comedy of Abjection in *Othello.*" *Renaissance Drama* 21 (1990): 3–22.

Brockbank, Philip. *Marlowe: "Dr. Faustus."* London: Edward Arnold, 1962.

Brown, Peter. *Augustine of Hippo: A Biography.* London: Faber, 1967.

Bryan, W. F., and Germaine Dempster, ed. *Sources and Analogues of Chaucer's "Canterbury Tales."* Chicago: University of Chicago Press, 1941.

Burke, Kenneth. *The Rhetoric of Religion: Studies in Logology.* Berkeley and Los Angeles: University of California Press, 1970.

Burlin, Robert. *Chaucerian Fiction.* Princeton: Princeton University Press, 1977.

Burrow, John. *A Reading of "Sir Gawain and the Green Knight."* London: Routledge, 1965.

Calderwood, James. *To Be and Not To Be: Negation and Metadrama in "Hamlet."* New York: Columbia University Press, 1983.

Calvin, John. *Institutes of the Christian Religion*. Edited by John O'Neill and translated by Ford Lewis Battles. 2 vols. The Library of Christian Classics: vols. 20–21. London: S.C.M. Press, 1960.

Carmichael, Virginia. "Green is for Growth: Sir Gawain's Disjunctive Neurosis." *Assays* 4 (1987): 25–39.

Carruthers, Mary. "The Wife of Bath and the Painting of Lions." *PMLA* 94, no. 2 (March 1979): 209–22.

Cassirer, Ernst, and others. *The Renaissance Philosophy of Man*. Chicago: University of Chicago Press, 1948.

Castle, Terry. "The Carnivalization of Eighteenth-Century English Narrative." *PMLA* 99 (1984): 903–16.

———. *Masquerade and Civilization: The Carnivalesque in Eighteenth-Century English Culture and Fiction*. London: Methuen, 1986.

Chadwick, Henry. *Augustine*. Oxford: Oxford University Press, 1986.

Chaucer, Geoffrey. *The Works of Geoffrey Chaucer*. General editor: Larry D. Benson. New York: Houghton-Mifflin, 1987.

———. *The Works of Geoffrey Chaucer*. Edited by F. N. Robinson. Cambridge, Mass.: Riverside Press, 1957.

Cheung, King-Kok. "The Dialectic of Despair in *Dr. Faustus*." In *"A Poet and a Filthy Play-maker": New Essays on Christopher Marlowe*. Edited by Kenneth Friedenreich, Roma Gill, and Constance Kuriyama, 193–202. New York: A.M.S. Press, 1988.

Clark, Katerina, and Michael Holquist. *Mikhail Bakhtin*. Cambridge: Harvard University Press, 1984.

Cohen, Brent M. "'What Is It You Would See?': *Hamlet* and the Conscience of the Theater." *ELH* 44, no. 2 (summer 1977): 222–47.

Cole, Douglas. *Suffering and Evil in the Plays of Christopher Marlowe*. Princeton: Princeton University Press, 1962.

Coles, Romand. *Self/Power/Other: Political Theory and Dialogical Ethics*. Ithaca: Cornell University Press, 1992.

Colmer, Dorothy. "Character and Class in the *Wife of Bath's Tale*." *Journal of English and Germanic Philology* 72 (1973): 329–39.

Cook, Jon. "Carnival and *The Canterbury Tales:* 'Only Equals May Laugh' (Herzen)." In *Medieval Literature: Criticism, Ideology, and History*. Edited by David Aers, 169–91. Brighton: Harvester, 1986.

Cox, John D. *Shakespeare and the Dramaturgy of Power*. Princeton: Princeton University Press, 1989.

Crane, Susan. "Alisoun's Incapacity and Poetic Instability in the *Wife of Bath's Tale*." *PMLA* 102, no. 1 (January 1987): 20–28.

Cress, Donald. "Augustine's Privation Account of Evil: A Defense." *Augustinian Studies* 20 (1989): 109–23.

Cunningham, Karen. "Renaissance Execution and Marlovian Elocution: The Drama of Death." *PMLA* 105, no. 2 (March 1990): 209–22.

Curry, Walter Clyde. *Chaucer and the Medieval Sciences*. 1926. Reprint. New York: Barnes and Noble, 1960.

David, Alfred. "Gawain and Aeneas." *English Studies* 49 (1968): 402–9.

Davies, H. Neville. "Jacobean *Antony and Cleopatra*." *Shakespeare Studies* 17 (1985): 123–58.

Davis, Natalie Zemon. *Society and Culture in Early Modern France*. 1965. Reprint. Cambridge: Polity Press, 1987.

Deane, Herbert A. *The Political and Social Ideas of St. Augustine*. New York: Columbia University Press, 1963.

Delany, Sheila. *Medieval Literary Politics: Shapes of Ideology*. Manchester: Manchester University Press, 1990.

Dinshaw, Carolyn. *Chaucer's Sexual Poetics*. Madison: University of Wisconsin Press, 1989.

———. "Eunuch Hermeneutics." *ELH* 55, no. 1 (spring 1988): 27–52.

Dollimore, Jonathan. *Radical Tragedy: Religion, Ideology, and Power in the Drama of Shakespeare and His Contemporaries*. Brighton: Harvester, 1984.

———. *Sexual Dissidence: Augustine to Wilde, Freud to Foucault*. Oxford: Oxford University Press, 1991.

Eagleton, Terry. "Bakhtin, Schopenhauer, Kundera." In Hirschkop and Shepherd, 178–88.

———. *Walter Benjamin or Towards a Revolutionary Criticism*. London: Verso, 1981.

Eliot, T. S. "Notes on the Blank Verse of Marlowe." In *The Sacred Wood*. 1920. Reprint. London: Methuen, 1960.

Ellis-Fermor, Una. *Christopher Marlowe*. 1927. Reprint. Hamden, Conn.: Archon, 1967.

Emerson, Caryl. "The Tolstoy Connection in Bakhtin." In Morson and Emerson, 149–70.

Evans, Bertrand. *Shakespeare's Tragic Practice*. Oxford: Clarendon Press, 1979.

Evans, Gillian. *Augustine on Evil*. Cambridge: Cambridge University Press, 1982.

Farrell, Kirby. *Shakespeare's Creation: The Language of Magic and Play*. Amherst: University of Massachusetts Press, 1975.

Felperin, Howard. *Shakespearean Representation: Mimesis and Modernity in Elizabethan Tragedy*. Princeton: Princeton University Press, 1977.

———. *The Uses of the Canon: Elizabethan Literature and Contemporary Theory*. Oxford: Oxford University Press, 1990.

Ferrari, Leo C. *The Conversions of St. Augustine*. Philadelphia: Villanova University Press, 1984.

Fichter, Andrew. "*Antony and Cleopatra:* The Time of Universal Peace." *Shakespeare Survey* 33 (1980): 99–111.

Field, P. J. C. "A Rereading of *Sir Gawain and the Green Knight*." *Studies in Philology* 68 (1971): 255–69.

Fisher, Sheila. "Leaving Morgan Aside: Women, History, and Revisionism in *Sir Gawain and the Green Knight*." In Baswell and Sharpe, 129–51.

———. "Taken Men and Token Women in *Sir Gawain and the Green Knight*." In *Seeking the Woman in Late Medieval and Renaissance Writings: Essays in Feminist Contextual Criticism*. Edited by Sheila Fisher and Janet E. Halley, 71-105. Knoxville: University of Tennessee Press, 1989.

Fiore, Peter. *Milton and Augustine: Patterns of Augustinian Thought in "Paradise Lost."* University Park: Pennsylvania State University Press, 1981.

Forster, E. M. *A Passage to India*. Edited by Oliver Stallybrass. Harmondsworth, U.K.: Penguin, 1961.

Fradenburg, Louise O. "The Wife of Bath's Passing Fancy." *Studies in the Age of Chaucer* 8 (1986): 31–58.

French, Marilyn. *Shakespeare's Division of Experience.* London: Jonathan Cape, 1982.

Frye, Northrop. *Fools of Time: Studies in Shakespearian Tragedy.* Toronto: University of Toronto Press, 1967.

Frye, Roland Mushat. *The Renaissance "Hamlet": Issues and Responses in 1600.* Princeton: Princeton University Press, 1984.

Ganim, John M. *Chaucerian Theatricality.* Princeton: Princeton University Press, 1990.

Gardiner, Michael. *The Dialogics of Critique: M. M. Bakhtin and the Theory of Ideology.* London: Routledge, 1992.

Gash, Anthony. "Carnival Against Lent: The Ambivalence of Medieval Drama." In *Medieval Literature: Criticism, Ideology and History.* Edited by David Aers, 74–98. Brighton: Harvester, 1986.

Gilson, Etienne. *The Christian Philosophy of St. Augustine.* Translated from the French by L. E. M. Lynch. London: Gollancz, 1961.

Ginsburg, Warren. "The Lineaments of Desire: Wish-Fulfillment in Chaucer's Marriage Group." *Criticism* 25, no. 3 (summer 1983): 197–210.

Gorfain, Phyllis. "Toward a Theory of Play and the Carnivalesque in *Hamlet.*" *Hamlet Studies* 13, nos. 1–2 (1991): 25–49.

Gower, John. *Confessio Amantis.* Edited by Russell A. Peck. Toronto: University of Toronto Press, 1980.

Greenblatt, Stephen. *Shakespearean Negotiations: The Circulation of Social Energy in Renaissance England.* Berkeley and Los Angeles: University of California Press, 1988.

———. *Renaissance Self-Fashioning from More to Shakespeare.* Chicago: University of Chicago Press, 1980.

Greg, W. W., ed. *Marlowe's "Dr. Faustus" 1604–1616.* Oxford: Oxford University Press, 1950.

Griswold, Wendy. *Renaissance Revivals: City Comedy and Revenge Tragedy in the London Theater 1576–1980.* Chicago: University of Chicago Press, 1986.

Gurevich, Aron. *Medieval Popular Culture: Problems of Belief and Perception.* Translated from the Russian by Janos M. Bak and Paul Hollingsworth. Cambridge: Cambridge University Press, 1988.

Hahn, Thomas. "Teaching the Resistant Woman: The Wife of Bath and the Academy." *Exemplaria* 4, no. 2 (1992): 431–40.

Hallett, Charles A., and Elaine S. Hallett. *The Revenger's Madness: A Study of Revenge Tragedy Motifs.* Lincoln: University of Nebraska Press, 1980.

Halverson, John. "Template Criticism: *Sir Gawain and the Green Knight.*" *Modern Philology* 67 (1969): 133–39.

Hanning, Robert W. "Sir Gawain and the Red Herring: The Perils of Interpretation." In *Acts of Interpretation: The Text in Its Context, 700–1600.* Edited by Mary Carruthers and Elizabeth D. Kirk, 5–23. Norman, Okla.: Pilgrim, 1982.

Hansen, Elaine Tuttle. *Chaucer and the Fictions of Gender.* Berkeley and Los Angeles: University of California Press, 1992.

Harwood, Britton J. "The Wife of Bath and the Dream of Innocence." *Modern Language Quarterly* 33, no. 3 (september 1972): 257–73.

Hawkins, Anne Hunsaker. *Archetypes of Conversion: The Autobiographies of Augustine, Bunyan, and Merton.* Lewisburg, Penn.: Bucknell University Press; London and Toronto: Associated University Presses, 1985.

Haynes, Jonathan. "Festivity and the Dramatic Economy of Jonson's *Batholemew Fair.*" *ELH* 51, no. 4 (winter 1984): 645–68.

Heng, Geraldine. "Feminine Knots and the Other *Sir Gawain and the Green Knight.*" *PMLA* 106 (1991): 500–14.

———. "A Woman Wants: The Lady, *Gawain,* and the Forms of Seduction." *Yale Journal of Criticism* 5, no. 2 (1992): 101–34.

Hick, John. *Evil and the God of Love.* 1966. Reprint. London and Basingstoke, England: Macmillan, 1977.

Hirschkop, Ken, and David Shepherd, eds. *Bakhtin and Cultural Theory.* Manchester: Manchester University Press, 1989.

Hieatt, A. Kent. "*Sir Gawain:* Pentangle, *Luf-Lace,* Numerical Structure." *Papers on Language and Literature* 4 (1968): 339–59.

Hills, David Farley. "Gawain's Fault in *Sir Gawain and the Green Knight.*" *Review of English Studies* n.s. 14 (1963): 124–31.

Hollis, Stephanie J. "The Pentangle Knight: *Sir Gawain and the Green Knight.*" *Chaucer Review* 15 (1981): 267–81.

Honderich, Pauline. "John Calvin and Dr. Faustus." *Modern Language Review* 68 (1973): 1–13.

Huppé, Bernard. *A Reading of the "Canterbury Tales."* Albany: State University of New York Press, 1964.

Ibsen, Henrik. *Peer Gynt.* Oslo: Gyldendal Norsk Forlag, 1991.

———. *Rosmersholm.* Translated from the Norwegian by James McFarlane. Oxford: Oxford University Press, 1969.

Journet, Charles. *The Meaning of Evil.* Translated from the French by Michael Berry. London: Chapman, 1963.

Kamps, Ivo. "Magic, Women, and Incest: The Real Challenges in *Sir Gawain and the Green Knight.*" *Exemplaria* 1, no. 2 (1989): 313–36

Kaske, Robert E. "Chaucer's Marriage Group." In *Chaucer the Love Poet.* Edited by Jerome Mitchell and William Provost, 45–65. Athens: University of Georgia Press, 1973.

Kean, P. M. *Chaucer and the Making of English Poetry.* London: Routledge and Kegan Paul, 1972.

Kelsall, Malcolm. *Christopher Marlowe.* Leiden: E. J. Brill, 1981.

Kermode, Frank. *Forms of Attention.* Chicago: University of Chicago Press, 1987.

Kernan, Alvin. *The Canker'd Muse: Satire of the English Renaissance.* New Haven: Yale University Press, 1959.

Kernan, Anne. "The Archwife and the Eunuch." *ELH* 41, no. 1 (spring 1974): 1–25.

Kinney, Clare. "The Queen's Two Bodies and the Divided Emperor." In *The Renaissance Englishwoman in Print: Counterbalancing the Canon.* Edited by Anne M. Haselkorn and Betty S. Travitsky, 177–86. Amherst: University of Massachusetts Press, 1990.

Kirschbaum, Leo, ed. *The Plays of Christopher Marlowe.* New York: Meridian, 1962.

Kirwan, Christopher. *Augustine*. London and New York: Routledge, 1989.

Kitely, John F. "'The Endless Knot': Magical Aspects of the Pentangle in *Sir Gawain and the Green Knight*." *Studies in the Literary Imagination* 4 (1971): 41–50.

Knapp, Peggy A. "Alisoun of Bath and the Reappropriation of Tradition." *Chaucer Review* 24, no. 1 (1989): 45–52.

———. "Alisoun Weaves a Text." *Philological Quarterly* 65, no. 3 (summer 1986): 387–401.

———. *Chaucer and the Social Contest*. London: Routledge, 1990.

Knights, L. C. *Drama and Society in the Age of Jonson*. 1937. Reprint. New York: Barnes and Noble, 1968.

Kocher, Paul. *Christopher Marlowe: A Study of His Thought, Learning and Character*. Chapel Hill: University of North Carolina Press, 1946.

Kott, Jan. *The Bottom Translation: Marlowe and Shakespeare and the Carnival Tradition*. Translated by Daniela Miedzyrzecka and Lillian Vallee. Evanston: Northwestern University Press, 1987.

Kuriyama, Constance B. *Hammer or Anvil: Psychological Patterns in Christopher Marlowe's Plays*. New Brunswick, N. J.: Rutgers University Press, 1980.

Kyd, Thomas. *The Spanish Tragedy*. Edited by J. R. Mulryne. London: Ernest Benn, 1970.

Ladurie, Emmanuel LeRoy. *Carnival in Romans*. New York: George Braziller, 1979.

Laroque, Francois. *Shakespeare's Festive World: Elizabethan Seasonal Entertainments and the Professional Stage*. Translated from the French by Janet Lloyd. Cambridge: Cambridge University Press, 1991.

Leggatt, Alexander. *Shakespeare's Political Drama: The History Plays and the Roman Plays*. London: Routledge, 1988.

Leicester, H. Marshall, Jr. "Of a Fire in the Dark: Public and Private Feminism in the *Wife of Bath's Tale*." *Women's Studies* 11 (1984): 157–78.

Levin, Harry. *The Overreacher: A Study of Christopher Marlowe*. Cambridge: Harvard University Press, 1952.

———. *The Question of "Hamlet."* London and New York: Oxford University Press, 1959.

Levine, Robert. "Aspects of Grotesque Realism in *Sir Gawain and the Green Knight*." *Chaucer Review* 17 (1982): 65–75.

Leyerle, John. "The Game and Play of Hero." In *Concepts of the Hero in the Middle Ages and Renaissance*. Edited by Norman T. Burns and Christopher Reagan, 49–82. London and Sydney: Hodder and Stoughton, 1976.

Lindahl, Carl. *Earnest Games: Folkloric Patterns in the "Canterbury Tales."* Bloomington: Indiana University Press, 1987.

Lindley, Arthur. "Lovelace and the Self-Dramatizing Heroes of the Restoration." In *The English Hero, 1660–1800*. Edited by Robert Folkenflik, 193–204. Newark: University of Delaware Press, 1982.

Long, Walter C. "The Wife of Bath as Moral Revolutionary." *Chaucer Review* 20, no. 4 (1986), 273–84.

Loomba, Ania. *Gender, Race, Renaissance Drama*. Manchester: Manchester University Press, 1986.

Luther and Erasmus: Free Will and Salvation. Edited by E. Gordon Rupp and Philip S. Watson. The Library of Christian Classics, vol. 17. London: S.C.M. Press, 1969.

MacIntyre, Alasdair. *Three Rival Versions of Moral Inquiry: Encyclopedia, Genealogy, and Tradition.* London: Duckworth, 1990.

Mack, Maynard. "The World of Hamlet." *Yale Review* 41 (1952): 502–23.. Reprint. In *Shakespeare: Modern Essays in Criticism.* Edited by Leonard F. Dean, 242–62. New York: Oxford University Press, 1967.

Malone, Kemp. "The Wife of Bath's Tale." *Modern Language Review* 57, no. 4 (October 1962): 481–90.

Malvern, Marjorie. "'Who Peynted the Leon, Tel Me Who?': Rhetorical and Didactic Roles Played by an Aesopic Fable in the *Wife of Bath's Prologue.*" *Studies in Philology* 80, no. 3 (summer 1980): 238–52.

Mann, Jill. *Chaucer and Medieval Estates Satire.* Cambridge: Cambridge University Press, 1973.

———. *Geoffrey Chaucer.* Hemel Hempstead: Harvester, 1991.

Manning, Stephen. "A Psychological Interpretation of *Sir Gawain and the Green Knight.*" In *Critical Studies of "Sir Gawain and the Green Knight."* Edited by Donald Howard and Christian Zacher, 279–94. Notre Dame: Notre Dame University Press, 1968. 279–94.

Marcus, Leah. *The Politics of Mirth: Jonson, Herrick, Milton, Marvell and the Defense of Old Holiday Pastimes.* Chicago: University of Chicago Press, 1986.

Margherita, Gayle. *The Romance of Origins: Language and Sexual Difference in Middle English Literature.* Philadelphia: University of Pennsylvania Press, 1994.

Markels, Julian. *The Pillar of the World: "Antony and Cleopatra" in Shakespeare's Development.* Columbus: Ohio State University Press, 1968.

Markus, R. A. *Sæculum: History and Society in the Theology of St. Augustine.* Cambridge: Cambridge University Press, 1970.

Marlowe, Christopher. *The Complete Plays.* Edited by J. B. Steane. Harmondsworth, U.K.: Penguin, 1969.

Maslen, Elizabeth. "The Dynamics of Kyd's *Spanish Tragedy.*" *English* 32, no. 143 (summer 1983): 111–25.

Maus, Katherine Eisaman. "Proof and Consequences: Inwardness and Its Exposure in the English Renaissance." *Representations* 34 (spring 1991): 29–52.

Matson, Wallace. *The Existence of God.* Ithaca: Cornell University Press, 1965.

McAlindon, T. *Shakespeare's Tragic Cosmos.* Cambridge: Cambridge University Press, 1991.

———. "Cultural Materialism and the Ethics of Reading; or The Radicalizing of Jacobean Tragedy." *MLR* 90, no. 4 (October 1995): 530–46.

McMahon, Robert. *Augustine's Prayerful Ascent: An Essay on the Literary Form of the "Confessions."* Athens: University of Georgia Press, 1989.

Meagher, Robert. *An Introduction to St. Augustine.* New York: New York University Press, 1978.

Mercer, Peter. *"Hamlet" and the Acting of Revenge.* Basingstoke, U.K.: Macmillan, 1987.

Miller, Robert P. *Chaucer: Sources and Backgrounds.* Oxford: Oxford University Press, 1977.

Milton, John. *Paradise Lost*. Edited by Alistair Fowler. London: Longmans, 1968.

Morson, Gary Saul, and Caryl Emerson, eds. *Rethinking Bakhtin: Extensions and Challenges*. Evanston: Northwestern University Press, 1989.

Murry, John Middleton. *Shakespeare*. New York: Random House, 1936.

Murtaugh, Daniel M. "Women and Geoffrey Chaucer." *ELH* 38, no. 4 (December 1971): 473–92.

Neely, Carol Thomas. *Broken Nuptials in Shakespeare's Plays*. New Haven: Yale University Press, 1985.

Oberembt, Kenneth J. "Chaucer's Anti-Misogynist Wife of Bath." *Chaucer Review* 10, no. 4 (1976): 287–302.

O'Connell, Michael. "The Idolatrous Eye: Iconoclasm, Antitheatricalism and the Image of the Elizabethan Theater." *ELH* 52, no. 2 (summer 1985): 279–310.

O'Daley, Gerard. *Augustine's Philosophy of Mind*. Berkeley and Los Angeles: University of California Press, 1987.

Owen, Charles A. "The Crucial Passages in Five of the *Canterbury Tales:* A Study in Irony and Symbol." *Journal of English and Germanic Philology* 52 (1953): 294–311. Reprint. In *Chaucer: Modern Essays in Criticism*. Edited by Edward Wagenknecht, 294–311. Oxford: Galaxy, 1959.

Pagels, Elaine. *Adam, Eve, and the Serpent*. New York: Random House, 1988.

Patterson, Annabel. *Shakespeare and the Popular Voice*. Oxford: Basil Blackwell, 1989.

Patterson, Lee. *Chaucer and the Subject of History*. London: Routledge, 1991.

———. "For the Wyves Love of Bath": Feminine Rhetoric and Poetic Resolution in the *Roman de la Rose* and the *Canterbury Tales*." *Speculum* 58, no. 3 (July 1983): 656–95.

Plummer, John. "Signifying the Self: Language and Identity in *Sir Gawain and the Green Knight*." In Blanch, Miller, and Wasserman, 195–212.

Poems of the Pearl Manuscript. Edited by Malcolm Andrew and Ronald Waldron. 1978. Reprint. Exeter: University of Exeter Press, 1987.

Porter, Henry C. *Reformation and Reaction in Tudor Cambridge*. Cambridge: Cambridge University Press, 1958.

Prosser, Eleanor. *Hamlet and Revenge*. Stanford: Stanford University Press, 1967.

Reed, Thomas L., Jr. "'Boþe Blysse and Blunder': *Sir Gawain and the Green Knight* and the Debate Tradition." *Chaucer Review* 23 (1988): 140–61.

Rendall, Thomas. "*Gawain* and the Game of Chess." *Chaucer Review* 27 (1992): 186–99.

Robertson, D. W. *Essays in Medieval Culture*. Princeton: Princeton University Press, 1980.

———. *A Preface to Chaucer: Studies in Medieval Perspectives*. Princeton: Princeton University Press, 1962.

Rowland, Beryl. "On the Timely Death of the Wife of Bath's Fourth Husband." *Archiv* 209 (1972–73): 273–82.

Sachs, Arieh. "The Religious Despair of Dr. Faustus." *Journal of English and Germanic Philology* 63 (1964): 625–47.

Sales, Roger. *Christopher Marlowe*. Basingstoke, U.K.: Macmillan, 1991.

Sanders, Wilbur. *The Dramatist and the Received Idea: Studies in the Plays of Marlowe and Shakespeare*. Cambridge: Cambridge University Press, 1968.

Scala, Elizabeth D. "The Wanting Words of *Sir Gawain and the Green Knight: Narrative Past, Present and Absent.*" *Exemplaria* 6, no. 2 (1994): 305–38.

Schibanoff, Susan. "The New Reader and Female Textuality in Two Early Commentaries on Chaucer." *Studies in the Age of Chaucer* 10 (1988): 71–108.

Schmidt, A. V. C. "'Latent Content' and 'The Testimony in the Text': Symbolic Meaning in *Sir Gawain and the Green Knight.*" *Review of English Studies*, n.s. 38, no. 150 (1987): 145–68.

Seaton, Ethel. "*Antony and Cleopatra* and *The Book of Revelation.*" *Review of English Studies* 22, no. 87 (1946): 219–24.

Shaheen, Naseeb. *Biblical References in Shakespeare's Tragedies.* Newark: University of Delaware Press; London: Associated University Presses, 1987.

Shakespeare, William. *The Riverside Shakespeare.* Edited by G. Blakemore Evans, Harry Levin, and others. Boston: Houghton-Mifflin, 1974.

Shepherd, Simon. *Marlowe and the Politics of Elizabethan Theatre.* Brighton: Harvester, 1986.

Shoaf, R. A. *The Poem as Green Girdle: Commercium in "Sir Gawain and the Green Knight."* Gainesville: University Presses of Florida, 1984.

———. "The 'Syngne of Surfet' and the Surfeit of Signs in *Sir Gawain and the Green Knight.*" In Baswell and Sharpe, 152–69.

Shuger, Debora Kuller. *Habits of Thought in the English Renaissance: Religion, Politics, and the Dominant Culture.* Berkeley and Los Angeles: University of California Press, 1990.

Shukman, Ann. "Bakhtin's Tolstoy Prefaces." In Morson and Emerson, 137–48.

Shumaker, Wayne. "Alisoun in Wanderland: A Study of Chaucer's Mind and Literary Method." *ELH* 18 (1951): 77–89.

Silverstein, Theodore. "The Wife of Bath and the Rhetoric of Enchantment; or, How to Make a Hero See in the Dark." *Modern Philology* 68, no. 3 (February 1961): 153–73.

Simmons, Joseph L. *Shakespeare's Pagan World: The Roman Tragedies.* Brighton: Harvester, 1974.

Simons, John, ed. *From Medieval to Medievalism.* Basingstoke, U.K.: Macmillan, 1992.

Sinfield, Alan. *Faultlines: Cultural Materialism and the Politics of Dissident Reading.* Oxford: Oxford University Press, 1992.

Sir Gawain and the Green Knight. Edited by J. R. R. Tolkien and E. V. Gordon; 2d edition edited by Norman Davis. Oxford: Oxford University Press, 1967.

Snyder, Susan. *The Comic Matrix of Shakespeare's Tragedies: "Romeo and Juliet," "Hamlet," "Othello," and "King Lear."* Princeton: Princeton University Press, 1979.

———. "Patterns of Motion in *Antony and Cleopatra.*" *Shakespeare Survey* 33 (1980): 113–22.

Stallybrass, Peter, and Allon White. *The Politics and Poetics of Transgression.* London: Methuen, 1986.

Stanbury, Sarah. *Seeing the Gawain-Poet: Description and the Act of Perception.* Philadelphia: University of Pennsylvania Press, 1991.

Steane, J. B. *Marlowe: A Critical Study.* Cambridge: Cambridge University Press, 1964.

Strauss, Barrie Ruth. "The Subversive Discourse of the Wife of Bath: Phallocentric Discourse and the Imprisonment of Criticism." *ELH* 55, no. 3 (fall 1988): 527–54.

Strohm, Paul. *Hochon's Arrow: The Social Imagination of Fourteenth-Century Texts.* Princeton: Princeton University Press, 1992.

Sturgis, Robert S. "The *Canterbury Tales*' Women Narrators: Three Traditions of Female Authority." *Modern Language Studies* 13, no. 2 (spring 1983): 41–51.

Surin, Kenneth. *Theology and the Problem of Evil.* Oxford: Basil Blackwell, 1986.

Taylor, Charles. *Sources of the Self: The Making of Modern Identity.* Cambridge: Cambridge University Press, 1989.

Tennenhouse, Leonard. *Power on Display: The Politics of Shakespeare's Genres.* New York and London: Methuen, 1986.

Thomas, Vivian. *Shakespeare's Roman Worlds.* London: Routledge, 1989.

Thundy, Zacharias P. "Matheolus, Chaucer, and the Wife of Bath." In *Chaucerian Problems and Perspectives: Essays Presented to Paul E. Beichner.* Edited by Edward Vasta and Zacharias Thundy, 24–58. Notre Dame: University of Notre Dame Press, 1979.

Tourneur, Cyril. *The Plays of Cyril Tourneur.* Edited by George Parfitt. Cambridge: Cambridge University Press, 1978.

Turner, Victor. *From Ritual to Theater: The Human Seriousness of Play.* New York: Performing Arts Journal Publications, 1982.

Walzer, Michael. *The Revolution of the Saints: A Study in the Origins of Radical Politics.* Cambridge: Harvard University Press, 1965.

Warner, William Beatty. *Reading "Clarissa": The Struggles of Interpretation.* New Haven: Yale University Press, 1979.

Watson, Robert N. "Giving Up the Ghost in a World of Decay: *Hamlet,* Revenge and Denial." *Renaissance Drama,* n.s. 21 (1990): 199–223.

Weil, Judith. *Christopher Marlowe: Merlin's Prophet.* Cambridge: Cambridge University Press, 1977.

Weimann, Robert. *Shakespeare and the Popular Tradition in the Theater.* Edited and translated by Robert Schwartz. Baltimore: Johns Hopkins University Press, 1978.

Weissman, Hope Phyllis. "Antifeminism in Chaucer's Characterization of Women." In *Geoffrey Chaucer.* Edited by George D. Economou, 93–110. New York: McGraw-Hill, 1975.

Welsh, Alexander. "The Task of Hamlet." *Yale Review* 69, no. 4 (June 1980): 481–502.

West, Philip. "The Perils of Pauline Theology: The *Wife of Bath's Prologue and Tale.*" *Essays in Arts and Sciences* 8 (1979): 7–16.

Westland, Joseph. "The Orthodox Christian Framework of Marlowe's *Faustus.*" *Studies in English Literature* 3 (1963): 190–205.

Wilson, J. Dover, *What Happens in "Hamlet."* Cambridge: Cambridge University Press, 1935.

Wilson, Richard. "'Is This a Holiday?': Shakespeare's Roman Carnival." *ELH* 54, no. 1 (spring 1987): 31–44.

Wurtele, Douglas J. "Chaucer's Wife of Bath and the Problem of the Fifth Husband." *Chaucer Review* 23, no. 2 (1988): 117–28.

Yachnin, Paul. "'Courtiers of Beauteous Freedom': *Antony and Cleopatra* in Its Time." *Renaissance and Reformation* 15 (1981): 1–20.

Zum Brunn, Emilie. *St. Augustine: Being and Nothingness.* New York: Paragon, 1988.

Index

DATE DUE

APR 15 1997			
MAY 0 8 2001			